FULL MOON TO FRANCE

Devereaux Rochester

FULL MOON

TO FRANCE

Harper & Row, Publishers

New York, Hagerstown, San Francisco, London

 For information address Harper & Row, Publishers, Inc., 10 East 53rd Street, New York, N.Y. 10022. Published simultaneously in Canada by Fitzhenry & Whiteside Limited, Toronto.

FIRST EDITION

Designed by C. Linda Dingler

ISBN: 0-06-013586-7

LIBRARY OF CONGRESS CATALOG CARD NUMBER: 76-26250

77 78 79 80 81 10 9 8 7 6 5 4 3 2 1

To Helen Allen
who insisted for years that I should do it.

To my aunt, Mary Louise Rochester,
who loaned me the money so I could eat
while I was doing it.

To Jeanine
who was always there in spite of many hardships.

And to the Combes family
who showed me friendship and concern.

FULL MOON TO FRANCE

Prologue

This was my war! I suppose that may sound pretentious since there have been so many later ones, and since, down the ages, mankind has always had wars. The cave dwellers of Europe fought with their neighbors over their hunting grounds, while along a broad river in the Middle East another, more advanced civilization was fighting when it wasn't reclining at ease, discussing philosophy or sacrificing virgins and harmless animals to its gods. And so it went until the time came for my father to sally forth. His was the war fought to end all wars. I don't know if he believed this, because while he was fighting I was being born in New York and on his return my mother and he divorced and I never knew him.

For me everything concerned with wars started in 1922 at Verdun.

"Now I wonder where that child can have disappeared to," my mother must have exclaimed then—words which were destined to become a leitmotiv for many years to come, despite long-suffering nurses and governesses. At that time I didn't hear them, for I had drifted off in search of more interesting matters than the description of the Battle of Verdun being droned out by a one-legged hero of that epic struggle. In the beginning I had been fascinated by the wooden peg that had replaced his lost limb, chiefly because it made a sucking sound on the cement floor of the Fort Douaumont. But in a short while this ceased to be interesting, especially as he refused to tell me—in spite of my nagging—how he had lost it and how he attached its replacement. And so I wandered away down murky corridors faintly lit by dirty electric bulbs. I was quite happy because I could still hear the guide's voice as well as the echo of my steps—quite happy until a turn in the corridor cut out all sound and I was alone. For a while I trailed along until I became conscious of the silence. I started to cry then, running panic-stricken. I don't know how long I kept this up, but when I reached a half-open iron door with a skull and crossbones painted on it, I slid around it because I heard voices on the other side.

When I entered—a small, terrified child sobbing in an unknown language—I was comforted by a helmeted poilu with a spade. Burying my face in his putteed legs, I cried until one of his pals stepped out of the shadows holding a hurricane lamp. Until then I had failed to see what they had been shoveling into hand trolleys. When I did, I screamed with horror. Heaped from floor to ceiling were bones and skulls with empty eye sockets. One skull still wore a helmet at a rakish angle, while some of the bones had traces of faded blue material stuck to them. The stench was overpowering. I fainted. This was my first introduction to man after death.

I didn't return to Verdun until 1937. It was late spring. I say late because in other parts of France the countryside was in bloom, an explosion of varied tints which made one happy to be alive. This was not the case in Verdun twenty-one years after the battle. No, here it was a diffident spring, as if nature was afraid to give free rein to its exuberance over the shell-pocked hillsides. Still, gorse abounded next to frail wild flowers nestling together near ivy-throttled trees whose roots had died when their growth set off mines or unexploded bombs.

Standing on a gun emplacement, the rusted barrel of the gun still pointing aggressively into space, I felt an idle breeze teasing at my skirts. It might have been carefree were it not for its plaintive whine—a whine which sounded like a lament for all the soldiers still lying in hastily dug graves. Maybe these bracken-covered resting places were fitting epitaphs to that war—the most murderous of all so far. These warriors slept, French and German alike, remembered only in faded photographs propped up on mantelpieces or pianos: *"A Maman, de son fils, Jules." "Für Mutter von ihre sonne, Ernst."*

But I was part of a new generation and I had just come back from Berlin, where my stepfather, Myron Reynolds, had gone on business.

I had never been in northern Germany before, and I had been startled by the massive architecture of its capital. At the end of three days I was uncomfortable, but not because of the buildings. The big monuments bedecked with swastikas seemed merely to serve as a backdrop for the tramp of marching boots, the songs of handsome, blond young men goose-stepping to the sound of martial music. I became bad-tempered, but it was only at the end of my stay that I had an inkling as to the cause of my ill-humor. It was the warlike atmosphere of the place that was setting me on edge. There were uniforms everywhere; the men who wore them were exquisitely polite automatons, efficient and cold, all heel-clicking and bowing, while in the background the snarls and yells of a guttural, rasping voice shouted over loudspeakers phrases that sounded both senseless and belligerent. I would have liked to ask someone to explain what I saw and heard and felt, but I had no one to turn to, since I distrusted the apparent friendliness of everyone around.

"Why are you looking so grumpy again?" my stepfather asked.

"I don't mean to be," I mumbled. "Sorry." And turned away. I wasn't able to tell him. He liked Germany and now admired the Nazis.

My generation . . . my generation . . . It would have its war too. But that thought didn't frighten me. On the contrary, I was thrilled. It would be an adventure. I was sure to be involved. I don't know how I knew this, probably because I wanted to be. I certainly knew that if there was a war I didn't want to stand by and continue my fruitless life. France would fight as she had always done. (Verdun was the proof of her courage.) And I had been brought up in France and loved it, if only in a distant, perhaps patronizing way. Anyway, we all knew the Maginot Line was impregnable. No German would cross the Rhine and goose-step on French soil. And perhaps the Belgians would remain neutral. But how could they if they were invaded? Then they would fight too. Yes, it would be like the last time. Eventually my country would come in and America had never been beaten. They didn't have a chance, those Nazis—those beautiful, godlike young men with their stern, hard faces.

I turned away from my cannon, tapping it affectionately. It was a museum piece in 1937. France and England had newer ones. Meanwhile, back to Paris and then on to Brittany, where friends were waiting to take me sailing and then to play tennis or golf.

1

I had two years . . . two years and three months. I lived them as I'd lived the years before. I jaunted to Bavaria, Vienna, Budapest, and I was in Greece on the first September weekend of 1939.

Looking back, that pleasure jaunt while the war clouds gathered seemed like the height of folly. In Vienna I had found friends loading an old Ford station wagon and a low-slung Mercedes with as many of their possessions as they could pile in—not many, because their house in Vienna was a large one.

"You're crazy! Go back to Paris," they said between sips of coffee, orders to workmen and the sound of nails being driven into crates filled with family portraits.

I shrugged this off and proceeded on my junket. But I wasn't the only one playing with time. In Athens on Monday, September 4, 1939, the American Embassy was bedlam, besieged by frantic Greek-born United States citizens clutching and waving their passports, crowding up against hastily erected barricades that separated them from a harassed official and a couple of secretaries.

When it was my turn to approach the barrier, I was stared at in amazement, my arm was grabbed and I was swept away into another room. I may have protested a little because I felt sorry for all those honest U.S. citizens who had come over to visit their relatives and were now stranded. The Statue of Liberty must have seemed to them like a lost dream.

I was still sorry and embarrassed that evening when I boarded a Turkish ship bound for Marseille. Obviously, Mother had been keeping the telephone wires humming, and at the time I took it for granted. At twenty-one, I was a spoiled brat and an American one at that. Nothing could happen to me as long as I had my passport. All over the world those red-and-gold booklets (I think they had gold on them somewhere) represented the most coveted and honored nationality.

The Turkish ship was crowded with French nationals, most of them young men returning to their homeland to fulfill their military obligations. There were a few English, also on their way home to be mobilized, but I think I was the only American.

Among the passengers were a young French couple on their honeymoon. On this antiquated, dirty vessel there were few cabins, and they were all occupied. I shared one with another girl and I remember agreeing with her to allow the young lovers the use of it at night while we slept on deck. In the beginning that was no sacrifice: those starlit nights were wonderful as we plowed through the Mediterranean. But as we drew farther away from Greece they became chilly. Sitting huddled in a lifeboat, which I'm sure would have sunk had it ever been launched, I smoked endless cigarettes, indulging—for the first time in my life—in some thinking. Constructive thinking I imagined it to be! On my arrival in Paris I would join an ambulance corps. It should be easy, I decided with my customary brashness. I wasn't going to wait until my country was at war; I wanted to enter the fray and right from the start.

When the news came over the radio of the sinking by a German submarine of a British passenger ship en route to Canada and filled with women and children, we were indignant. Afterward we started to think of ourselves. The Italians could easily do the same to us. After all, we were carrying future soldiers. It would be a way for Italy to enhance her prestige—a declaration of solidarity with her partner.

Of course it was ridiculous, but in close confinement, with news spluttering spasmodically over an ancient radio, anything seemed possible, and, like the others, I spent many uncomfortable moments staring out to sea on the lookout for a periscope.

In sight of Marseille we cheered, and I stayed on deck until the last moment. I think we had already berthed when I went below to finish my nightbag. Suddenly, without a knock, the door was opened and a young man stepped in. He was a youngish, serious-looking chap and by the stamp of his clothes and his crew cut I knew he was American.

My fellow passenger and I gawked at him while he stared at us, embarrassed. It had been the steward who had flung open the door. Finally my cabin mate spoke in French protestingly.

"I'm sorry," he mumbled. "I'm looking for an American girl who boarded this ship in Piraeus."

I stopped fiddling with my nightbag and stepped forward.

"I have instructions to detain you on this ship until you can catch an American vessel coming from Naples and bound for the States."

"But I don't want to go to the States," I objected. "I live in Paris. My mother is there expecting me."

"I'm sorry, all U.S. citizens are to be repatriated."

I protested. I think I even cried. I also probably lost my temper. To no avail. I was to stay on board until the American ship arrived.

While this conversation was going on, my cabin mate slipped away, leaving me alone with this old-young man, perfect product of the State Department.

"But surely you'll let me telephone. . . ."

He snorted and I found this quite startling. Maybe he was human after all!

"There's a war on. It hasn't done anything to improve the French telephone service. You'll just have to wait here."

"But it's hot and dirty. Can't I go ashore?"

"No."

"But I must!" I cried. Then suddenly I blurted out: "I need some sanitary napkins. Oh, how can you do this to me? I *must* go ashore! I need some sanitary napkins!"

Obviously, the young man had never been faced with such a problem, and for one horrible moment I thought he was going to ask me what I meant. When he blushed, I was relieved.

"If I let you go ashore, will you give me your word to come back?"

With tears streaming down my cheeks I sobbed: "I give you my word of honor," while with one hand behind my back I crossed my fingers.

Then I charged ashore and ran for the nearest train—a very crowded one, but I was to learn that trains would always be crowded during the war years. Crowded, cold, uncomfortable and sometimes frightening.

I got to Paris, and I began to hammer on doors, clamoring to join an ambulance corps. With my cylinder-shaped gas mask banging against my legs, I climbed stairs, stood in line in front of the Red Cross building or one of its affiliates, begging to be accepted as a driver. It was disappointing, frustrating. No one wanted me. No one seemed to have any use for an American longing to become a heroine for La Belle France. But then there were so many longing to do the same thing and it was a French war, even if it appeared to be a stagnant or "phony" one. Certainly the newspapers of that period seemed interested only in vaunting the fine food and wine supplied to the troops compared to the provisions their fathers had received.

On November 30, Russia attacked Finland. Amazed and thrilled, Europe watched that little country stand up against its huge neighbor. A French contingent of Red Cross drivers set off for the front, together with an American one. But there was still no place for me.

January 1940 found me skiing at Alpes d'Huez, disgusted and tense, filled with spiteful contempt for this war I couldn't get into. But when spring came, the picture changed overnight. In twenty-six days the Nazis overran Denmark, Holland, Belgium and northern France, and the British army in France fled from Dunkirk for England.

Disaster gave me the chance I craved. I joined the American Hospital Ambulance Corps. Filled with pride and joy because of my uniform, I strolled into Mother's salon expecting to be congratulated. Instead her response conveyed "Better late than never." She and a distant cousin had already volunteered for nursing duty with the American Hospital.

I was terribly proud of the Chevrolet ambulance I was assigned to, a Chevrolet that bore the number 8. Until a few years ago one could still faintly see the ambulance numbers—eleven of them—painted along a wall at the bottom of a grade on the west side of the American Hospital driveway.

Each ambulance had two drivers, and my teammate was an elderly American lady, a member of the American colony. I had met her before the war, but only for a few minutes. I was brash, impulsive and quick-tempered. She was slow, cautious, bossy and proud, and she had been in the earlier war. Obviously, we were not meant to get on.

I remember my first important outing somewhere north of Paris where a factory was being bombed. It was night and we stayed in the shelter of a small wood, for hours it seemed, waiting for the German planes to finish their job before we moved in to rescue the wounded. While the sky lightened and the German planes streaked away, I and some other youngsters fretted, believing our job was to move right in and start our work. But my co-driver was in command of this convoy and ordered us to wait, and so she and I naturally came to words. After that she ignored me, leaving me to clean up the mess on the floor of the ambulance when we returned to our base hours later.

I was horribly sick, mixing my vomit with the blood and excrement on the floor, but because she stood by, with an expressionless look on her face, I persevered with my sponge, water and Lysol. I hated her (today she is dead) and refused to speak to her for many years after everything was over, although I often saw her at the American library.

In early June the sadly mauled French army was to make a stand—it would be its last—on the river Loire, and part of the American Hospital staff, with some of the ambulances, were ordered to Angoulême, a cathedral town not far from Cognac. I was to drive my own car, accompanied by Number 8 ambulance, but my unloved teammate was to remain in Paris. Her place was taken by another American woman, younger and more likable. My mother and the distant cousin were in the car with me, dressed in their Red Cross uniforms. They were auxiliaries sent to help the few qualified nurses the hospital in Paris had loaned us—most of them French women, some of whom had fled from French towns now occupied by the Germans.

Our convoy took more than six hours to get beyond Saint-Cyr, normally an hour's drive. Beyond that, the going was no less difficult because up north the Germans were moving closer to the capital, capturing every airfield to lengthen their flying range. Along the roads cluttered with troops, civilians in cars, wagons and baby carriages, the German Stukas swept down, machine guns stuttering, sirens wailing—a devilish assault that added to the terror and confusion of the refugees, many of whom had been on the road from northern France for days.

In this chaos, this spectacle of a defeated nation fleeing in panic, Mother suddenly remembered she had forgotten to lock the door of the apartment and began to bemoan the fate of her silver. Dulled by fatigue and horror, I snarled at her: "The world is dying—an epoch has ended—and all you can think of is your silver!"

I regret my words, for I'm sure now she was trying to blindfold herself in order not to see what was going on around us. On top of everything, and wildly incongruous in the circumstances, the two small dachshunds she had brought with her were ill. One died of a heart attack before long, and I was obliged to leave it in a ditch—a ditch where other animals had died. I don't remember seeing any human being there, only a worn-out horse, sides heaving, eyes glazing over, blood oozing from a gash in its shoulder.

In Angoulême the so-called hospital we were to take over was an abandoned school and unspeakably dirty, and it took several nights and days to get it clean enough to unload from the ambulance the equipment supplied by the American Red Cross. Set on a hill, it overlooked the road to Cognac and it was about half a kilometer from the center of the town.

In the beginning we all tried to believe that the miracle of the Marne would be repeated—that this time there would be a miracle of the Loire. In the end, when the trains started rolling in with the wounded, we were all too tired to think of anything—except a few hours' sleep, cleaning out the ambulance, grabbing scraps of food before rushing to the station to reload. In Paris we had been trained to wait for the stretcher-bearers. Now there was no question of that. The few we had were at the hospital helping with other chores. I think I grew up then, listening to the groans and screams of the men we sometimes mishandled, staring stony-eyed over my wheel as I dodged between refugees who were still fleeing southward among groups of demoralized soldiers throwing away their equipment. We were no longer behind the lines, but at the front.

Then, on June 25, in the long wooden hut partitioned by packing crates, one end occupied by the French nurses and the other by us, one of my comrades turned on her radio and a thin, sad voice said: "Français, je haie les mensonges qui vous ont fait tant de mal." Marshal Pétain, the victor of Verdun, was announcing the armistice.

Some of the off-duty nurses crowded in, and when the pathetic speech was over many of them burst into tears. Others glared at us. "If only America had come in, this would never have happened," they said in scorn. We were tired, taut. There was almost a fist fight, with some of our British colleagues joining in on our side.

After that, doctors and nurses slunk away, followed by the lightly wounded soldiers, the fortunate ones in cars, their tanks often filled with stolen gas, the others on purloined bicycles or on foot. I myself lost a reserve can of gasoline I had stashed away, and the doctor who stole it was quite frank about it. I was furious. But now, as I look back, what were a few liters of gasoline if they saved him from four years in a prisoner-of-war camp? At that time all sorts of rumors were flying about and no one really knew just how much of France was to be occupied.

When everyone who could leave had gone—including some of the more seriously wounded, who were miraculously evacuated in broken-down trucks—we were left alone with our American Red Cross equipment and ambulances. Alone to watch the last soldier straggle down the road, the last fleeing refugee hobble his way southward. Silence descended then—a great silence. After the chaos it was uncanny—as if the world was waiting on the brink of the great unknown. I decided to walk into the town. Yes, walk, because of the gasoline shortage.

As I rounded the corner of the hill leading up to the town, a motorcycle with a sidecar came slowly toward me.

For a second I was puzzled. I had never seen anything like it before—no vehicle I knew was painted such a drab blue-gray. But what surprised me most of all were the rider of the machine and the occupant of the sidecar. They were dressed from head to foot in sheaths of green and yellow and their faces beneath potlike helmets were masked by enormous goggles. They looked like men from Mars, but I knew they weren't. I'd seen those helmets before —in Berlin.

As I stared at them I can't say I particularly hated them or even felt any fear. No, at first I was only startled, perhaps even disappointed. I had never expected they would arrive in this silent, leisurely manner. Now, looking back, I can't see how they could have come any other way, certainly not with a blaring band. Maybe it was the ease with which they arrived, as if they were at home, that began to anger me.

I think it was this attitude of the German troops that in the end confirmed my hatred for them. Yet, in their tactless, oafish way they tried to gain the friendship of the population by helping old ladies across the roads and by carrying their shopping bags. (In those days there was still something to put in one.) I saw this occur several times, watching with a grin the expressions of amazement turn to alarm when the heel-clicking erupted like a rifle shot. Sometimes this startling noise went with a resounding, arm-outstretched "Heil Hitler!" The movement was so rapid that it was in its own way a miracle of co-ordination, and for four years never ceased to amaze me.

When the Germans finally allowed us to return to Paris and to keep our equipment, since it was the property of the American Red Cross, the journey was one of detours, burned-out villages, overturned civilian and military vehicles with their contents spilled, while over everything hovered the sweet, sickly smell of decay and death.

Because of all the detours, I ran out of gas in the town of Vendôme. At our departure the ambulance had been well supplied by the Germans, but they hadn't been so generous to the accompanying cars.

I came to a stop at the Kommandantur, located in the town hall and now sporting a huge swastika instead of the familiar tricolor, and I leaned on the horn.

"What shall I do?" I cried to my teammate as she came toward me from her ambulance.

"Go in and ask them. They're the lords and masters now," she answered, cocking a thumb at the building. "After all, they can't eat us. I'd give you some, but mine is almost all used up. Those damn detours! I wonder if it was the Germans or the French who blew up all the bridges over the Loire. Probably both. I'll come with you. Do you speak German?"

"A little," I replied, staring at the helmeted sentry standing in front of the door. "Supposing they won't let us in?"

"Tell them who we are—members of the American Red Cross. Maybe one day they'll need us. You never can tell. Come on. Let's go! And don't forget your mother and aunt are nurses—American nurses. The dog is the hospital mascot. Come on." And with that she ran up the steps with me tagging behind.

The sentry didn't stop us—merely continued to gaze out into space with a blank stare like a cigar-store Indian.

"Cute, isn't he! Full of expression too! I prefer Horse Guards. Never seen one without those fuzzy hats they wear," and then beneath her breath, "Wish I could see one . . . and now."

In the end, after much palavering, much scrutinizing of our papers and permits, two spare cans of gas were reverently pulled out of the town-hall safe. Had I dared, I would have burst out laughing.

When we got back to Paris, Mother found the apartment locked and the Germans in full charge. (We lived almost directly opposite the Hotel Majestic, which they had completely requisitioned.) And on the table in the hall we found a letter from my stepfather. He had left Paris to close the house in Brittany, but he had been unable to get though and had doubled back, only to take flight again in a car borrowed from the Rolls-Royce garage in Neuilly just before they shut down. Shortly before Orléans, the borrowed Rolls broke down and the luggage as well as some bibelots belonging to Mother had been looted by refugees.

In the occupied city, I went back to work at the American Hospital as a driver for the American Red Cross. There were few wounded to transport in those midsummer weeks of 1940 except those in isolated field hospitals in need of more sophisticated attention from Paris doctors. But on several occasions we were sent up to Château-Thierry and once we went as far south as Châteauroux, crossing the Loire on a pontoon bridge. That trip took us through the little town of Angerville, where my stepfather had parted company with the Rolls-Royce, and I stopped in at the Kommandantur to explain the situation to a very pleasant young German officer. He took me to an abandoned lot filled with cars.

"We saved it! We saved it!" he kept repeating to me in English, pointing to the once beautiful machine. "She is a mess inside and out. She will have to be towed back to Paris."

I wondered how I was going to find the gas to do this and told him so.

He shrugged his shoulders. "It's a beautiful car. Such a pity. Maybe your Embassy could help."

Some such solution must have been found, because the car was finally towed back to Paris and returned, much the worse for wear, to its rightful owner.

Just outside Angerville there was an airfield, built, I suppose, by the Germans. We were held up for a while by a military convoy and, as I wasn't driving, I had a full view of the planes and the surrounding woods. There were a lot of planes and I automatically began to count them until something strange in the way the sunlight hit them stopped me.

"Hey! Look at those planes!"

"Hell! I don't want to look! I've had all the planes I want—German or otherwise! Let's go! That military cop with his red disk is waving us on. I'll make my dinner date after all."

Later, just as we were entering the suburbs of Paris, she asked: "What's up? Worrying about the Rolls?"

"Yes, wondering how I can get it back." It was a lie. I was thinking of those planes. They had been wooden.

I slept on my problem and the next morning went to the Embassy to see a family friend, to whom I told my story.

He listened to me in silence, sometimes with a thoughtful smile. Oh, Lord, I thought, it's no good. We're neutral and the State Department wants us to remain that way. It's no good. He's just listening to me because he's a friend of the family.

Slowly, tactfully he moved me toward the door, but before he opened it he said: "Are you thinking of going home?"

"No."

"Pity. I think you should. Things are going to get rough. I won't forget what you've just told me." And patting me on the back, he dismissed me.

I couldn't have been the only one to notice the wooden planes beside a forest where the real ones had to have been hidden, but sometime after that Angerville was bombed by the RAF.

It was in the course of another trip that we came on freshly dug graves, French helmets stuck on rough crosses. Farther on we found hundreds of unopened letters with army postmarks. Most of them were too dirty and mildewed to read, and even if we had been able to post them it was unlikely they would reach their destinations. Postcards with just enough space for the briefest message were the only communication allowed now.

Here too I found in a trench a box filled with Croix de Guerre decorations. I remember fingering one, running it through my fingers, tears suddenly springing to my eyes. It was such a simple thing, just a badge for someone to wear all his life as proof of his courage. Now they were forgotten in the damp earth along with the men who might have worn them. I left them there with the mud-stained envelopes, the broken wine flasks. In time the ribbons would rot . . . unless the Germans found them first.

On the day I was sent alone to Compiègne—my co-driver was down with the grippe—the ambulance was loaded with medical supplies, blankets, canned foods and huge, round loaves of brown bread. My orders were to deliver them to a prisoner-of-war camp set up around the barracks on the outskirts of the town.

It was a sinister place and I knew because of the bread I was bringing that the departure of the prisoners for Germany must be imminent.

I was stopped at the gates; the German authorities said my papers were not in order and that I needed not only another permit but a German armed escort as well. Annoyed, I retraced my route and found the German headquarters, situated as usual in the town hall on a huge square completely empty of vehicles; not even a German one in sight.

It was a gray, damp, foggy morning with the first autumn chill in the air. It took some time to get my piece of paper duly typed and stamped with seals, the swastika emblem held in the claws or the beak—I can't remember which—of a hovering eagle.

When I came out, accompanied by a helmeted soldier with a rifle, and climbed up into the ambulance, a small German car filled with officers—a sort of bug-looking contraption—drove up beside us. In a way it reminded me of a Marx Brothers movie. One of them got out and marched over to me, pointing to a sign in French and German indicating that parking was forbidden.

I stared around at the empty square with an idiotic expression as he began to rave and rant. Finally I slipped the ambulance into gear and, as I pulled out, said in German: "Everything is always forbidden in Germany, but here we are still in France." In the rear mirror I could see him taking down my license number.

The camp was awful and I knew by the wan faces of the prisoners that many of them must be suffering from dysentery. The stench of bad drains and bad food hung over everything. The uniforms of the men were in tatters, and some of them hobbled around because their boots were either too small or too large. Only a few had overcoats; the others trailed over their shoulders torn and soiled khaki army blankets. The Germans in their clean green uniforms elbowed their way roughly among them.

When I drove in, the prisoners crowded around, yelling out questions, and when I jumped down, some of them surreptitiously shoved letters into my pockets. The guards drove them away and my iceberg escort suddenly came to life and pushed his way to the open doors of the ambulance. When I had left Paris I had thought I was well supplied. Now, looking around at the yelling men, I knew I'd brought chicken feed.

Suddenly a French officer appeared. Although he was unshaven, his uniform was still fairly clean. By the stripes on his sleeves and the red on his kepi I knew he was a medical captain. He began to speak in fluent German to the noncommissioned officer standing there, who in turn barked his orders to several of the nearest soldiers.

They started to unload while I stood by with the French officer at my side.

"We were expecting three ambulances," he said out of the corner of his mouth. "We have nothing. Many of the men are sick. The barracks are filled. Rumor has it some of us are leaving for Germany tomorrow. What's the news?"

"England is still fighting in spite of the blitz. And two months ago some French general in England called on every Frenchman to join him."

"Can't you remember his name?"

"No. I was only told about him. He calls himself the leader of the Free French. They beam a program over the air every night, but the Germans jam it. They've even forbidden the population to listen to the BBC. All the guns, even air rifles, have to be turned over to the local Kommandantur on pain of death. There's an eleven-o'clock curfew in Paris. I'm sorry there's only one ambulance. We're running low on stocks. They say an American Red Cross boat is expected in Marseille."

"It will be too late. They want us to die. I wish you could remember that general's name. We heard part of his speech over our radio before they smashed it. I'm always hoping for news from the townspeople here. We've tried talking to them through the barbed wire, but they hate us. Blame us for the defeat, and they're especially afraid because two men escaped last week and the villagers were held responsible. That's why you have a guard. I'm going to try and get away, but I don't know how. It's sure to be a long war. I have some letters. I'll fling them behind your seat. Will you post them?"

"Of course. But only if they're for the occupied zone."

"I know . . . I know . . . but you'll understand when you open the satchel. Look out! Move away. We're being watched."

I was tired that night when I finally turned into the Avenue Kléber on my bicycle; my car had long since been laid up and the only vehicles seen on the streets now were German. On the other hand, there were bicycles all over the place. It was quite a sight to see smartly dressed women of all ages peddling madly down the Champs-Elysées or across the Concorde. Everyone vied to have the smartest saddlebags and I know of one woman who sacrificed her horse's saddle to have a bicycle saddlebag made by Hermès. Her reasoning was simple: "Since they've taken my horse, of what use is the saddle now?"

When the Hotel Majestic was taken over by the Germans, all the streets leading to it were barred, including part of the Avenue Kléber. Our apartment lay in this zone, and every time we passed through this barrage of barbed wire we had to show a special pass. Needless to say, this discouraged many people, and they moved away. Mother was going to do the same as soon as she could find another apartment, but for the moment we were the only civilian residents left in the building and were completely surrounded by Germans.

As I peddled slowly home, beneath my tiredness, desire for a bath and a drink I was conscious of a nagging worry. What would be the result of my row with the German officer? It was so much on my mind I forgot the satchel of letters I had found squeezed behind my seat in the ambulance. Fortunately, the guard knew me and let me through without searching my saddlebags. It was only when I reached the foyer that I realized what a reckless fool I had been.

Naturally, the elevator was out of order and I had to trudge upstairs. Halfway up, the satchel burst open and all the letters fell out. I started to pick them up on my hands and knees, helped by an elderly German who had been coming downstairs—probably one of the secretaries whose clattering machines we could hear from our apartment. He worked very carefully, even making stacks of them and fastening them together with rubber bands. Thanking him profusely, I resumed my way, my heart hammering.

When I walked into the apartment, I heard loud voices in the salon. There, surrounded by German officers, sat my stepfather. I think I must have blanched, remembering my row of the morning.

"It's all right. Come in and have a drink," he said, starting to introduce me.

There were four of them, together with a painter friend of ours.

Without a word I turned and went out of the room, still clutching my satchel.

I found Mother in her bedroom lying down.

"This is an outrage! Isn't it bad enough having them in the same building?"

"They're friends of your father's."

"Friends!"

"*We're* not at war, darling."

I tried to explain my day to her. For a while she listened and then she began to cry.

I went into the bathroom to get a damp cloth for her eyes, and it was then that I saw it.

Swimming leisurely in the tub was a fish.

"What's that?" I shrieked, rushing back.

"It's only a carp, dear. The cook brought it from the market in a bucket. The fishmonger is closing down."

"And you propose to take a bath with that swimming around you?"

"No, no, of course not. Do sit down, dear. It makes me nervous watching you prowl around. I'll put it in the bidet."

And that's how I really started to live under the occupation: Germans in the salon drinking the last of the whiskey, my mother crying in anger, and a carp in the bathtub that we weren't yet hungry enough to kill.

2

Unlike American men, American women residents of France were not picked up to be interned until September 1942.

I was in the country at the time, although the German authorities had forbidden us to leave Paris. To enforce this regulation they made us sign our names once a week in a black ledger at the Commissariat of our quarter. How other residents living elsewhere handled this I don't know, but in our case the French police turned a blind eye if somebody else signed instead.

I returned to Paris as soon as I heard the news. Some friends were in touch with the American cousin who shared the smaller quarters we had rented after my stepfather left for the States, and from them I learned that the Germans had erupted into our apartment at six A.M. That was their customary time, and the number of people picked up at that hour for more dangerous offenses than being American doesn't bear thinking about.

Of course, we had been expecting them for some time, especially after the British women had been moved from their camp in Besançon to a larger camp at Vittel, where the famous spa had been cordoned off with barbed wire. Apparently Mother had behaved like a slighted queen or an avenging angel when they arrived, raising Cain in German, English and French because she would not stir without the cabin trunk she had packed with linen and blankets. The two minor Gestapo officials—the real thugs were reserved for more important matters—corraled two German soldiers innocently wandering down the street and managed to lug the trunk down six flights of stairs, with Mother traipsing behind dressed in boots and wearing every piece of warm clothing she possessed. How they wedged the trunk into a Citroën with Mother and the two Gestapo agents, I have no idea. But I was told people hung out of windows while passers-by stopped to watch.

I certainly had no intention of holing up in Vittel as an internee, and the obvious alternative was to head for the unoccupied zone. For ten days I was shunted from one friend's house to another, waiting until arrangements could be made for the false French identity card I would need, and although I was in good hands I was wretched. I was alone for most of the day because my friends worked, and I was forbidden to answer the doorbell or the telephone without a prearranged signal. My suitcase remained packed—including my toothbrush—in case I should have to make a run for it.

It was a very brave thing that these friends did. Giving shelter to a citizen of a country at war with Germany was a criminal offense carrying a prison sentence. It didn't carry the death penalty as did helping aviators who had been shot down, escaped prisoners of war or Jews, but once in the hands of the Germans one never knew when freedom would smile again.

Finally the day for my departure came. I was to go that evening, but I first had to take the gloss off my new French identity card, which I did by putting it in my shoe and striding around the apartment. My American passport, which I loved (and not only because of all the stamps and visas on it), was taken by a friend who promised to wrap it in oilcloth and bury it at her country house not far from Paris. When I gave it up I felt bereft.

I was to leave from the Gare d'Austerlitz. It was a lovely autumn evening, and as I stared around, taking in the smells and sights of the capital, I wondered bleakly when I would see it again. The two women who accompanied me were Red Cross drivers in uniform. Wedged between them and trying to look like a suitcase —my actual suitcase was to follow me later through an arrangement made with a railroad employee—my khaki army satchel slung over my shoulder, I waited near a ticket booth for another American girl, Renée, who had dodged being picked up by escaping through the tradesmen's entrance of her apartment house. We knew one another well—our parents had been friends in New York before we were born—and I'd heard that her mother and one of her sisters had not been so lucky, but that her father was free because he was too old for internment and her youngest sister was too young for it.

Renée turned up and we smiled ruefully at one another. After what seemed like a long wait—the hands of the clock creeping closer to departure time—our passeur arrived. I did not know then that it was advisable to board a train just before it pulled out so as to avoid last-minute inspection by German police.

The passeur was a woman named Minette. A schoolteacher, I believe, from a small town called Ruffec not far from the imposed armistice frontier, or ligne de démarcation. She had a pleasant, vivacious face, a short, stocky body, and no one could take her for anything but a country woman, especially as she spoke with the twang of the southwest. I wished I looked like her because I felt that I stuck out like a sore thumb—that no one could take me for anything but an American.

I had thought my friend Renée and I would be traveling alone, but this was not the case. Minette was escorting eight other people—all Jews. It was, of course, sheer folly, especially as among them were a very spruce elderly man and his overdressed, stout wife. Perched on her high heels, she looked like some exotic bird. She carried an umbrella and I think she wore a frilly hat. The two of them hardly looked prepared for a clandestine escape, and yet, listening to them talk in hushed voices, I thought they must be Dutch, which meant they'd already been in flight for some time and were now on their last lap to freedom.

They sat opposite me in the first-class compartment Minette had insisted on our taking while she traveled in third to watch over the rest of her charges. They made no attempt to speak to Renée and me. In fact, we all behaved as if none of us knew why we were there. It was just as well. I was in no mood for conversation. I wasn't afraid—I just felt lost, as if someone had punched me in the middle and left me in the roadway. I mistrusted my French identity card; I suspected it looked as phony as I did myself, and I was sure it would never stand up under questioning because my French was far from perfect. Indeed, if the truth must be told, it was lousy, not only because of my accent but because I'd never bothered to improve my vocabulary and would break into English whenever I was at a loss for a word. It had improved since America's entry into the war and my constant association with French friends, but I still had a long way to go before I could pass as a French girl. On top of all that, my physique had nothing French about it. I was too tall and my gestures were too brusque. Unlike Renée, who had been educated in France, I had been brought up first in Austria and then by an English governess, ending up in an English school.

No, there was nothing French about me. I would never get across the demarcation line. Somewhere along the way a gendarme or, worse still, a civilian in the pay of the Germans would stop me and question me, and I would have to give myself up and join Mother in Vittel. I ought to have done it in the first place. Our Embassy friend had been right. We should have gone back to the States.

From now on I would hang back from the others. That way I would be less trouble. Renée was sure to get through. And the others? They risked far more than I did. They would give a small fortune to be in my shoes—even in Mother's. Vittel was nothing compared to what awaited them. But what *did* await them? All we really knew was that they had been made to wear those yellow stars that set them apart like lepers from the rest of the population. At the start of the occupation there had been quite a few of them shuffling through the streets. After a while they only crept out at night before the curfew. Then one day they disappeared. Picked up. Women and children, the old and the young, thrust pell-mell into busses by rough soldiers using rifle butts . . . It was monstrous. If I hadn't seen it, I wouldn't have believed it.

I stared across at the two elderly representatives of this persecuted race and then turned away, embarrassed. The woman was quietly crying.

I closed my eyes. I didn't want her to know I had seen her. Besides, I think I was very close to tears myself. Would things ever be the same again? No, of course not. Partir, c'est mourir un peu. . . . I should have made Mother return to the States. I had been selfish . . . selfish. What a bitch . . . bitch . . .

I awoke to find Minette standing over me, tapping my shoulder; Renée was smiling at me.

The Dutch couple were on their feet, the woman fiddling with her numerous parcels while her husband lifted down two battered suitcases, in one of which something squeaked.

"We're arriving. You're to get off last," Minette said.

I never knew why she said this, but when the train came to a clattering stop, Renée and I watched her leave, the Jewish couple trailing behind her.

It wasn't until the last of the passengers had filed by our compartment that we stood up. As we headed for the door, I heard "Ruffec!" shouted down the line for the last time.

A long line of people was milling on the platform, eerie beneath the shrouded blackout lamps.

Suddenly someone shrieked, started to cry hysterically, pleadingly. Abruptly two German soldiers shouldered their way through the throng, thrusting people aside to make way for an officer and a plain clothesman dragging a woman between them.

"They've caught someone. It happens every time there's a contrôle," an elderly man muttered, glaring at me before scuttling away.

I looked around. On my right was the station, while to my left was the train, shadowy figures moving through it. I knew they were soldiers because the station lamps were reflected on their helmets.

Obviously, there was no help from that quarter.

I turned and looked behind as Renée watched. The line was moving faster. It worried me. Gradually I edged my way backward, creeping closer to the end of the station, hugging the shadows until I saw a low white fence with a flower bed planted in front of it.

Then I made a dash; Renée followed. In one bound we cleared the fence, but we weren't quick enough to escape the notice of two soldiers, who shouted and started after us.

Making the most of our head start, we ran until we came to a large open doorway flush with the street. Running in, we hid behind the door and listened to the Germans pelt by.

"We'd better not move," Renée whispered. "Why did you bolt?"

"Because of the controle. I don't trust my identity card."

We stayed there a long time, to let our eyes get accustomed to the darkness. We decided we were in a barn with piles of hay stacked on a sort of balcony or loft above our heads. Opposite us was a ladder, its rungs distinguishable in the lighter dusk coming from the street. I started to feel a tickling at the back of my nose and wondered how long I could keep from sneezing.

Suddenly we heard the Germans returning.

They came into the barn, talking angrily, and started to search it. One even climbed the ladder and prodded the hay, viciously driving his bayonet into it. Finally they left, without looking behind the door.

Although we knew we were safe, we still didn't stir. We didn't know where to go. I started to sneeze.

In the end Renée crept out and, at the back of the barn, discovered a door leading to a courtyard with the silhouette of a large house towering over it. Creeping toward this, we found an open window which we slid through, landing in a stone-flagged room with a thick door at the end of it—a splinter of light shining beneath it.

It was only by placing my ear against the keyhole that I could hear the murmur of voices beyond the door. At first I couldn't make out what they were saying because they all seemed to be talking at once. But finally I recognized Minette's voice and I lifted the latch. The door was locked. For a while we were stumped. Maybe there were Germans in there? We knocked softly, so softly that no one heard. We knocked again and this time there was a sudden lull in the conversation and the lamp was doused.

It was Minette who opened. To my astonishment, she was delighted to see us instead of being angry at our sudden flight. And she didn't seem surprised that we had miraculously stumbled on the right rendezvous. "Your scamper caused a diversion—no one was left at the contrôle!" she said. "Come with me!"

She led us to a bedroom where there was a double bed and a couch. A woman lay on the bed fully dressed. At our entrance she sprang to her feet in fright. Minette reassured her and she moved from the bed to the couch.

I fell asleep but not for long. Wondering what had awakened me, I listened. Everything was quiet, the silence pressing heavily on my ears. And then I heard it. Squeak . . . pause . . . squeak . . . pause . . . In regular intervals above my head. Where had I heard that noise before? I lay puzzled. Suddenly it stopped. Silence drifted back, but it was just as bad, the old story of the traveling salesman who drops one shoe before remembering the people on the floor below. A shoe! That was it! The train! The Dutch couple! The man reaching for the suitcases in the rack! But why weren't they sleeping? I began to stir, disturbing Renée, who whispered angrily at me. (I don't think she has forgiven me to this day.) After a while she dozed off again, but I was still awake when dawn clawed at the shutters.

Early in the morning Minette took us into a kitchen where a gray-haired woman offered us coffee—the customary brew of acorns that had replaced the real stuff and was the only thing we could obtain on our ration cards. I noticed it was better than usual and supposed it was because of the milk. It had been many months since I had tasted any. Thick, wonderful slices of bread lay on a plate beside a huge lump of butter, but we didn't dare help ourselves until the woman gestured toward it. Then we set to. And how good it was! I'll never forget that lump of butter. I've never tasted any like it since.

About ten Minette called Renée and me into the courtyard; somewhere she had managed to find bicycles. With a few provisions stuffed into our satchels, which in turn were stuffed into our saddlebags and then covered with baskets (my basket held a squawking chicken; Renée had its mate, a surly cock), we sallied forth, Minette leading the way. I don't remember what animal she had as camouflage.

I can't say I enjoyed cycling through the village. (In those days it was only that.) As I recall, the main street was macadamized and a crowd of villagers mingled with Germans around the market place. Head down, I stared at the back wheel of Minette's bicycle, praying no one would notice us.

Presently we left the main road and bowled along a hedge-lined dirt lane which led to a farmhouse. There we left our traveling chicken coops in the hands of a fat woman who barely looked at us.

Although it was October it was still warm and soon we were hot and thirsty. I was just beginning to think we would never get to where we were supposed to go when we turned down a cart track and stopped in a copse.

"Stay here out of sight until nightfall. Don't move. The Germans aren't far. Two men will come later to guide you over the line," Minette said cheerily. Then she vanished.

For a while we slept. It was the mosquitoes that woke us, swooping down like a squadron of Spitfires. For a time we resisted them, but the more we killed the more there were. In the end we smoked, hoping no German was near enough to smell us. Afterward we took out our provisions. To our amazement, there were hard-boiled eggs, ham, cheese and a bottle of wine. We hadn't seen so many goodies in a long time.

We slept again and this time when we awoke the sun was slanting through the trees. It was evening.

I suggested that one of us crawl out to look around, but Renée was against it. And she was right, because a little later we heard a car moving at low speed. Of course, it could have been a doctor, but I didn't think so. It was probably the Germans—Minette had said the line wasn't far. Maybe they were patrolling the road. Hurriedly, I drew the bicycles farther into our shelter.

Slowly darkness fell and with it the mosquitoes vanished. Somewhere a train hooted. It could have been anywhere. Sounds travel strangely at night.

We started to worry. Had we been abandoned? Maybe everyone had been arrested? Maybe the car we had heard had been carrying our fellow fugitives back to Ruffec? Where was Ruffec? About fifteen kilometers . . . ? We had cut across so many lanes and roads that long before reaching the copse I had lost my sense of direction. We argued over this in whispers but without conviction. In the end we fell silent. I felt beaten. Frightened, too. No maps. Nothing. We were lost. Abandoned.

I soon found myself starting at every noise. Even the tick-tock of my watch sounded loud. I looked down at it and saw it was past ten. It was then that I made up my mind we would have to do something. But what? Suddenly a screech owl dived from the tree above us, reminding me of the Messerschmitts during the fall of France. Then came the dying scream of its victim.

I don't know what time it was—at that point I forgot to look at my watch—when we heard footsteps coming down the lane. I stiffened. Renée put her hand up to her mouth. The night bird flapped away.

Suddenly a torch flashed, blinding us. When it was switched off, two men were there. We scrambled to our feet.

They didn't say anything—just stared at us. Finally one gestured to us to pick up our stuff. While we did this he flashed the torch low on the ground. When we finished, still without a word he beckoned us to follow him.

We walked for ten minutes in silence. Once Renée stumbled against me and muttered: "Talkative, aren't they!"

Suddenly the man ahead crouched down while the one behind shoved me in the small of the back. I turned on him resentfully, but he merely motioned to me to do likewise.

For a while we crawled and I was grateful for the woolen stockings my friends in Paris had made me wear. Still, I couldn't help wondering how long they would last.

Abruptly we stopped behind a hedge.

"They're over there," the man in front whispered, peering over the hedge. "Don't stumble any more."

I tried to get a glimpse of his face, but all I could see was the back of his head. I turned my attention to the other one and got a shock. His face was hatchet sharp, and with a corner of his sheep-lined duffel coat pulled up, he looked like someone out of a gangster movie.

When we started to move again, we headed away from the direction our guide had been staring in and, crouching, advanced across an open space. It must have been well past midnight when we finally reached a building silhouetted against the night sky. Its wooden doors were padlocked and one of the men drew out a key . . . turning the well-oiled lock easily. They pushed us inside.

Suddenly I heard screams. By the light of a storm lamp set between the shafts of a haycart I saw six figures in every stage of dishevelment. Amazed, I stared and started to sneeze. Then I focused on the source of the screams until my eyes caught sight of a round alarm clock carefully placed on the seat of the haycart. I giggled, sneezed again and then giggled some more. These Jaz clocks were the ugliest, most efficient, noisiest instruments ever invented by a clockmaker.

The six figures proved to be the Jews Minette had escorted down from Paris. They were all there except the Dutch couple. I don't know how they had reached the barn, but they were indignant about the way they had been treated. I was too, but I consoled myself with the thought that all Renée and I risked was internment in Vittel. I hated myself for thinking this, but I couldn't help it, and I fell asleep on a pile of hay still thinking it.

I awoke early—very early—to the sound of the alarm clock, and by the light creeping under the door and through the roof I saw that the clock was blue. I've wanted one ever since, but I'm afraid that model has long since ended up in a trash heap. Pity.

I went over to the door. It was locked. This was getting worrisome.

Renée joined me, picking hay out of her hair. "I heard the men say they had to lock it because of the farmer. But the door on the other side is open, and there's a brook nearby. We're to be careful if we go there."

"Why?"

"The Germans are close."

"But I thought we were over the line."

She shrugged. "Only just. They're coming back tonight."

"Christ! More than twenty-four hours to cover a few kilometers!"

We stayed in the barn all that day except once when I went out a cobweb-covered door I'd discovered. I had seen a woman passing through the yard with a pail of milk, but when I asked her for some she walked by me without a word. Later I heard the door being boarded up. Everyone had provisions and we all shared them, but none of us had water and long before nightfall we were thirsty.

Toward evening we started taking turns peering through the slits of the door that looked out on the brook. I could see a steep embankment leading down to a small, meandering stream. Beyond it were clumps of poplars. In normal times I would have found the scene charmingly bucolic, but since we had only a limited view we worried about what might lie right and left of it. Once I thought I saw some figures through the trees, but since I wasn't sure, the only result was a nagging worry and I wished I hadn't mentioned it. Shortly after seven I slipped out, hugging the shadow of the barn, two canteens draped around my neck. I lay still for a time, surveying the lie of the land and whispering to the others a report of what I saw.

The barn was next to a road; a stone bridge crossed the stream. Beyond were woods, while on the other side were fields in which cows were lying. Since we were on top of an embankment, once I got down to the water no one could see me except from the road and the bridge.

"Keep watch while I go down. Whistle if you see anything," I said to Renée.

I filled three canteens before I saw anyone. When I did I was on my last trip. I saw the two men before Renée did, which was just as well because the gurgle of the water would have drowned out her whistle. I flung myself flat, face hidden between two rocks. And how I wished the rocks were larger, for both men were in uniform—one in the blue of a gendarme, the other in feldgrau —the Germans' field-gray.

I lay there for what seemed hours while my hands began to get cramped from lying in the water clutching the canteen. I didn't want to relax my grip and let the thing float away and strike the rocks.

It did indeed seem like hours. I tried to think of other things —of happier times before the world went awry. But thinking of them only made me wonder if I would be shot at. No, they'd hold me for interrogation. What would happen to the Jews if I talked? Of course, there was only one canteen. I could say it was mine —that I had stopped for water while waiting for nightfall before crossing the border on my own. Why hadn't those gangsters taken us directly to the nearest railroad station as had been agreed in Paris? God, but my hands were cold! This stream must come from the North Pole! Would those men never go away! What could they be talking about? The German laid down his rifle and was handing over a package. Black market! Cigarettes against brandy! That was it! Black market! Would they never go?

Suddenly I felt the canteen slipping from my fingers, heard it scraping, bumping against the rocks. The men looked up. One came toward the bridge parapet. I no longer felt my hands, which I dared not pull out of the water. Instead, goose pimples broke out over my body, while my face, still pressed between the rocks, felt hot.

"Wer gehst da?" the German called.

Damn fool! Did he think I'd answer?

"Nix—rien," the gendarme cut in. "Probably an animal."

After that their voices became a murmur, finally dying away with their footsteps.

I was so relieved I was almost in tears when I returned to the barn.

It was dark when we heard the padlock turn. Someone flashed a torch. It was the Dutch couple—the woman exhausted and on the verge of hysteria. Like us, they were shoved in without a word of explanation.

We were now ten—ten frightened, frustrated people.

Renée and I tried to figure out what was happening and what we should do. We were stumped. I started to feel more and more like a squirrel on a treadmill and finally buried my face in my coat to hide my tears.

Suddenly the door opened again and this time three men entered carrying a storm lamp.

While the others were firing questions, I examined them, deciding I had never seen three more unpleasant characters. Then, to my amazement, the one who had led us the night before (I recognized his voice) told Renée and me to gather up our things. When we asked why, he said we were the only ones he was going to take.

"We don't go without the others," I snapped.

"You have no choice."

"We're Americans. All we risk is internment. We'll give ourselves up and when we're interrogated we'll tell them everything."

The man stepped forward and I thought he was going to strike me. I wondered how I would stand up to that. To my surprise, I felt everybody solidly behind me.

Of course the long and short of it was money—more of it.

"We'll discuss that when you've taken all of us," I retorted, turning back to the others, who were already beginning to collect their possessions.

The crossing was a nightmare, chiefly because of the Dutch couple. Renée and I straggled behind, helping the woman. It wasn't so much her parcels that slowed our progress as her pace. Obviously, she wasn't accustomed to walking anywhere but on a sidewalk, and her shoes did nothing to help matters. At one moment she lost one, and while her husband put down his suitcases to look for it, Renée and I held her up; she looked rather like a fat cow trying to give birth to a reluctant calf. I remember her crying a lot and fiddling with her umbrella. Now, I've always thought these things the most stupid instruments ever invented by mankind—the most stupid and the ugliest—but that Dutch woman's umbrella was the most hellish of all umbrellas. Even unopened, it somehow impeded our progress almost as much as her parcels, which Renée and I had managed to drape around ourselves.

The passeur drove the pace mercilessly, so that we three were frequently far behind and I was obliged to prod the woman, sometimes even kicking her. Renée and I were both coldly angry and utterly exhausted; left to ourselves, we would have lain down in a copse to wait for daylight.

The end came just when I knew we could go no farther. By then we were dragging the woman.

The end was a macadamized road and blessed oblivion in a loft filled with hay. We climbed a ladder to it, but how the woman made it I don't know. I suppose her husband helped her since he could now lay aside his suitcases.

I awoke late, and as I looked around at all my people—yes, my people because, willy-nilly, I felt responsible for them—I felt proud, happy. We'd made it! At least, I hoped so.

To my surprise, Renée was awake—to my surprise because until now she had seemed to have a capacity for sleep which I envied.

"Don't make any noise," she whispered. "Crawl over to the edge and look." When I did I saw that in our exhaustion we had gone up not only one story, but two.

Normally, I would have hated looking down such a drop. But this time the spectacle below was so amazing it drove away my fear of heights.

Below us, at the foot of the stairs, was a room with tables, chairs and a zinc bar. Leaning against this were two gendarmes, drinking and talking to one of our passeurs, who was now acting as barman.

I crawled back.

"Well, what do you think?"

I was too shaken to answer.

"Well?" Renée persisted.

"I don't know. I don't know," I answered miserably. And I had slept thinking we were safe!

"We must be in a bistro. In any case, we're across. Maybe we should give ourselves up."

"Don't be a fool! Let's wait and see."

And wait we did, until noon, with me gnawing my nails in an

effort to forget how much I wanted to go to the bathroom.

At noon two of our lovable passeurs climbed up the ladder. Staring at us contemptuously, they demanded money. The sum made us gasp.

"Why do you want more money? We're in the unoccupied zone," someone said. I think it was the Dutchman.

"You're between the two zones, and according to the armistice terms, the gendarmes are obliged to hand you back to the Germans."

"A sort of no-man's-land," I suggested in the mildest tone I could muster.

"Yes."

"You were paid to take us to the nearest railroad station," I said. "Nothing was said about this."

"It's only since last week that the clause was put into effect. Three gendarmes were arrested because of Jews."

"Even if we give you the money, how will you get us to the station?"

"I have a truck, but you'll have to pay for the gas."

"And where do you expect to find that?"

"I'll buy it. The Germans barter theirs against other things."

Behind me everyone was arguing. The price was, of course, outrageous and I was sure most of my companions couldn't pay it. I knew I couldn't.

"How about some food?" I suggested amiably. "Warm food might help," I said, while Renée eyed me warily. I wished I could reassure her.

The man stared at me. His companion rubbed his chin. It made a horrible scraping sound. Finally he shrugged, and presently we filed down the ladder through the bar into another room, low-raftered and filled with tables. Obviously, we were in an inn. Probably a black-market restaurant where no food coupons were required.

When I entered, the first thing I saw was an old fly-stained map hanging on the wall. I made straight for it, but before I could reach it one of the men barred my way, shouting to his companion to take it down.

I was furious and raised my hand. He grabbed it and guided me firmly to the center of the room where the others were already seated.

The meal was delicious and not only because we were hungry, but because the fish and meat which followed the thick vegetable soup were food of a sort we had not seen for a long, long time. We devoured it silently and it wasn't until we had finished that we started discussing our situation.

I was for giving a quarter of the sum and so was Renée, but the others were all against it and I can't say I blamed them. Except for the Dutch couple, Renée and myself, they looked like simple people. God, how I hated those gangsters! I was also starting to have my suspicions concerning Minette. Something of my fury must have shown on my face, for the chief passeur, sitting at a table near us nursing a bottle of wine, rose and called to someone at the back of the room.

Presently a young chap entered with a shotgun. I'd never seen him before.

Drawing up a chair opposite me, he sat with the gun cradled between his legs as he slowly rolled a cigarette.

Our arguing came to an end.

I asked the woman who had waited on us for the bill. She was a silent creature whom I guessed to be the mother of the shotgun individual as well as the wife of the chief passeur.

"We'll divide," I murmured. No one disagreed.

To my surprise, it came to very little. In any case, I wouldn't have cared one way or the other because on the slip of paper, printed in indelible ink, was an address.

Back in our loft, we argued with the two men, or rather I let the others argue. Instead, I smoked, my feet dangling into space. My attitude obviously puzzled the men because until then I had been the spokesman for the fugitives. Renée ignored me pointedly. She and I had hastily hatched up a scheme between our retiring to a filthy lavatory and climbing back up to the loft. I would let everyone argue themselves to exhaustion before I said anything.

I had time for two cigarettes before things started getting out of hand. The passeurs were turning mean, sticking to their ridiculous price and using insulting language which reduced two of the women to tears and the Dutch woman once more to hysteria.

Carefully stubbing out my cigarette, I stood up. Pretending great calm, which I was far from feeling, I said: "We'll give you half the price. Not one franc more and only when you've delivered us to the nearest station."

"Yes. That's reasonable!" the Dutchman exclaimed, patting his fat wife.

"*I* give the orders here," growled the passeur I had seen behind the bar.

"Not any more you don't."

He shrugged. "You can't do anything. You don't even know where you are."

I tried to smile, but I'm sure it was only a grimace.

"I've already told you that my friend and I are Americans. We don't risk a thing—either from the gendarmes or the Germans. But you do. Plenty. If you turn us over to the authorities, we'll tell them you practice extortion. This bistro—" and I named it —"will then be shut and your family will go to jail."

After that it was easy. In a very short time we were loaded into a canvas-covered truck. As we drove away I felt pity for the owner's wife, but only because she was such a good cook!

3

I was in Mougins above Cannes when the North African landings took place. But when the Germans invaded the whole of France, remaining with my hosts—friends of friends of mine—seemed too much of an imposition, so I decided to go to Lyon, where Renée was.

When I arrived I saw dismay written on her face. My heart sank. I wasn't wanted by anybody but the Germans.

"Why didn't you stay South?" she demanded.

I explained wearily, but as I talked I saw a strange expression in her eyes. I stopped in the middle of a sentence.

"Your French has improved. What have you been doing?"

"Reading out loud—listening to myself, correcting the broad a's—rolling my r's."

"You've done pretty well, but if you really want to pass as a French woman, don't barge into people's houses demanding a bath. Wait until it's offered. Baths are a luxury with the gas and electricity cuts."

"I hope I didn't take someone's turn."

"Yes, mine. I won't give you any more of my soap, though."

We laughed.

The soap situation was just as bad as the food problem, for it too was rationed. I don't think anyone who has lived through the occupation will ever forget the small, leaden cakes we were generously allowed once a month. The soap was a dirty gray color, packed with sand, clay and some chemical substance supposed to do the cleaning but it rarely did unless you were willing to take your skin off in the process. Like everything else, it could be obtained on the black market and once I bought a couple of cakes obviously made by the Germans because they were embossed with the swastika. Since they were of better quality, I scrubbed the emblem off onto my skin and regretted that my finances hadn't allowed me to buy more!

"What do you intend to do now?"

"Go to England."

"And how do you expect to do that?"

"By returning to Paris."

"You've lost your sense of direction—forgotten your geography! The Pyrenees lie south."

"And I suppose you expect me to stand there in front of them crying 'Open Sesame! Stand aside, crags and valleys! Here I come!' "

"And you think you'll find a way in Paris?"

"Yes."

And because I believed this I returned to Paris.

Through relatives of Renée's future husband I was given an address in Châteauroux where I might contact someone who in turn would take me—rather like an animated parcel—into the occupied zone. Yes, the occupied zone because, in spite of the occupation of all France, a German permit was still needed to pass from one zone to another. The Germans continued to require this for months, either from habit or viciousness, in order to make traveling as complicated as possible. Personally, I thought—but much later—that it was done to give their Gestapo agents—French and German—time to take up their positions and infiltrate their spies among the population.

I was received with suspicion at the house in Châteauroux, and rightly so. But in the end I was taken to the station and left in a hut near a freight yard.

Night was falling and it was bitterly cold. After a while a cheminot—a railroad worker—poked his head through the door to tell me he would fetch me around ten and not to stir until then.

As proof of his friendliness—which I wouldn't have doubted anyway because of the grin which flashed from his soot-stained face—he left me some wine and food and told me to light a small brasero with some kindling and coal. The coal was soft stuff that smelled abominably. Still, it warmed up the place, and since there were drafts everywhere, I was saved from the poisonous fumes.

He returned shortly after ten just as I was starting to look anxiously at my watch. I followed him out, stumbling over railroad tracks and cross ties. Finally, he helped me to climb onto an antiquated freight car with a sort of sentry-box contraption at one end of it. What purpose this served I don't know, but it was equipped with an iron wheel on top of a pole which jutted out of the floor, and there was a wooden seat behind it.

Seated on this, I crossed the two zones once more, loving every moment of the chugging journey in spite of the freezing temperature.

Somewhere in the early hours of the morning we stopped and my cheminot suddenly appeared, rather like a jack-in-the-box. He told me to get down. Speechless from cold, I stumbled after him, clambering over steel girders and old tracks, crouching between freight cars to avoid a German patrol searching for clandestine passengers. My memory of that trip is of stark, raw beauty enhanced by moonlight playing with deep shadows.

When I was settled again in a hut only a little less cold than the outdoors, he handed me a cracked mirror and a towel of dubious cleanliness and motioned to a bucket of water.

Standing next to the storm lamp he lit, I stared at my reflection and burst out laughing. My face was black.

We stayed there for quite a while drinking coffee—the real stuff—which he told me proudly he had stolen from a German freight car going south. We laced it with brandy—from the same source—and we were soon warm. My young-old man—it was difficult to know his age because of his soot-encrusted face—told me this was his last trip, that he was joining his family in Savoie. When I asked him why, he shrugged.

"You can't go on forever! I'll be caught one day and that won't do my brother any good."

"Your brother?"

"He's a prisoner in Germany. I send as much as I can. But with my nest egg now I'll return to the farm to help my mother for the duration." And leaning over, he offered me a cigarette—a German one.

A thief! That's what he would be called. But was he? Had he been stealing from freight trains all his life? I didn't care and in any case it didn't matter. He was taking what belonged to him—to every Frenchman. Relieving the victors of their spoils was his way of loving his brother and proving his hatred for the occupiers of his homeland.

"They're fools! They haven't a chance against the Russians and the Americans," he said, staring at me.

"Not a chance," I replied calmly. "How much do I owe you?"

"Nothing. It's my last trip. At five I take a new lot of freight back to Châteauroux. After that—pfft! I'll wake you when I leave and show you how to get to the station. There's an express for Paris at six." And with that he threw me a tattered blanket and doused the lantern.

I was sleeping soundly when he woke me some hours later with a tepid cup of coffee.

"It's four thirty! It's four thirty!" he said, shaking me, his breath steaming in the light of the lantern. "There's a bus on the square at five thirty. Mingle with the people when they get off it. In that way you won't be noticed if there are any Germans. There's a fire in the waiting room. It's very cold. Let's hope the latrines are frozen."

"Latrines?"

"Yes. Stand in the shelter of them until the bus arrives. They stink."

"How will I find them?" I asked, suddenly frightened at the thought of being once more on my own.

"By the smell."

"But if they're frozen?"

"The smell never freezes. Just follow your nose."

And that's just what I did shortly after five. Fortunately, I didn't have long to wait because it wasn't cold enough to freeze the latrines! In fact, I heard the water gurgling quite happily and I gagged. The mixture of tepid coffee laced with brandy on an empty stomach wasn't settling the way it should. But I forgot all that when the bus showed up.

I could hear it coming from a long way off, for gone were the days of silent engines. This thing was a wood-burning terror with a boiler fitted on one side of it. Chugging and rattling through the sleeping town, it arrived in front of the station trailing sparks in its wake.

These contraptions were called gazogenes, and when they worked they were fine, noisy things, startling not only humans but the animal population as well. But because they were temperamental they occasionally exploded; as a result, whatever you did —riding or just standing beside them—was something of a risk.

In the stove-heated waiting room, I fell asleep and dreamed I was back in my Latin class with two pet white mice. Poor Miss Chism! Her shrieks had been shrill. After that I was dispensed from Latin, which was just what I wanted. Amo, amas, amamus . . . I once had a boyfriend who quoted Virgil after making love. I never gave him the chance to do it again!

I awoke with a start, hearing something about an ear. It took me some seconds to realize it was *my* oreille that was being talked about. This was especially surprising as under my nose was a bréviaire with lovely Gothic characters. I was in the arms of a curé.

"Votre oreille, Madame. It's very dirty."

Dirty ears! Me? I sat up and stared at a rotund little man with a jolly face and pop eyes like a fish. I suppose his soft, round figure was the reason I had slept so well. But dirty ears . . . My God! Coal dust!

He was right, of course. Not one but both my ears were filthy. Retiring hastily to an equally dirty washroom, I scrubbed them with ice-cold water, which drove away the last vestiges of sleep. Afterward I washed my handkerchief without any soap. This froze my hands. No wonder we had chilblains in those days.

"Thank you, mon père," I said later, shoving my damp handkerchief into my suitcase and taking out another one. "Forgive me for leaning on you."

"That's all right. Have you your ticket, my child?"

"No."

"I'll get it when I get mine. We're so near the zone a pass is needed. My cassock helps all kinds of sinners."

Three hours later I was in Paris. The capital was grim and silent, shivering with cold and hunger under a gray sky. As I drove through it on a sort of rickshaw, pulled by a muscular gentleman on a bicycle, I saw long queues of drab people standing in front of food shops. The only cars were German, and crossing the Concorde and looking up the Champs-Elysées was like looking at a familiar yet unfamiliar portrait which a giant hand had pushed out of perspective. It was heart-rending, but never had the city seemed so beautiful. With no hoots from irritated taxi drivers, no dodging between busses, it seemed to sleep under its gray sky while its gray, down-at-heel inhabitants shuffled along indifferently between groups of feldgrau soldiers and officers in steel-gray coats falling to their heels.

I stayed a week in Paris, avoided by people I had thought were friends, helped by others and finally succored reluctantly by one in whose friendship I had had the utmost confidence. Looking back now, it reminds me of the hand-washing of Pontius Pilate. Somewhere then the realization of what fear can do to people—even those I had thought fearless and above reproach—stirred within me like an evil thing. The Gestapo was knocking at doors daily, arresting, taking hostages anywhere, everywhere, in the Métro, in the cinemas, along the streets. Lightning raids struck at any time and the word "rafle" became a synonym for fear, uncertainty. Yet most of the citizens stood together, slinking down side streets to give warning of where the raids were taking place, shouting from their bicycles: "Rafle, Rue X!"

At the end of a week my friend decided to send me to Rouen, where someone knew someone who knew of someone who might be in touch with another someone who could get me to England! To explain my presence in a city so near the coast, I was secretly enrolled in a French ambulance section commanded by a girl younger than myself, who had found the courage to bypass the Paris office whose screening I might not have survived because of my accent and identity card. I met this girl for the first time on the platform of the Gare Saint-Lazare, picking her out of the crowd because of her uniform. I too was in uniform—my American hospital outfit with all the tabs off—and I prayed all the way down that this unknown person in contact with some other unknown person would materialize as soon as possible.

Since the start of the war Rouen had suffered greatly from bombardments, first by the Germans during the lightning war of 1940, and afterward by the RAF and the American Flying Fortresses. All the quarter lying near the docks along the Seine was flattened, but most of the population had refused to leave. They lived without any sanitary facilities in cellars and in hovels made from blackened beams and planks. As there were no streets, wooden signs stuck on piles of rubble read: "The Dupont family live past the pump next to the old stove. Don't lean on or displace the beams!"

This was Rouen in 1942, but the city which had burned Joan of Arc was really only starting its long agony and what I saw was just the beginning. When the end came after June 1944, more than three thousand lay dead in its rubble, thirty thousand were homeless, ten thousand houses destroyed, two churches reduced to dust and fourteen other churches and monuments severely damaged—the whole surrounded by a hundred and forty acres that had been completely leveled.

The office of the ambulance unit was in the garage which housed the fire engines. It was a poky little place with just enough space for a desk, two chairs and a couch propped up on bricks. On the wall was a telephone connected to the town hall. Next to it, a map of the city stuck with different-colored flags indicated the whereabouts of each ambulance.

We were lodged by the municipality in an apartment on the other side of town behind the Place du Vieux Marché, where Joan of Arc was reputed to have been burned. Every time I crossed this square it reminded me of Mother—not because she had been burned, but because of La Couronne, the famous restaurant. She had loved it and often driven down from Paris for a meal with visiting Americans. Now it was frequented only by Germans—high-graders with their mistresses, collaborators and their sleazy accomplices.

Our job consisted in driving the sick and the old to and from the hospitals and in picking up the wounded and dead during air raids.

On one occasion we evacuated a lunatic asylum located near two freight yards that were targets of the Allied bombers. Two of the largest ambulances were set aside for this job and I was in one of them, but not as the driver. I suppose I had been chosen because I was the strongest of the six girls who composed the section. Four women from the asylum were assigned to our ambulance, and like lost creatures from another world they stumbled inside, dressed in sacklike dresses that reached the floor, and staring wide-eyed, touching everything and then springing back as if expecting to be hurt. I helped one of them because she seemed more lost than the others, but when I touched her arm she started to whimper. It was like trying to succor a wounded animal. In the end she crouched by my feet, fingering, with soft cries, the material of my uniform.

Before leaving, a pair of handcuffs were thrust upon me by one of the sisters in charge of the asylum. I stared at the things in dismay, wondering what I was supposed to do with them.

At first everything was all right and my uneasiness disappeared. They were nothing but four harmless creatures in a world of their own. Yes, everything was all right, until the air-raid sirens started to wail. Then all hell broke loose. The gentle creature crouching beside me sprang to her feet shrieking, knocking me sideways so that my helmet rolled away to be pounced upon by her companions. I tried to grab it, but I had to defend myself from her flailing arms. I finally remembered the handcuffs and tried to catch her; by then she was spitting and frothing at the mouth.

I think I started to yell, but my voice was drowned out by the clump of falling bombs and the explosions of anti-aircraft guns. At one point my face was lashed by a fingernail and I felt the taste of blood. I lunged with my fist and—more out of luck than anything else, because the ambulance was plunging and bouncing all over the road—caught her on the side of the jaw. To my amazement, she went limp, rather like a deflated balloon. Quickly I slipped one of the rings of the handcuffs over a bony wrist, snapping the other to one of the ceiling hooks for the stretchers.

After that I turned my attention to the others. One had fainted and was lying huddled in a corner while the two others were fighting over my helmet. The strongest finally captured it and began to gnaw it like a dog with a bone. The other watched her with a sly expression, a small pool of urine dribbling down beneath her long dress.

I pulled away, stanching my cheek, while out of the corner of an eye I watched the handcuffed one coming around, her free arm flailing like a windmill. I moved out of her reach, but there isn't much space in an ambulance, and as she regained consciousness, her twisting, squirming body obliged me to duck. I wondered how long the hook would hold and what would happen when she got free. Those handcuffs would then become more dangerous than the bombs falling outside. Finally I crawled into the corner near the woman who had fainted. To my astonishment, she was stiff. I thought she was dead. I began to bang against the partition nearest the driver, but I had to make a hell of a racket before the girl who was driving heard me.

"Can't stop!" she shouted. "Hang on! We're almost there!"

And hang on I did because there wasn't anything else I could do.

The bolt on the ceiling gave way and I started to get ready for another onslaught. Suddenly we stopped and the doors of the ambulance were wrenched open and I fell into the arms of a German male nurse.

"Terrible . . . Terrible la guerre!" he exclaimed later, in the small room where he was dressing the cut on my face while my boss hovered over me. I knew it wasn't my face that was bothering her but my contact with the German, and I smiled at her reassuringly, knowing I had nothing to fear from this man with his bullet head and china-blue eyes. He was only an elderly minor member of the Wehrmacht medical corps and to him I was only a French woman and the French were defeated.

With this thought I started to thank him. Suddenly the door opened and a man in a doctor's white coat entered, followed by an officer in uniform. I stared across at him and stiffened. He had black tabs on his collar and a big swastika armband.

SS! What was he doing here? My dressing was finished and my dull-witted German was ill at ease. Watching his fingers clumsily packing away his cotton wool and iodine, I knew he longed to be gone. What a fool! What a weak fool! Why didn't they do something—get rid of these smooth thugs? Easier said than done, a voice whispered within me. But what was the SS man doing here, talking in a low voice to the doctor? Suddenly a thought struck me—a horrible thought. They liquidated the insane! I had nothing to fear. I could leave. They wouldn't even notice my departure.

I crept away with the stolid German, hating him but myself even more.

Outside I grabbed the arm of my companion.

"What do you think we can do?" she snarled, shrugging me off.

She was right, of course, but for days every time I felt the scratch on my face I remembered those poor, demented creatures. Then, after a time, I lost my sense of guilt, even the contempt I felt for myself.

Old Norman houses with their overhanging beam-raftered façades are beautiful to look at. Nice to photograph but not to live in. The twisting stairs are so narrow it's impossible to get a stretcher up them.

One day my co-driver and I were called to one of these four-hundred-year-old houses to fetch a man who had died. The proprietor wanted his body removed. Normally speaking, an undertaker would have done this, but the man was a pauper—in fact, he had died of starvation. We were assigned the task because the trucks and fire engines were elsewhere.

The man was old, tall and smelled—not yet of decay, but of age, dirt and hunger. Yes, hunger because this too, like everything else, carries an odor—a sour, fetid smell. It was bitterly cold in the room under the eaves. He was dressed in a pair of thin trousers with a turtleneck sweater, stiffly seated at a plain deal table, head down on his arms.

My co-driver and I tried every possible way to unfold the stretcher, but all to no avail. It simply wouldn't shrink and the stairs wouldn't widen, and in the end I carried the corpse slumped over my shoulder. I wish I could say I felt pity or chagrin for the old man who had died in that cold, cold room alone and unmourned in a house that had been a tourist attraction, but I think I was starting to lose my sense of feeling. The memory of him lingers, though. It doesn't haunt me. I just remember him and try to console myself by thinking that remembering him is worth as much as a first-class funeral. In any case, maybe his dignified, lonely end was better than lying wounded beneath the house after a bombardment.

One noon, when all the others had gone to lunch and I was on duty with a girl named Bridget, the telephone rang.

She answered and her protests stirred me from a book I was reading between nibbles at a butterless sandwich.

"It's impossible, Madame. We cannot come without an order from the police. Impossible." And she put down the receiver rather sharply.

It was so unlike her to be jolted out of her customary placidity that my curiosity was aroused. Setting aside my habit of keeping to myself, I asked what it was about.

"Some woman has a sick person on her lawn and wants him removed."

"Lawn?" the word sounded strange in this bombed city.

"She seems hysterical, but the words came strong and clear. The police station doesn't answer and she thinks we're the fire brigade."

"Well, we're in their garage! I'll see if anyone is around."

When I returned a few minutes later, she was again on the telephone.

"We'll have to go. She sounds desperate—elderly, too. She could have a heart attack if something isn't done."

Well, we went. As it wasn't far, no one could upbraid us for wasting gasoline. It was also in a quarter untouched so far by any bombings.

The house was a big place with a many-paned façade. In its day it must have been nice. Not a château or a manor—just high middle-class. It sat back surrounded by trees with a badly kept lawn in front of it. All the shutters needed paint and several swung aimlessly in the wind.

Lying in the driveway was a man clutching a satchel to his chest. He was dead. As we were wondering what to do, two women rushed out at us, shrieking angry, disjointed sentences. They didn't use any bad language. Oh, no! They were the genteel kind whose gentility was sadly perturbed at the moment. Not accustomed to having dead men on their lawn, they took it as a personal insult. They, the house, the garden were vestiges of another époque. I am sure that in summer they played croquet in straw hats!

After listening to their sarcastic remarks concerning our uniforms and our ambulance, I couldn't but wonder if the war hadn't bypassed them. Maybe they only remembered the Franco-Prussian one!

In the end Bridget and I were so annoyed and shocked by their lack of feeling that we told them to shut up so we could ask some questions. Meanwhile I picked up the man's satchel. It was just as well, for rigor mortis was setting in and I had to wrench it from his grasp. In so doing, the catch snapped open and a bundle of banknotes fell out.

"What was this man doing here?" I asked, stuffing the notes back.

They didn't reply, only stared at the money. I began to feel ill at ease. Everything was so damp and dismal, and with the dead man at our feet the sense of impropriety turned to evil. At that moment the air-raid siren started to wail.

"Well, what was he doing here?"

"He is the gas collector. He threatened us. Imagine, threatening my poor sister, who is ill!"

I looked at the "poor sister" and decided she looked surprisingly well, especially for these days. On top of everything, she was staring at the satchel with a very crafty look.

"I don't think he threatened you," Bridget said. "I think he was just doing his job—collecting bills."

"It wasn't our fault if he was taken ill," they whined.

In the end, between the air-raid alarm and our sense of discomfort, we decided to bundle the man onto a stretcher and drive him to the morgue. We took the satchel and his papers to the police station, where Bridget gave a full report of the incident while I sat in the ambulance smoking endless cigarettes and praying I wouldn't be called in to corroborate the story.

Naturally, there was a sequel. It couldn't be otherwise. Both Bridget and I were summoned to the office of the Commissaire. Accompanied by our boss, annoyed but understanding, we went.

"There are laws in France—in every part of the world—concerning the removal of corpses!" he greeted us. Then, after demanding our papers, which he looked at a long while in silence, he leaned back in his chair and stared at us musingly.

After a while Bridget started to explain in her plodding way: "The women weren't easy. In the first place, they told us the man was ill and that it was our duty to transport him. When we arrived he was dead, and with all that money—"

"What about that money?"

"We didn't dare leave it," I cut in, suddenly very sure of my French. "We couldn't separate because of the air raid."

"Why?"

"Because we're supposed to be together during a raid. Otherwise one of us would have stayed while the other went for a policeman."

After that there was a long pause while our papers were again scrutinized. I noticed that he was checking my driver's license—just as false as everything else—against my identity card and I wished I was a hundred miles away!

"You are going through a period of instruction?"

I nodded. To my astonishment, Bridget did too.

"Rather near the coast for that! I would have thought Paris more suitable. Well, I suppose what you did was for the best! But in the future don't go around picking up corpses without a permit or an authorized person with you." And he shoved the papers back to us with a strange smile.

As far as the law was concerned, the incident was settled, but not in my boss's mind.

Back in the office, she called me aside. "The man we hoped might help you has been arrested. I won't be able to keep you much longer. Next week a big shot from Paris is coming on inspection. I think—"

I never knew what she thought, because she was called to the telephone.

I'd always known, of course, that this would happen. In my heart of hearts I hadn't held much hope concerning the "friend of a friend." Still, I had been, if not happy—how could one be happy surrounded by so much unhappiness?—at least contented. Contented to be doing something worthwhile.

Later I was sent out on a call with Bridget.

"What is it this time?" I asked.

"An accident! We're to call at the police station for the permit to transport someone to the morgue."

"Oh, don't let's forget that!" I exclaimed.

Bridget turned and stared at me. I had the impression she wanted to say something. She didn't, however, and I suppose she found driving in the twilight and rain difficult. I know I found it so. Blackout lamps on wet streets are hell. I started to crank the ambulance horn.

It wasn't until we were in front of the morgue an hour later that she spoke to me.

"I'm getting sick of this. How would you like to go to Switzerland? . . . Look out! Look out!"

I had almost dropped my end of the stretcher—not that it would have changed anything for the old woman who had been knocked over by a German truck. Bridget had spoken in English—and very good English.

"Ah, ladies! You again! I've been wanting to see you!" the morgue attendant exclaimed.

Now, what could this bouncing, gnomelike man with his jovial face want to see us about? We stared at him as he slid his new "customer"—he always called them that—onto a trolley.

"The one you brought me the other day—the gas collector."

"Oh, God! Not him again!" I wailed.

"But yes, Mademoiselle. He was a canny one! I wouldn't have believed it if I hadn't undressed him. . . . We have to do that for the relatives, you know. Before the war we washed the clothes, but now . . ." He shrugged. "Nobody will claim this poor one," he added, handing back our blanket. "Nothing here. But the other one . . . Ah! That's another matter! Come and see."

And leaving his latest "customer," he skipped over to one of the cold-storage bins and hauled out the gas collector.

In spite of my aversion, I stared and then giggled. Oh, our nice, neat old man with the satchel full of money! The sight of him now was indeed an epitaph to a bad day!

Our gas collector was arrayed in black silk underwear with a cheap necklace around his scrawny neck.

4

The air-raid siren was wailing when we left Rouen.

In Paris we went to a "safe house"—the expression was Bridget's. Later I learned to use it as easily as she, even though it kept me puzzled about her. With her fair hair, clear complexion, china-blue eyes and heavy body, she could be German. But somehow I knew this wasn't so, just as I knew she wasn't English either. Not entirely, anyway. Maybe only her mother. In any case, whatever she was, I knew she wouldn't tell me because in her lackadaisical way she was secretive, avoiding skillfully the few questions I had put to her and never speaking in English again after her proposition at the morgue. Come what may, we were linked together. Switzerland and not England was our destination, though what we would do once there—if ever we crossed the frontier—was beyond me.

The safe house proved to be a ground-floor apartment behind the Chamber of Deputies on the Place du Palais Bourbon. The lady who greeted us seemed familiar, but I couldn't place her and that fact annoyed me the whole evening. I knew she was either American or English because of her accent and, since her name was French, I supposed she was married to a Frenchman, like the distant cousin who shared Mother's apartment. The association of ideas awakened my homesickness. I was suddenly unhappy, and

I suppose it showed because I found myself being closely observed by my hostess.

Rising from the couch where I had been sitting, I decided to ask her where we had met, but she cut me short: "Bridget, I think your friend is tired. You can sleep on the couch, Mademoiselle." And with that she started pulling off the slipcover. "I'm sure you have everything in your rucksack. Very convenient things, but not like prewar luggage." And, smiling, she left with a wave and a pleasant "Bon soir."

I stared at my rucksack—acquired somewhere during my travels—with distaste and affection. Distaste because nothing ever came out of it neat, affection because it contained all I had.

During the night I thought I heard voices, but since the sound was only a discreet murmur I soon fell asleep again.

The next morning Bridget seemed more stolid and vague than ever, but the circles beneath her eyes made me wonder if she had slept. I was soon to know.

"I have some bad news," our hostess said complacently over a meager breakfast of black bread and saccharin-sweetened apple compote. "The passeur I had in mind has left his home. He was going to be arrested."

"But surely the demarcation line no longer exists. It was announced in the newspaper weeks ago."

"Do you believe the newspapers? The trains are still checked. Your description might be posted," Bridget said.

"My description! What nonsense! The Germans have other things to do!" And I stared at her. Suddenly I understood. *She* was the one who feared a German check-up! This revelation so amazed me I felt like a pricked balloon!

"I have a map—a detailed Michelin of the region surrounding Macon et Chalon-sur-Saône. I've pinpointed a spot on it where I think you'll be able to cross," our hostess said.

And that is just what we did, landing in a small town where there was a factory. Mingling with the workmen coming off the job, we left the town and headed for a village whose church steeple cut the night sky. From the map we knew we were not far from the demarcation line, and our intention was to ask the curé of the village for guidance through the back lanes so we could catch the express at Villefranche for Lyon. Bridget seemed very sure there would be no check-up at Villefranche, and she was bent on getting there because it suddenly developed that she had someone to see in Lyon.

We reached the village a little after six and made for the church. Inside, people were waiting to go into the confessional. It was then that I realized it was Christmas Eve.

Kneeling in a back pew, we waited until we were the last. Only then did Bridget disappear into the ugly black box. She was not long. To my surprise, when she returned her pallor had vanished and she was flushed with anger.

"What's the matter?" I asked, following her to the corner where we had left our rucksacks.

"Let's walk to that wood you noticed on the map. We're on our own now. I hope you can read a map!"

It was dark, but a pale moon and my pocket torch helped me.

Once in the wood, we tramped down a footpath which I knew from the map led to the road our hostess in Paris had identified as the dividing line between the two zones. I said then: "Let's rest. It's past eight."

Settling ourselves in the shelter of a couple of trees, I asked my companion what had upset her.

"The curé told me he couldn't help—that he had received orders from his bishop not to assist Jews. And on Christmas Eve!" she finished lamely.

"But that's awful! I've a good mind to go back and tell him what I think of him!"

"Don't be a fool! It's true many of the clergy have been arrested for helping them. At least he was frank. And told me that after the wood there are fields and then a large copse."

I peered at the map, starting to swear. "We're too far off to the right. I think I saw a path farther back. It's not marked, but it seems to run in the direction of the fields. I think it's going to be a longer walk than we expected."

And so it was—more than three hours. To make matters worse,

the pale moon left us and it started to rain. Only a thin drizzle at first, but cold enough to be snow, and I think it did snow for a while.

When we reached the road, we found a hut above it. It was a filthy place, smelling abominably. At one point of its existence it must have housed a he-goat. Still, it was better than nothing.

After resting I crawled out and stumbled down the track. I was standing at the edge of the road when I heard a car. I dropped flat, knowing it could only be a German vehicle at this hour. To my horror, it slowed down. Had I been seen? No. It passed, stopping a few yards farther down and above the sound of rain on macadam I heard German voices, saw the black mass of a house with a ray of light streaming from an open door.

I heard cheerful greetings and then the sound of singing came from the house. "O Tannenbaum! O Tannenbaum!" Blast them, they were celebrating! Wryly, I remembered a Christmas spent in their country with snow falling on skis stacked upright in front of a châlet door!

Soon I heard a sharp "Heil Hitler!" Surely that greeting on this night was the ugliest I had ever heard!

Then the car started up and roared away, and I remembered: "the silence surged softly backward now the plunging hoofs were gone." Stupid and amazing to recall a poem by Walter de la Mare at such a moment.

I began to inch my way closer to the house and I then saw the other road, perpendicular to the one I was on. Across it stretched a wooden fence like those at railroad crossings, and next to the fence I could just make out the faint silhouette of a sentry box.

I decided to return to Bridget. As I turned, the door of the house opened again and in the beam of light a man stepped out and marched, none too steadily, toward the sentry box. The changing of the guard! Smiling, I crept back to Bridget.

A half-hour later we slid beneath the barrier. The rain had ceased momentarily, and we heard snores—loud, heavy ones. It was then that I blessed Christmas Eve and good French brandy.

After that the rain came down in sheets. At every step we wondered how long our shoes would stand up to such treatment, for they were not of pre-war quality. To make matters worse, the canvas straps of our rucksacks started to shrink, pulling on our shoulders and making every moment agony.

Just when we could bear it no longer, we saw the glimmer of a light, and without hesitation we went toward it.

It was coming from a small house, and as we approached, I heard a radio. Since the broadcast was being scrambled, I knew someone in that house was listening to London—probably a Christmas Eve program by the Free French, beaming messages only the Resistance fighters could understand. People listening to it weren't likely to be collaborators.

I knocked.

The radio ceased immediately. At the same moment a dog started to bark. Above his snarls came the familiar voice of the speaker from Radio Paris reading the late news—the official German-censored news which was all we were allowed to listen to.

I knocked again, laying my rucksack against my legs as protection against the dog.

The door was opened to us by a middle-aged man in shirt sleeves and wearing a skimpy beret. For a few seconds he stared at us in silence, one hand grasping the collar of his dog.

I stretched out a hand toward the animal, which backed away, wagging its tail uncertainly. Not much of a watchdog, but when he gets older he'll be a tough customer, I thought.

"We're lost," Bridget said. "We saw your light."

Suddenly our arms were grabbed and we were pulled into a large room that evidently served as a kitchen, dining room and parlor.

"Don't say anything," he growled, but not unpleasantly. "A few minutes more and we would have been in bed. Agathe, we have visitors!" he cried to the woman sitting next to a buffet on which stood a small radio.

They were kind. Agathe made us undress to our slips and then wrapped us in blankets, while her husband took our shoes and scraped the mud off them before caking them with grease and placing them on the open door of a wood-and-coal-burning oven. Later they gave us some hot soup with red wine in it. To my surprise, I found this concoction good and nourishing—certainly the equal of brandy or marc for heat calories.

Afterward, we talked. They were small farmers with two cows, a horse and several pigs. Their only son was a prisoner of war in Germany. They were eager to learn all that was going on in the occupied zone—as it was still called—but their curiosity was never disturbing. They behaved as if it were a normal occurrence to have two wet, bedraggled girls come knocking at their door in the middle of the night.

After a while they went into their bedroom, but not before tucking us into a couple of sagging armchairs in front of the stove. The dog remained with us, sleeping on an old dirty carpet near a woodpile. We slept with our feet in the oven next to our shoes.

It was still dark when I woke to the rattle of crockery.

Down the center of the table the woman was setting four bowls, plates, knives and spoons. Presently her husband came in with a loaf of bread tucked under his arm and carrying an earthenware crock filled with wonderful yellow butter, newly churned.

There was no sugar for the awful wartime coffee, but instead we had honey, which the farmer told us he traded from a neighbor in exchange for his cigarette ration.

"I ironed your blouses, Mesdames," his wife said. "Turn around, Jules, so the ladies can dress."

"I won't look, old woman. It's their shoes I am interested in. I was once a cobbler. I'm going to fit a piece of leather in each of them. It should hold for some time."

After we had eaten, Bridget asked how far it was to Villefranche.

"I have to go into town. I'll leave you on the outskirts. If you're going to Lyon, you'll have plenty of time to catch the express."

When we offered money to these dear people, they turned it down, and before we climbed up into the cart Agathe kissed us soundly on both cheeks: "My son would have it this way! We live in hard times. I don't know who you are or what you are doing, but I know you're carrying on the fight as the General in London asked us to do. Here's some food," and with that she slammed the door and vanished into the house.

Trotting down the road in the old cart behind the rump of a brown horse, I found myself crying. The General in London . . . My son would want it that way. Vichy France was still France.

We reached Lyon in the afternoon. The express from Paris was only three hours late. I supposed German convoys held it up—that was the usual explanation. I had heard the story of a traveler trying to reach a sick relative. Stranded in a backwoods station, he decided to walk to the nearest village to catch a bus. There was none—it had exploded the day before. He bought a bicycle, but there were no tires for it. He then wore out his shoes returning to the railroad station just in time to see his train puff away, hitched to a German convoy loaded with explosives and pursued by the RAF.

The station of Perrache in Lyon was bedlam, everyone having decided they wanted to go somewhere at the same moment. There were lots of skis and skiers—lots and lots of them—and they all had rucksacks. This made walking a dodgy business, and I wondered how Bridget thought she would locate the man she wanted to see. I was reminded of the time I dove for a lost ring in the bay of Saint-Malo! But she managed it by standing firmly beneath the main clock. At the time I thought she was crazy. It seemed like trying to swim in a whirlpool. I remember being swiped across the face by a pair of skis balanced on the shoulder of a man determined to talk to someone behind him. Instead of apologizing, he swore at me.

When I recovered, Bridget had disappeared. A sort of claustrophobia descended upon me. I had to escape the crowds, the noise. . . . Ruthlessly using my rucksack, I shouldered my way out, even hitting a German in the process. He gave me a polite "Excuse me."

In the waiting room I sat down on a tin trunk, staring around wild-eyed, wondering what to do. Head for the frontier on my own? It was a ghastly moment. I would buy a map. . . . Suddenly, I saw Bridget standing by the door that was swinging frantically back and forth. My God! Couldn't she pick a quieter spot to have a chat?

Deciding to join her, I rose from the trunk just before its owner came to reclaim it.

When I reached her, her companion had vanished.

"Come on! Hurry! We've only a few minutes to catch the train to Annemasse."

In the train, sitting on my wooden third-class bench, I stared at her. She looked tired and also very tense. I would have had to be dim-witted not to know what she had been doing. Espionage to me was something in a story by Somerset Maugham, exciting but not what I had been brought up to practice. Or else it was very glamorous or vampish like Mata Hari. But at the moment Bridget looked like a tired young girl, very down-at-heel, who carried an old French name which she could not shed no matter how hard she tried. But then, this war wasn't like any other. I tried to remember what I had read about the last one, but it wasn't much. Apart from a scrap of paper that represented Belgian neutrality . . . Verdun, which was linked with Pétain, who today imagined he was holding France together in Vichy . . . the miracle of the Marne . . . the Rainbow Division . . . the Escadrille La Fayette . . . and of course, Rupert Brooke . . . there wasn't much. Why Brooke? Because my English teacher had had a passion for his poetry and I'd had a passion for my English teacher, who had a lovely voice, was Welsh and taught me to love reading. All these things seemed very far from Bridget on the bench of a third-class compartment in a cold train heading for Annemasse on the Franco-Swiss border! And yet the strangest people seemed to be doing the strangest things these days. Nice people, useless people, the bad and the good all doing something—making fortunes on the black market, engaging in sabotage and being shot as terrorists. Yes, ordinary humdrum people, ex-gangsters, pimps, whores . . . Everyone was doing something. Not always on the right side? Didn't the Germans wear "GOTT MIT UNS" on their belt-buckles? In time of war God's name is often invoked. I hoped . . . no, I *knew* He would be with me. But in the meanwhile Bridget had given up her bourgeois life and was on the run, with every chance of being shot if she was caught. I wouldn't suffer that fate, since all I had been doing for the last three months was avoid internment, and suddenly I felt stupid, useless. I leaned over and tapped her knee: "We'll make it," I whispered.

For a moment a hint of panic flashed through her china-blue eyes. Perhaps I should have shut up. I had reminded her that maybe we wouldn't.

In Annemasse, by the manner in which Bridget led the way through the town filled with barbed-wire entanglements, I knew she was following verbal instructions. They must have been very precise and her memory very good because we were soon standing before the back entrance of a large building. I guessed it to be a hotel because of the crates, empty bottles and garbage cans cluttered around. Through a window giving onto this spectacle we saw a woman in a white apron standing over a huge stove.

Bridget knocked on the window. The woman turned and stared. For a moment she hesitated and I think it was because of the mixture she was stirring with a wooden spoon. The sight made me hungry; anyone who hesitates with such an anguished expression must be a good cook. In the end she left her stove, swept out of our vision and suddenly stood in the doorway, motioning us to a passageway and a door on which was printed WC.

For a moment I thought we had come to a dead end and momentarily blessed the respite. A few seconds later when I came out, Bridget had disappeared, but the woman was still there, beckoning me to a winding staircase; at the top of the stairs was a door, which she opened with a flourish. Entering, I found Bridget in the embraces of a large woman.

"Well, I'm glad you made it!" she cried in English with a nasal twang. "And this is your friend—the American. Happy Christmas!" And she embraced me, too.

Well, the long and the short of it was she was an Australian married to a Frenchman who owned the hotel.

The room was filled with gaudy furniture. In a way, it reminded me of a Western movie. There was only one bed—a huge one, bedecked with blue velvet drapes held by angels in the last stage of elephantiasis.

Laying down my rucksack, I stared, wondering which gold-legged chair I dare sit on. As I gazed around, my eyes encountered someone glaring at me. I naturally glared back until I realized I was glaring at myself. What a spectacle! My hair was a frilly mop because of the rain, my face a pasty color and my raincoat would have done honor to a tramp!

Scowling, I turned away from this depressing sight. Instead I concentrated on the mirror. It was worthwhile. Enormous, bordered by gold sequins set in an oval gold frame held by two angels—also suffering from elephantiasis but with their wings pockmarked by a mysterious malady—it was a sight to behold.

I was fascinated. How had these things arrived in a hotel in Annemasse?

Suddenly I heard a word that brought me back to reality. It was BATH.

Swinging around, I saw the Australian lady pointing to a door.

In one bound I plunged through it. After the angels and gold it was distressingly anodyne. But it was a bathroom—a real one with real pipes. Timidly I turned a tap. There was a sinister hissing, banging sound and then water, steaming hot. I've never seen such a beautiful spectacle!

Later, after soaking kilometers of tiredness out of our limbs and washing our hair, we were hungry. At which point our hostess appeared followed by the woman in the white apron carrying a loaded tray.

"Sorry there isn't much turkey, but I've added roast beef. My husband can't come because he's busy with the Germans in the bar, but he sends you this bottle of champagne to celebrate the news."

"What news?"

"Admiral Darlan has been assassinated in Algiers. It may only be a rumor. Radio Geneva will confirm tomorrow. Funny thing," the Australian mused, "I don't see how it will make any difference. I have a feeling he was going over to the Allies."

I shrugged. Darlan meant Vichy, and anything connected with that puppet regime was an abomination to me. Darlan was a political admiral who had ordered the French fleet to abide by the armistice terms—namely, to stay out of the war. In return, Hitler had promised he would make no demands on the fleet. But when the Germans invaded all of France, their first objective had been Toulon, where the fleet was anchored. Rather than surrender, it scuttled itself. The fleet—the proud fleet which the Allies might have captured and used—was sunk, and much of the blame could be laid at the door of that political admiral.

"Well, cheers! To the invasion!"

"To the invasion and may it come soon!"

"Have a good dinner. Sleep as late as you like. Don't open the shutters. This room is supposed to be empty. That's why I keep the lights so dim. I'm going to turn them off now and leave you a candle. Don't walk about except in bare feet. Tomorrow I'll arrange with a passeur for your crossing. I have some Jews waiting. Maybe you can go with them."

The following day, around noon, I was standing by the window trying to look into the street through the slats of the shutters when a man pounced into the room, stared at us and disappeared.

We were surprised, but since there was nothing we could do, I returned to my attempted scrutiny of the street. It was a difficult pastime because the only way to see through the slanted shutters was to hang head downward from the ceiling. Since I saw no way of doing this without becoming a bat, I contented myself with what I thought was half a curé in half a soutane talking to half a young man clad in half a pair of ski trousers. Later, this faded away and half a German appeared. The trouble with him was he wasn't dressed in the usual way. Instead of a helmet, he sported half a cap with half a feather stuck in it. This was so startling I squirmed and wriggled around.

"Why bother? Get away from that window! Your shadow might be seen!"

I swung around to face a tall man dressed in a short sheepskin coat known as a Canadienne. They were very warm, those things, and I had long ago decided to buy one on the black market as soon as I could afford it.

Bridget came out of the bathroom.

"We'll take you over tonight, but you'll have to pay."

We nodded, but I wondered if it was going to be the same

racket as in October? Then, on second thought, I decided not. This man appeared cold, efficient, and he spoke like a cultivated person. He didn't strike me as an amateur or a thug.

"It's not going to be easy. There are a lot of you. Since you represent the Allies, we'll accept less than for the Jews."

For a moment I wanted to argue. It seemed so damned unfair.

"I have to make everyone pay. We use the money for other purposes."

"Purposes? What purposes?"

"Surely you know."

After that I shut up. I *didn't* know. I had no idea.

"Do we pay now or later?" Bridget asked.

Damn fool! And have them vanish in thin air! What a stupid girl!

"Later. I might go off with the money."

I stared at him, wishing I could like him, but I realized there was no one I truly liked or trusted these days. Of course, I was unfair—the Australian who was risking her life harboring Jews . . . the kindly farmers . . . Christ, what a bloody life!

"What were you staring at?" the man asked.

"At a German who isn't dressed like one."

"He must be from the Jaeger regiment that's passing through before going up to the mountains."

"I thought the mountains around here were Swiss."

"There's always a border somewhere. The Austrian ski troops are equipped to guard it. Are you satisfied now?" And with that he stalked out, leaving me crestfallen and puzzled.

That evening, shortly after seven, he visited us again, only this time he was looking angry.

"Three more have turned up. I've said no!"

"I won't give up my place!" Bridget cried. "I must cross as soon as possible."

"Who are they?" I asked, not really expecting him to answer.

"I don't know. They were sent by a man I thought had been arrested."

"Turn them away and get us out of here as soon as possible," I snapped, feeling frightened.

"She's right! Turn them away!" Bridget almost shouted, beginning to stuff things into her rucksack.

Ten minutes later we were in the street after a hurried goodbye to the Australian. She was already starting to remove the traces of our passage from her gaudy bedroom.

At the corner of the street, a boy on a bicycle met us.

"Go past the church! Turn sharply left! Walk until you come to a railroad. Follow the tracks to the crossing-keeper's house. It's empty. The others are there. Be sure to turn left, otherwise you'll walk into a German outpost."

And with that he vanished whistling, his blackout lamp casting shadows against the walls of the houses.

It was a cold, clear night with a bright moon majestic and aloof in the star-studded sky. This time we wouldn't be soaked, only frozen.

We pretended to stroll, trying not to think of the two figures behind us. They were Germans, of course, wearing, instead of jackboots, brogues with crepe soles so as to have the advantage of surprise as they patrolled this frontier town.

They were talking—a desultory conversation. We decided to do the same. I began to tell Bridget of the dinner we would be having at Tante Agnes'—the old lady had promised us fish caught by my cousin Jean, who was a great fisherman! I talked so much of this damn fish and how it was going to be basted in white wine and herbs, I made myself hungry! Bridget played the game, too—vaunting the culinary talents of her mother, who, I'm sure, didn't know how to cook an egg! It did the trick, but not quite as we expected. The men were drawing closer, listening to our boasts. Any minute now and they would be asking us for recipes, maybe taking out a pencil to jot down the secrets of Aunt Agnes' chef-d'oeuvre! I decided to let Bridget keep doing the talking.

Suddenly they turned away, barking a cheerful "Gute Nacht!" and we found ourselves next to the church. After that we were soon in the country, and we walked down the railroad tracks until, around a curve, we came upon the house—a stark, hideous silhouette in the moonlight.

For some moments we crouched next to it doubtfully. Everything seemed too easy to be true.

Finally we went toward the open door.

It was dark inside, darker than outdoors, cold too—a damp, clammy cold. We heard furtive movements and could see a staircase.

The varied tints of darkness are amazing. There's a gloomy, wet darkness, filled with the noise of rain dripping from branches, from old gutters. There's the darkness of moonlight, as it was then, bristling with frost. There's a comfortable, homy darkness, filled with the familiar smells of a room in which the furniture cracks and chortles to itself. Then there's the cloying blackness of a house pretending to be empty, insidious, falsely humble like Uriah Heep, hypocritical, so that even the sound of a mouse in the wainscoting is a relief. There's also the darkness of happiness, of listening to the loved one sleeping, which is like a melody of the stars.

We saw our new companions by the moonlight streaming coldly through the dirty windowpanes. There were a lot of them—at least ten grownups, several children and one baby, asleep for the moment.

When we joined them, they didn't seem surprised to see us; I suppose they had been told about us. In any case, it didn't matter. This was no social occasion, although one portly gentleman was bent on introducing us to as many as he could, calling them all by their Christian names. Bridget and I begged him to be quiet—we even lied, telling him he could be heard outside. Then they settled down, but the children continued to be restless, and one even tried to play hopscotch with his shadow until he was cuffed by an old woman swathed in shawls. I don't know what nationality they were. They may have been German, because they spoke French with a guttural accent.

The wait was interminable and cold, and I got sleepy. But just as I was dozing off, the baby woke and started to cry. Its mother fed it from a bottle to which she may have added some brandy, because after a comfortable burp the baby slept again.

Poor, poor people! How many weary miles had they come? How many frontiers had they crossed, drugging a baby to save it for a better life—a better world? Yes, poor, poor people, but please stop moving around, stumbling over parcels and suitcases. Every sound you make shortens your chances for living in that better world!

When the passeur turned up, accompanied by another man, I was on edge. So was everyone else.

We finally left Indian file, clattering like a company of Horse Guards—my God, but they had a lot of parcels! But fortunately we didn't have far to walk—so short a distance, I couldn't believe it when we straggled down into a deep ditch and stopped.

"Switzerland is over the top! Separate when you walk across the field to the road. The Swiss are getting fed up with refugees. Now give me the money," the passeur said brusquely. We did so. I handed mine over reluctantly—so reluctantly it was snatched from me.

Abandoned by our guide, our companions stared at the steep incline of the ditch, bewildered.

Finally I scrambled up it, only to discover a broad barrier of chevaux-de-frises at the top. I slid back and everyone began talking in loud whispers all at once. Bridget and I tried to silence them, but to no avail. Finally Bridget went up the ditch and I handed suitcases and parcels up to her. I don't remember handing the baby, but I do remember a couple of saucepans!

With coats and blankets laid across the wire, they were able to crawl across the top of it. After that they clustered together, sorting out their belongings and leaving Bridget and me in the ditch to fend for ourselves. Tearing our stockings, scratching our legs and hands, we finally made it just in time to see them disappear across the moonlit field, bunched together like cattle.

Keeping a few meters apart, Bridget and I started across the field too.

Suddenly two figures dashed forward, springing from God knows where, yelling in German. I knew they had rifles because one passed so close to where I had flopped down I could hear the creak of his leather belt and the flap of his bayonet scabbard along his thigh. They ran after the scurrying fugitives, who scattered in all directions, shrieking. I watched, horrified, powerless, barely lifting my head above the dried stumps of last year's crops.

They caught them by the road where we could no longer see them, which somehow made the whole episode worse and made us more conscious of our ineffectiveness. Those passeurs! If they had been near me, I would have done them some violence, but they were far away, jubilantly counting our money. There is no way to describe my feelings at that moment. I only remember the sickness in the pit of my stomach, and that at one moment I covered my ears to shut out the cries of the children, the shrieks of the women, the harsh, guttural shouts of the soldiers.

We lay there for a long time, no longer conscious of the cold. Finally a car drove up and after that there was silence. Yes, a wretched, shocked silence, not broken even by night animals hunting. Perhaps these furtive creatures thought there had been enough hunting for one night—that only stillness was licensed to crawl back, whimpering. Above us the moon, enormous and imperious, rode high in the sky. I hated it. If it hadn't been for the moonlight, none of this would have happened.

In the end, Bridget and I rose to our feet and, staggering with stiffness, headed for the road. We didn't speak. On our way I stumbled and picked something up. At first I didn't know what it was. Then I recognized it. It was a gollywog. I hadn't seen one since my own childhood, and although I certainly didn't want it, I stuffed it into my pocket.

We lay in a ditch beside the road; I was very tired. Something kept trying to surface in my mind, but each time I tried to seize it, it glided away.

"What's that glow in the sky?" Bridget whispered.

"Geneva, I hope."

"It seems very close."

"Lights are deceptive at night. Let's move on. The road seems clear. Maybe those swine have all gone to bed. After all, they've done a good night's work!"

We walked down the road, hugging the shadows, watching the glow in the sky.

At a crossroad, we stopped because of a wooden signpost. It was so tall and the lettering so faded we couldn't make out what was written on it.

Suddenly my mind froze—I had pinpointed my elusive thought.

"Hey! We're not in France! The signpost! They don't have those in France. Look out! There's a bicycle coming." And I pulled her down into the ditch.

After that we walked, ducking bicycles, arguing, looking for the familiar red-and-white French milestones. There were none and the bicycles passing us were more and more numerous. Hardly any had blackout lights. I was sure we were in Switzerland, but I was also sure the soldiers had spoken German. Had it been German? Every so often we stopped to rest, flopping into ditches, our rucksacks cutting painfully into our shoulders.

In the end we were overtaken by a man who rode silently up from behind.

"Halte! Police de frontière!"

My first reaction should have been fear, but I was exhausted. I don't think I even cared any more.

"Vos papiers."

We handed them over. He stared at them and then shrugged. I was surprised. I hadn't thought they looked so phony. I'd had them so long I'd grown accustomed to them. Besides, I even liked my name of Denise.

"Are we still in France?" Bridget asked.

"France! No. Can't you see the lights of Geneva?"

"But the soldiers—they spoke German," I said.

"Switzer Deutsche."

"It's Switzerland!" Bridget cried, bursting into tears. I think she would have knelt down and kissed the soil if it hadn't been for the weight of her rucksack, and only then did I realize how frightened she must have been since our departure from Rouen. I hated to remember all the times I had been impatient with her.

"I'm not French," she cried between her sobs while the Swiss policeman helped her out of her rucksack. "I'm not French . . . not French. I'm English and my friend is American."

"Ah! The Allies!" and deliberately, solemnly, the man studied our papers again, even flashing his torch to examine them better. "They're a good imitation. The French are becoming expert forgers. Well, welcome to Switzerland, Mesdames! Have you heard the news?"

"No."

"Darlan has been assassinated in Algiers."

"We were told in Annemasse it might be just a rumor."

"It was confirmed by Radio Geneva and they never take stock of rumors. Have some chocolate. Eat it while I attach your rucksacks to my bicycle."

"Where are you taking us?"

"To the police station."

"But why? Surely . . .?"

"You've entered Switzerland by fraud. Come."

At the police station we saw our fellow travelers lying sprawled on wooden benches. One was stretched out on the floor in front of a stove, his arm around a child. Both were sound asleep.

The only one who seemed awake was the sociable gentleman. "Did you find a doll?" he asked, hurrying over to me.

Wordless, I stared at him.

"You know—a small rag doll," he pleaded.

Remembering, I dragged the gollywog out of my pocket.

"I was out when they took her away," he mumbled, turning the limp toy over and over in his hands.

The upshot of it all was that we were interned the next day for entering the country illegally. But it wasn't for long. Shortly after we arrived at the internment camp, a strikingly handsome man turned up, wearing a Swiss officer's uniform. He looked at our papers carefully but amiably and immediately released Bridget and me.

5

There's nothing more humiliating than to consider oneself a heroine and have no one share this opinion. That was my case when I arrived in Geneva.

I had thought naïvely that the American Consul would greet me with open arms and be only too eager to hear the latest news from France. To my dismay, I found he couldn't have cared less. In fact, the only thing that interested (and outraged) him was my claiming to be American—an American without a passport, because I had adopted a false French identity. An identity card I now no longer possessed because the Swiss secret service had confiscated it when they interrogated Bridget and me.

In other words, I was banging at the door of the American Consulate without proof of what I professed. At first I was furious, but I suppose they had good reason for their attitude. There were so many would-be Americans wandering into Switzerland at the time.

I was also practically penniless; my expenses in a third-rate pension were being paid by the Swiss secret service who assumed they would be reimbursed by the Consulate once my status was cleared. Naturally, this caused contention between the Swiss and the Americans, and by the end of a week, I had wondered many times if I wouldn't be sleeping on the sidewalk. I imagined myself on a bench in the park by the lake, found frozen to death by an oh so clean Swiss policeman!

Meanwhile Bridget had found a job at the British Consulate (I had been right: she was half English), but only because she had been working for them in Paris. This provided her with papers which entitled her to a working card as well as a temporary residence permit. I had nothing but a sheet of typewritten paper from my skeptical Consulate saying I claimed to be one of their nationals. I also had a stamped card from the Swiss police—just like a streetwalker! "En carte" they were called in France!

I envied Bridget, who left every morning for work and didn't return until evening. I even felt resentful. I had no idea what her job was, but I wished I was in her shoes. I began to hate everything, especially the shops bulging with goods that were being enjoyed every day by these kind people, so slow and easy-going, so proud of having remained the last beacon of light in Europe.

"Sour grapes" is the only expression I can find to describe my attitude as I roamed the streets—never far because my card did not authorize it. Which was just as well because my shoes were in a sorry state. Looking up at the mountains covered by eternal snow, I remembered prewar days when I had passed through this city on my way to ski at Caux, Saint-Moritz or Gstaad. They were still there, those resorts, filled but now by stolid Swiss deploring the fact that their hotels were empty because of a stupid war which brought only penniless refugees or spies who did nothing for the tourist business. I looked up at those mountains, concentrating my gaze on Mont Blanc because most of it lay in France. If I retrieved my French identity card, I could return to France and make my way south to the Pyrenees. It was a crazy scheme and impossible to accomplish because I had no money and the Swiss were adamant about not returning my card. But I wanted badly to be doing something—something which would allow me to say: "I too did my share."

Of course, cables had been sent to the States—cables reluctantly paid for by the Consulate. Days went by, but nobody replied, least of all my stepfather and his lawyer-brother who were supposed to look after my mother's business affairs. I dare say those two shabby characters and my sister found it more convenient to let me stew. With time, they must have thought, the

Americans and Swiss would get sick of me. And so they did. The Americans were the first.

One day I was refused entry to the Consulate but, at the same time, I was invited to the Consul's home to have tea with his wife. This was so amazing it flummoxed me completely. After vainly trying to put a shine on my shoes and remove the stains from my clothes, I took a tram to the address on the formal card, grimly resolved to balance a cup of tea gracefully while eating as many sandwiches as I could.

My hostess was a kind woman, unbelieving and amazed that an American should have preferred to stay in Europe at war rather than go home. Of course she asked me about my family, and although I was expecting it, nothing could have embarrassed me more. You see, I knew very little about them because when Mother married my stepfather they had promptly left for Europe, trailing her two daughters from her previous marriage.

As I told my story I tried to keep the weariness out of my voice. It's tiresome trying to explain who you are!

"But surely you must know where your sister is?" the good woman prompted, dazed.

"I haven't seen or heard of her since 1936. When I last saw her she was living in Hollywood. Lake Hollywood Drive, above the dam. She's remarried. I don't know her name," and to give myself some sort of countenance, I continued to munch steadily. This also gave me time to decide whether I should add that the last time I had heard of her she was on her third husband with little likelihood of ceasing her collection. Deciding finally against sharing this information, I said: "There's seven years between us. I'm the youngest and we were never very sisterly, not even when we were in school in Austria."

"Austria!" And the Consul's wife made that poor country sound like the entrance to hell.

"Yes, we went to the Convent of the Sacred Heart in Pressbaum near Vienna," I said, deciding not to mention my previous school in Salzburg. I didn't think she would approve that part of my varied education. Personally, I couldn't have blamed her. I hadn't approved of it myself. It had been one of Mother's less bright notions!

"Have you no relatives in the States?"

"Oh, yes. A great aunt. Mrs. Aimee Hanson. She lives in Westhampton, Long Island. I also have two aunts and an uncle on my father's side. But I don't know where they live. I've only seen them once or twice."

"And where is your father?"

I didn't answer immediately. Instead I wiped my fingers on a tea doily, feeling more and more like Orphan Annie. "My father died in 1937. In New York, I think. I never knew him."

I suppose I must have sounded a little fierce because after that, for a while, my hostess talked of other matters.

"Can I get to England from here? I was in school there and have a lot of friends."

The Consul's wife shook her head sadly. At least, it seemed like that, but I wondered if it wasn't connected with the ravages I had made in her tray of dainty sandwiches.

"Only with diplomatic papers, and *you* haven't any papers at all. Why do you want to go to England? They're having a difficult time."

"Because they're fighting and I don't want to sit the war out here."

"What do you do with yourself all day?"

"Nothing. I walk. But not much of that."

She didn't ask why and I was grateful. I had no desire to have her offer me a pair of her cast-off shoes! It was stupid pride, of course. Anyway, her shoes probably wouldn't have fitted.

"I'm sure things will straighten out. You must be patient. My husband is checking your status, but the war makes things take longer. By the way, do you remember the name of your dog?"

This startled me so much I almost dropped my teacup, which was the last thing I wanted to do.

Although I'd always hated tea parties, my long-suffering English governess had taught me how to behave at one. I don't know what she would have thought about the amount I had eaten, but

I'm sure she would have overlooked it. From tea parties I had drifted to cocktail parties, which I also loathed. Loathed because I'd never been able to drink, eat and carry on an intelligent conversation with my mouth full.

"Dog? Why, yes . . . " I stammered. "She's an Airedale. My stepfather gave her to me when we were on a trip to India. Her name is Durban." And I lowered my head to hide my sudden tears. Durby, dear Durby! She wasn't young. I would probably never see her again. Maybe she would just fade away, starve to death waiting for my return. Drat the woman! She had forced me to remember the trusting eyes of an animal I loved.

"I want you to meet a very nice Swiss lady who works in the library. I'm sure she could give you odds and ends to do, like replacing books on the shelves. It will help pass the time."

And that's just what it did, but in such a solemn, dull way I sometimes wondered if I wasn't dreaming.

And then one day, when I'd just about given up hope of ever knowing anything but silence among book-lined shelves, I was called down to the Consulate.

I naturally thought my family had decided to admit I existed and were sending me money. At least I could stop looking like a scarecrow. But, to my amazement, I was handed a railroad ticket for Berne and a few Swiss francs—very few—and told to present myself at our Embassy the following day at eleven thirty. When I wanted to know whom I was to ask for, I was told I would soon find out and not to be late.

The next day I caught a spotless train for the capital of Switzerland and, on the dot of eleven thirty, entered the U.S. Embassy.

After walking down corridors and crossing offices filled with human robots hunched over typewriters, I was ushered into a cell-like room and told to wait. Presently an exceedingly well-groomed secretary came in. Checking my paper from the Consulate, she led me into a large office with a plain deal table cluttered with telephones and files. Seated behind this was a man in his late forties who waved me to a chair opposite a window so the light fell straight into my eyes.

"You claim to be an American?" he growled.

"I am."

"Do you know who I am?"

"No."

"I'm Allen Dulles, in charge of everyone claiming to be an American."

"I *am* an American," I protested, staring across at this falsely benevolent-looking man. "Dulles. Allen Dulles?"

He nodded, smiling. It would have been a nice smile had it reached his eyes. "Tell me about yourself."

I was tired, fed up with repeating myself. I must have told my story badly because I soon felt I wasn't getting across to this man with the small gray mustache and clipped voice. Dulles . . . Allen Dulles . . . Wasn't he something to do with the FBI? What interest could I have for such an organization? Did they take me for a crook?

"Aren't you connected with the FBI, Mr. Dulles?"

He burst out laughing. This puzzled me because I didn't think I had said anything funny.

"Not quite. But I sometimes have dealings with them. Would you be willing to return to France?"

"Yes."

"What could you do back there?"

"That's for you to say, Mr. Dulles." Now I knew who he was. He was something called the CIA, but what that was I didn't know.

After that he stared at me and this made me feel dirtier and even shabbier than ever.

Suddenly he leaned forward and pressed a bell. Seconds later a man appeared.

"You!" he exclaimed, staring at me. I was so taken aback I burned my fingers with the match I had struck for a cigarette. Then I recognized him.

It was the young consular official from Marseille to whom I had given the slip on my return from Greece in September 1939.

"You gave me your word of honor!"

I am afraid I laughed.

"I crossed my fingers, and my mother *does* live in Paris and Dinard."

"Well, look where you are today!"

I bristled, conscious once more of my shabby appearance. What a horrible coincidence!

And yet was it? Now I was recognized. There could be no further doubts over my nationality.

"Despite my appearance, I don't suppose Mr. Dulles has called me here to quibble over my word of honor. I'm sure I could be useful back in France. I know the country and its present conditions."

"Return to Geneva, Miss Reynolds. Or is it Rochester? I will provide you with funds to refurbish your wardrobe—sensible things. The Consulate will tell you where to go. I'll see if I can employ you as a courier in our French organization." Then Mr. Dulles dismissed me with a casual wave. In fact, everything about him was very casual.

All the way back in the train I kept on repeating to myself: "I've been recognized. I've been recognized . . . Courier to France! What on earth could that be? I'll ask Bridget." And I was so happy in that spotless train that some man leaned over and offered me a cigarette.

The following day I knew Berne had phoned, because when I got to the Consulate everything had been arranged and I was taken to a tailor by one of the secretaries to order two skirts and matching jackets. One was a lovely pale gray, the other dark blue. They were simple, but, to my disgust, I had to give in to the new fashion—very short skirts, long jackets. Dressed this way and perched on wooden clogs set on square heels, most women looked like cranes. To lessen this impression I bought several gaily colored blouses, and, best of all, I became the owner of two pairs of shoes. The secretary told me to wear them regularly so they would have a worn look. Courier to France! And I laughed as I watched the salesgirl dangling my old ones at arm's length as if they were vermin. I took them home, nevertheless.

It was a good thing, too, because I developed blisters.

"Why not try putting water in them?" Bridget suggested.

"What good will that do?" I cried, shaking talcum powder over my sores.

"I've been told it helps. I didn't invent the idea," and before I could protest she poured a glass of water into my new shoes.

After this treatment they had a worn look.

In ten days my clothes were ready. By then it was the early part of February and the siege of Stalingrad had turned into a victory. I started to fret and worry about being too late, too late to participate in the turning tide. It couldn't be much longer now. The word "invasion" was on everyone's lips. In the spring, summer at the latest.

I went down to the Consulate every day, but they never had any news for me, until the morning when I was told that the courier work was too risky, that someone else had been chosen for it.

"I'll go back—identity card or not. I'll hitch a ride south to the foot of the Pyrenees. The cheminots are all in the Resistance. I'll go back!" I stormed.

"You're crazy!" Bridget told me. "Why don't you stay still? Try and find a job. Maybe the Consulate . . . After all, they're giving you a sort of allowance."

"The Consulate! Bah! A bunch of old hags frightened of their shadows who spend all their time gossiping and going to cocktail parties! Frumps, the whole lot of them! The Consulate! I say merde to it and the CIA as well!"

Perhaps just to shut me up, Bridget said she would speak to her boss about me. I didn't think there was much hope from that quarter, but I let her go ahead. I'd met him once, and he was at least a pleasant man. Meanwhile I collected my allowance, rationed my cigarette-smoking, gave up drinking wine and beer because they cost extra and the Consulate didn't believe wine was necessary for one of its indigent citizens. Between the Consulate, the CIA and my family, I was in one hell of a temper. I think if I could have got my hands on my stepfather and his lawyer-brother, I would have strangled them.

The day before I planned on leaving on my own, I wrote

Mother, telling her all that had happened to me since we had been separated. It was intended for her to read should I not get through the rest of the war, and I took much malicious pleasure in telling her about the deliberate silence of her brother-in-law.

Just as I was finishing, Bridget came in and stared at my rucksack and my belongings heaped on my bed.

"I still think you're crazy."

"I'm not going to sit out the war without doing something. In England or North Africa I could at least drive an ambulance. Don't you wish you were coming with me?"

"God, no! I've spoken to my boss about you."

"And I suppose he thinks I'm crazy too! I'll make for Lyon, borrow some money from Renée and then head south."

"You won't do anything of the sort. . . . Oh, stop glaring at me! You leave tomorrow night. In front of the station, between the pastry shop and that cigarette shop you're always staring at, there's an alley. There'll be a car there. It's the Swiss secret service. They'll drop you off at a spot near the border northeast of Saint-Julien."

I sat down, suddenly feeling weak, and lit one of my rationed cigarettes.

"That's not all. You're to memorize all I'm going to tell you because if you're caught, nothing must be found on you."

"Do I get my identity card back?"

"No."

"Why not?"

"I didn't ask. I was just told you wouldn't get it. Now listen. . . . "

And listen I did, repeating the name of my destination: Chaumont, near Frangy. The man who lived there was called Clément Blanc, but before getting to him I would meet someone next to the cemetery—a man called Jules. He would give me the all-clear sign by pronouncing the word "rain" three times. "Rain" was the signal and it must be repeated three times before I would be shown on my way.

I was so flabbergasted that for a minute I couldn't speak.

In the end I burst out: "It's ridiculous! The whole set-up sounds like a cheap adventure story for children! Supposing I land in this place at night?"

"You're not to. It must be in the afternoon or the evening of the following day."

"Where am I to sleep?"

"That's your business."

I started to protest, but she cut me short by disappearing down the corridor in the direction of the toilet.

"It's crazy . . . crazy! They're all mad," I muttered, looking down at a small piece of paper with a cutting from a Michelin map glued to it, which showed Saint-Julien and Chaumont and a series of red X's drawn over the rambling frontier.

"That's a hell of a walk," I said when Bridget returned. "It's almost twenty kilometers."

"Well, you have the night and most of the day to do it. What do you think the Pyrenees are going to be? How are your feet?"

At nine the following night, I said goodbye to Bridget and crept down the back stairs so the owner of the pension wouldn't see me. The Consulate could pay for the extra week that had started at noon that day.

In the alley a small, inoffensive-looking sedan was parked. When I came up to it, the door opened and I slid in next to the driver.

The man behind the wheel was the Swiss officer who had questioned us in the internment camp. Only this time, instead of the high-peaked kepi and the pale green uniform, he was dressed in a black skiing outfit. I decided he looked just as handsome as he had the first time.

"Aren't you happy with us, Mademoiselle?"

"I won't be happy anywhere until I feel I'm doing something useful. We're going to win and I don't want to be sitting in your lovely, neutral country when the victory bells ring."

"The victory bells are still a long way off. Stalingrad, North Africa are only the beginning."

"Give me back my identity card."

"I can't. Someone else is using it. You'll get another one where you're going. Only it will take time. Time for spring to come to the Pyrenees."

"I may not make it," I replied, feeling waves of doubt sweep over me.

"You will. I've had our patrols stopped for an hour on this part of the frontier to give you time. After the wires—yes, a long, high wall of them that you can slide under—you'll find a dirt track. Don't take it. Cross over it into the vineyards and keep on going for as long as you can. When you reach open fields you're out of no-man's-land and you should find a barn to shelter in until daylight. There are still German patrols."

"Do you do this sort of thing often?"

He didn't answer. Instead he said: "I've brought some French cigarettes. Better give me the ones you have."

Of course. How right he was. I should have thought of it. American cigarettes don't smell the same as Gauloises.

With the cigarettes were food coupons.

"You'll need them. There are a lot of them, but Blanc has a family to feed."

We were silent for a few minutes. I was worried about not having an identity card. If he could supply ration cards and French cigarettes, surely he could give me one?

"Why are you doing this for me?"

"Maybe because you're one less mouth to feed," and he grinned. He was really a handsome chap. "Maybe I envy you."

"Envy me?"

"Yes. I don't like the Germans either. Every day I hear echoes of what they are doing. I believe the Allies will win, but not as soon as you think. Now we're almost there. I'll come with you up to a few meters from the wires. Don't slam the door when you leave the car. I'm cutting my lights and engine."

The wires were impressive, at least three meters high. A stark black fence against the dull night sky. I'd never seen anything like it before and said so in a whisper to my companion, who was crouching with me in the shelter of some bushes.

"They're not as bad as they look. Don't move," he said, glancing at his watch. "Our last patrol is coming. Don't speak. I'll push you when you can go. Good luck."

Walking down rows of vineyards is not easy, especially at night. To make matters worse, it was an up-and-down job because the land wasn't flat. I can't say my crossing back into France was a brilliant exploit and I'm sure had someone seen me—which God forbid—they would have taken me for a drunken hunchback. When I came to ditches or hedges separating one owner's land from another, I had to search for a break and, once I was through, retrace my steps so as to remain in line with my initial direction. It was exhausting.

Once I came to a road just a little better than a track and stayed in a ditch bordering it before I decided to cross. When I was across I heard the tramp of boots and the clatter of metal against metal. I dropped flat, pushing my rucksack into the shelter of a stunted vine and blessing my dark clothes. Afterward I lay for a long time listening until I was certain the noises I heard were only night sounds. Finally I moved in the direction of a clump of trees. That German patrol—I had no doubt it was German—must be relieving their sentinels and a new sentry wouldn't be sleepy like his predecessor.

I felt more secure in the clump of trees, and when I saw a path I moved down it until I came to a road—a macadamized one. Instead of reassuring me, it left me as insecure as I had been back in the vineyards. But for a different reason. Where did the damn thing lead to? If I took the wrong direction, I might walk straight into a German outpost.

I huddled down behind a tree and started to cry. What was I to do? Finally I groped for my flask and swallowed some brandy and after a while I dozed. When I woke, although I was stiff from cold, I no longer felt so miserable and I decided to edge my way toward the road in search of a milestone. My God, how I blessed those red-topped kilometer markers!

The first one I saw was on the other side of the road.

Damn! I'd have to cross.

I found my luck had held. "FRANGY. 10 KILOMETERS." At first I couldn't believe it and switched on my torch just like doubting Thomas.

After that things were easy, and when I spotted a dark mass of buildings on a hill, I headed toward them until I stumbled into a barn—not, unfortunately, before waking a dog that barked and snarled angrily on the end of his chain. Once in the barn I had my usual sneezing fit, which made me wonder if I was going to sneeze my way through the war. And later, much later, I awoke with a light in my eyes.

"Who are you?" a man asked not very amiably.

"It was cold."

"Heading for Switzerland! I've a good mind to turn you over to the gendarmes!"

"Please don't do that."

"Well, get out." And the angry farmer reached for a pitchfork.

I stood up, picking hay out of my hair while the man eyed me warily.

Finally he threw the fork away. It landed with a clatter, startling some chickens.

"This damn war! Merde!" he snarled, thrusting his face into mine. "Merde . . . Merde . . . !"

"I didn't declare it. I'm sorry I've mussed up your hay. How far is it to Frangy?"

"Frangy! I thought you said you were going to Switzerland."

"*You* did," I replied, repeating my question.

"Well, it's none of my business."

"I'll be on my way," and I started for the door.

"Stop! I want my wife to see you first. She's furious about the dog. She doesn't sleep well. His barking woke her."

"I'm sorry about that too. But it's the first time in my life I've ever been glad about a chain on a dog."

"Why?"

"I don't like dogs on chains."

This remark so amazed him he took off his beret to scratch his head. He was bald. In fact, I don't remember ever seeing anyone quite so bald. His skull was pink as a baby's bottom and this somehow gave him a benign expression.

"Come!" he said, grabbing my arm and yanking me away despite my protests about my rucksack. "Come on! Don't argue. I'll bring it later."

After sliding past the snarling dog, to which he gave an amiable kick, he bustled me into a huge common-room with a roaring fire. Here I was greeted by a stout woman, arms akimbo, surrounded by staring children of various ages.

"What! Another one!" she exclaimed belligerently. "Gaston, you're to lock the barn door! Not a wink of sleep did I get!"

A tall, gangling boy laid a hand on her arm in a warning gesture.

Everyone continued to glare at me: two girls in their early teens glared curiously, their brother suspiciously. Only the young ones approached me in a friendly way. I saw then they were twins—a boy and a girl.

"I'm sorry I woke you, Madame."

"She says she is glad the dog was chained," her husband said with a rough laugh. He turned down the wick of his lamp; it was almost daylight.

"Well, Germans or no Germans, I'm going to let him loose at night!" the woman announced, taking a coffee-grinder off a shelf and handing it to one of the girls.

I was astonished. What could the dog have to do with the Germans? Surely love of animals was one of their few good qualities? Why the tone, as if she were defying the whole German army?

Suddenly the boy darted out, slamming the door. His father hesitated and then followed him with a resounding "Merde."

I wondered what to do. I would so much have liked something hot to drink, but I didn't dare ask. I turned away.

"Don't move. Please don't move, Madame," one of the girls whispered, a sense of urgency in her voice.

I froze and the door burst open. The dog charged in, followed by the father angrily remonstrating with his son. The boy was watching the animal, with a crooked smile.

As for me, I was quaking. I knew that if I made one false move, I would be chewed up.

"I wonder if you could give me some hot water. I have some Nescafé in my rucksack. I'll gladly share it with you," I said, trying to keep my voice as even as possible.

"Nescafé! Where did you get that? Black market!" the mistress of the house sniffed.

"No. Not the black market. In Switzerland."

"Switzerland! I don't believe it."

"Would you get my rucksack, Monsieur?" I turned my gaze toward her husband.

This was a critical moment. The lean cur was sniffing around my feet.

It was the boy who went out, and his father, with a sigh of relief, yanked the dog away.

"Oh, don't do that, Monsieur!" I exclaimed, trying hypocritically to keep the joy out of my voice.

They all stared at me again.

"If he had wanted to bite me, he would have done it immediately," I said, trying to persuade myself that what I said was true.

"He hates the Germans," the girl who had warned me said.

"So does most of the world," I snapped.

After that they made a pretense of accepting me, probably because I shared my precious Nescafé with them.

The dog roamed around the kitchen, sniffing at me now and again. Once he stopped to stare, his forelip quivering. I saw his eyes, brown-flecked but not mean. I resolved that before leaving I would pat him.

Presently the girl twin came to me with a torn book.

"Can you read us a story?" she lisped, climbing onto my lap.

Slowly turning over the worn, thumb-marked pages, I noticed how faded the pictures were. Some had been torn and clumsily glued together.

"Would you like to hear a new fairy story?"

They nodded and I helped her brother climb onto the oak table while the dog watched us silently, sitting on his haunches.

"Once upon a time there was a beautiful country filled with happy children. One day this lovely land was invaded by a horde of dragons. They were very fierce dragons who spat fire . . . look

. . . just like this one." And I pointed to a particularly repulsive one in the book, which had a dreadful squint because one of his eyes was badly glued together.

"Yes, just like this one! Only there were hundreds, thousands of them. They swarmed all over the place, and because they were very greedy, the poor people of this once-happy land had to feed them. Meanwhile the King of the country wept as he paced the drafty corridors of his spider-infested castle. With him lived his daughter, the beautiful Princess Marianne. She was the light of his life, but he rarely saw her alone because wherever she went she was accompanied by Slyness and Echo, who were spies of the dragons. They spied on the Princess and her father because they were afraid they would escape. Yes, escape and tell the outer world what was happening in this once-enchanted land. Fortunately, the Princess had two friends. A parrot and a faithful dog —a dog like yours. . . ."

"Boldo?"

"Yes, Boldo. One day she told her faithful Boldo to leave her —and go forth out of the land to other kingdoms across the sea and tell the truth. Now, as everyone knows, dogs cannot talk, but Boldo was a clever chap and he persuaded the Princess to let the parrot go with him. The Princess was very upset to lose both her companions and wept with her father. He because of the sorrows of his people, who were more and more unhappy, she because Boldo and her parrot, Trumpet, had left her. She also feared for them on their journey through the once-lovely land now infested with dragons.

"But Boldo and Trumpet managed to slip out of the once-happy land and reach the country of the great. Here, Trumpet called in sweet tones, in buglelike sounds, to the people across the water to come and free the once-happy land.

"In the end, they came with a great fleet of ships and a tremendous screen of umbrellas."

"Umbrellas!" the twins exclaimed.

"Yes, umbrellas of all colors so as to make the sky like a rainbow."

I paused for breath and suddenly caught the boy staring at me with a musing look, while his two sisters by the fire were openly smiling.

Turning then, I saw the mother of this brood, saucepan in hand, also watching.

"Would you like something to eat?" she grumbled. "After all, we accepted your coffee."

I hope it won't keep you awake, I almost said, but didn't. Instead I spent half the morning with them answering questions about Switzerland. What did the Swiss think about the Germans? When would the Allies land?

To this last question—the most important for all of us—I replied: "No one knows. But it won't be long now." And I put all my conviction into my voice to silence the remembered doubts of the Swiss officer. "Not long. It can't be much longer," I repeated fiercely.

"I hope so. My boy is sixteen and next year he'll be called up for work in Germany. To the Service de Travail Obligatoire. I don't want that to happen," his mother said.

"I won't go," her son said, fondling his dog, which looked up at him, whining with contentment. "I'll join the others in the mountains."

I wanted to ask him what he meant, but didn't dare. Instead I nodded solemnly. I think they thought I was some sort of crazy journalist or fabulous spy and I had no desire to change their attitude. I was right too, because one of the girls cut in:

"You should tell Madame about the convoy that went by yesterday. It was larger than usual."

Once again they all paused over their various occupations to stare at me.

"Well?" I asked.

"Usually, once a week, a couple of trucks go by to relieve their comrades and bring fresh provisions to the outpost down the road. Sometimes they stop to ask for butter and eggs. That's how one of them was bitten by Boldo. After that, their officer ordered us to keep the dog chained or he'd be shot. Well, this time there were four trucks all filled with men, several ambulances, two motorcycles and some officers in those cars that look as if they are going backward."

"When was this?"

"Two days ago. Another went by yesterday. Do you think they're going to invade Switzerland?"

I shook my head. That beacon of light was far too precious a place for their spies and financial dealings. Apart from Portugal, it was the only free country left in Europe—really free—because, from all I had heard, Spain wasn't a sure place either.

"I must go," I said, rising. "How far is it to Frangy?"

"I'll drive you there. I have to go anyway. Go and harness Colette," the father said to his son.

They all came out into the courtyard to bid me farewell, even the dog; I braved a pat, as I'd promised myself I would, and he thanked me by backing up, surprised, faintly wagging his tail.

Trotting down the road, Gaston plied me with questions, some of them personal. He seemed especially intrigued by my presence in occupied France. I let him ramble along, flicking his whip across Colette's rump.

"Yes . . . This war is not like the last one. Only men fought then—not women. It's not right."

Presently, over the brow of an incline, jutting out of the valley floor rose a steep, stone-encrusted ridge with the ruins of a castle at one end.

"What's that?" I asked.

"Chaumont."

Of course. How stupid of me! I must learn to read maps more carefully. But, my God, how was I to get up to the place? It seemed impregnable.

"It's a village, I suppose? Nothing much left of the castle?"

"There's a road on the Frangy side. From this end there's only a footpath."

"Please let me off before the footpath. I don't want you to be seen with me."

"So it's Chaumont you're going to! They're a strange lot up there. It's the jumping-off spot for the back of the world! Before the war they tried to make a tourist attraction of it because of the view. Now even the Germans hardly ever go there."

The climb was a steep one, and the first building I came to was part of the castle ruins. As it was lunchtime, I stayed holed up in it until two o'clock, thinking my contact wouldn't be expecting me sooner. (Even in occupied France the luncheon hour was still sacred.) The time slid by quickly because I dozed, but when I woke I was impatient to find the man who was due to parley with me about the weather. I saw no one in the few alleys of the village. The farmer had been right. The place was the back of nowhere, and it took me a little wandering before I located the cemetery about a hundred meters from the village, down a rough track running parallel to the face of the mountain.

Wondering what to do, I stared at the rusty iron gate surmounted by a cross.

Perhaps I should go in—pretend to look at the tombstones? Suddenly I heard steps behind me and swung around to face a lean old man carrying a spade. It gave me quite a shock, for I hadn't heard anything.

"Have you any relatives in there?" he asked. "They're difficult to locate. We've had a hot summer and the place is overgrown with weeds."

He paused to watch me through malicious eyes while I wondered what name to give a relative buried in this God-forsaken spot.

"We need rain, of course."

I nodded. That's one. Would he continue or was it just idle chatter? If so, I'd better be on my way.

Slowly he leaned his spade against the cemetery wall and removed the unlighted stub of a cigarette dangling from his lips, carefully crumbling the last shreds of tobacco into a tin box he fished out of his corduroy trousers.

"Yes, the place is full of weeds. Few people care about the dead any more. If we don't get rain, we'll have snow."

The second time. Maybe I was on the right track after all.

"Snow is all right until it turns to sleet," I hazarded.

"How right you are. After that it freezes and people break their legs. But it won't freeze—not tonight. So far the winter has been mild."

Following this slow declaration, he hauled out a shabby pouch and started to roll another cigarette. The situation was maddening, especially as I wondered if he wasn't laughing at me.

"No, it won't snow. We'll have rain," and this time he stared across at me before licking down his cigarette.

Although I was sure he had said the word three times, I didn't speak. Supposing he was just a countryman trying to while away the time.

"Can't you count, Mademoiselle, or are you still sleepy?"

"What do you mean?"

"I saw you on the footpath. Quite a steep climb. I've been watching you ever since you arrived, even when you were asleep."

I shrugged. I didn't like the idea of this man watching me sleep. Not that I'm a prude. It's just that sleep is such an intimate thing.

"Continue down the track until you come to a duck pond with a stream running through it. The house is on the left a little farther on. You can't miss it. It's the only farm on this side of the mountain. The land is rotten."

"Am I expected?"

He laughed, looking me over: "You are and you aren't." And picking up his spade, he pushed open the gate of the cemetery.

Jules was the gravedigger.

6

Wind, rain and the sound of water dominated Les Daines, reminding me of *Wuthering Heights.* Its inhabitants were strange, too. Clément Blanc greeted me coldly, even suspiciously, and so did his wife, a stern-looking woman. Even their two small daughters eyed me strangely. Of course they were suspicious, and they continued to be even after they heard from Switzerland, through the underground, that I was reliable and that they should supply me with an identity card.

After a while I gave up trying to charm them and, strangely enough, it was from then onward that I was accepted. Laurence Blanc and I found things to talk about when her husband was absent, which was very often. On rainy days—and there were many—I started to teach the eldest child English. In my stupid, careless fashion, I hadn't realized these people were proud and that I brought into their lives a world they had never known. They also couldn't understand why anyone who had had the chance of remaining in Switzerland should wish to return to France and to attempt the risky passage over the Pyrenees.

"Why didn't you stay where you were? You were safe," Laurence said.

"But there's a war on."

"You're not a man. It isn't as if you were going to be called up to go and work for the Germans."

Her words made me feel stupid. Lying awake at night in the

garret beneath the leaking roof and listening to a grandfather clock ticking away the hours, I was frustrated. Only the Flying Fortresses, winging their way to Italy, gave me a sort of bitter consolation. I was proud of their strong, steady sound, although I lamented the suffering they were destined to inflict. Many times I left my bed to watch them, one by one, slowly blotting out the stars in the indigo sky. I didn't have to open a window—the hole in the roof was enough. It even served as a telescope beneath which I squirmed and turned until they were out of my vision.

Later, on their return flight, some of that even roar was changed, and once I saw a glowing red mass pitch earthward like a blazing comet.

After that I didn't get up to watch any more. I knew Clément listened, too, because one night he told me to go back to bed.

At Les Daines there were few books, but even had there been hundreds, there was no electricity, no candles, only carbide lamps. These were the most extraordinary contraptions I have ever seen. Their heavy, cylinder-shaped bodies—which sometimes exploded —were divided into two parts. The bottom was reserved for the carbide, looking like jagged pieces of stone (a poor description, for no self-respecting stone smelled like cheap wine and garlic on a sour stomach). The top section was a water reservoir into which was drilled a small hole to allow the water to drip onto the carbide, thus causing a chemical reaction and releasing gas which rushed up through a metal tube onto a copper wick on the outside of the lamp. When enough of this evil-smelling stuff spouted forth with the hiss of an angry snake, you struck a match with a prayer! The wick gave out a bright, almost blue light and when the damn thing worked, it was fine. But to achieve this required constant attention, especially as the carbide was not always of good quality. In fact, there were times when I found splinters of real rock and the only way to tell them from the carbide was to gauge their weight. Smelling was no good either because the odor pervaded even the stone. The stuff was sold by the kilo, and I knew the fragments of ordinary rock were just another feature of the black market.

My job was to keep these lamps in order and after a while I

became quite proficient. At least, I supposed so because no one complained—no one except me, who never seemed to get the smell off my hands, probably because of the soap shortage.

There were other pastimes at Les Daines like going out with the children to prevent the sheep from straying to better pastures or discouraging them from climbing to the top of the mountain where they might break their legs. The children and I could risk broken limbs or pneumonia, but not the sheep!

In this God-forsaken spot there was always a mean, cold wind, and sometimes snow flurries landed on my bed when I was asleep. Some mornings I would wake up feeling like Father Christmas after a heavy night with the elements.

I was curious about the top of the ridge which sloped up steeply from the platform to which we clung, and because I was bored with playing Joan of Arc, I borrowed a pair of Blanc's old boots to climb it. Perhaps I expected to find Shangri-La at the summit? I never found anything; it was like trying to scrabble along the spine of a porcupine, and the rocky scree defeated me long before I reached the crest.

On my return I was greeted by Blanc, just back from one of his trips. "Practicing for the Pyrenees? It's a good idea, but I didn't think your feet were so big!"

"They aren't. I stuffed paper into your shoes."

"Don't waste it. We need it for kindling. Come into my room. I want to talk to you."

He sounded tired, but it wasn't until a lamp was lit that I became alarmed. His face had a yellow tinge, and instead of lighting one of his inevitable cigarettes, he sank into his sagging armchair with a low moan which he tried to mask by swearing.

"Are you all right?"

"No. I must have caught cold or eaten something," and with that he laid his head down on the rough deal table that served as a desk.

I called his wife.

The long and short of it was jaundice, so it wasn't until the following day that he was able to talk to me between hideous bouts of nausea. I learned then that he had brought with him three Allied aviators who had been shot down, and that I was to take them over the border to Switzerland in Blanc's place.

"Do you think you can do it?"

Because I didn't know what to say, I shrugged. I was also frightened. Later, in my room, I was excited. This was certainly better than playing Joan of Arc among the sheep.

The following day Blanc said: "The truck will take you to within three kilometers. After that there will be a boy to guide you to the wires. Make arrangements with him for the return journey."

It meant I was really going. A twinge of dismay hit me. Supposing the boy didn't show up or the truck broke down? I knew the penalty for this kind of work. This time, if I was caught, my non-internment alibi had little chance of standing up. I'd look swell trying to explain my three aviators to a lot of Germans. The best I could hope for was to run into one of the Italian patrols that guarded sections of the Swiss border and then declare my real nationality. Although America had been in the war for over a year, they were sometimes inclined to be merciful to American citizens. But they had no pity for the underground, and the chances of survival were even less if you were a Frenchman or an Englishman.

Blanc's wife said: "If you get back, try and bring some oranges. The kids need fruit. The apples are giving them the colic."

You could hear the truck coming a long way off. A steep road climbed from the bottom of the farm, at the foot of which a stream had formed a large pool where the ducks used to gather and frolic. Well, the truck stuck there that night. The ice didn't hold up and the water oozed around the worn tires, and the more the driver raced the engine, the lower she sank. The noise sounded deafening and I knew it could be heard down in the valley. Of course, there weren't any Germans there or Italians either. They were in Annecy twenty-five kilometers away, but there were plenty of curious people who sometimes did as much harm as a collaborator.

We went to the rescue with sacks of sand and snow shovels. The aviators accompanied us and it was then I saw that one of them was limping. It was easy to see in spite of the dark. Pausing, I waited for him to catch up with me.

"What's the matter?" I asked in English.

"Oh, nothing much. That bullet wound I got when I was shot down hasn't quite healed and with the cold and everything . . ." His voice trailed off.

I turned toward the others. The driver had stopped his engine and was waiting for us. Behind me I heard the Englishman say: "Don't worry, Miss, I'll be all right."

It didn't take long to clear the truck and I ran back to the farmhouse to pick up my rucksack. When I returned, the boys were installed. They weren't taking any of the miscellaneous junk they'd collected in their travels. Seemed better to leave it for the others who might come on after them. Besides, Switzerland was the land of plenty!

In the truck there were empty crates that still contained packing straw. I made the men lie down behind them, and I did the same. Close to the canvas top there was a hole I could see through.

Later, when the truck stopped, I noticed the sky was clearer and a few stars had come out. Next to me, the man with the bullet wound began to shake. I grasped his hand and it was hot with fever. I knew then that he wasn't scared, but I was. Something was choking up inside of me. I wanted to scream.

Up front the driver was talking in French. Once I heard him laugh. That made me mad. Blast him! What was there to laugh about when we were like canned sardines in the back of his truck? Had he betrayed us? Had he driven toward Annecy instead of the frontier? And then I heard a thick voice from the road say: "Roulez," and I laughed and so did the others: "Scram!" They knew what that meant, poor wretches! In the last few months they must have heard it many times.

I squeezed the wounded man's hand reassuringly before releasing it. I couldn't tell them it was my first trip—that the other times I had been alone, only responsible for my own skin.

When the truck finally stopped for good, the hands of my watch read 10:15. I was the first one to leap down onto the road, but there wasn't anyone there—nobody except us and the driver.

I hid the men in the bushes. The driver was in a hurry by then. I suppose he was relieved to be seeing the last of us. Whatever it was, he didn't waste time or words, and when I asked him about our earlier stop he said laconically: "Pal of mine," and drove off.

The silence after his departure was heavy. At first I couldn't hear anything, only the boys whispering as they crouched in the bushes next to me. Presently they fell silent as the cold began to eat into us. Then there was a rustling sound and the sharp snap of a twig. I thought it was the boy and tensed myself to meet him. Things were turning out better than I had expected, but after a few seconds an owl flapped out of a tree on heavy wings. One of the men said: "Blast that bird! I thought it was something else," and at that moment two bicycles came along the road, their blackout lamps flickering unevenly. We all sank deeper into the bushes while I felt my heart leap into my mouth. Supposing the boy never came? What then? Where was I? The Franco-Swiss border was long and I couldn't be expected to know every inch of it.

"I think there's someone walking along the road," the man with the bullet wound said.

A sudden hush fell. The seconds drew on. I was about to lose hope when a stone rattled behind me and a figure loomed a few yards ahead, clearly silhouetted against the lighter background of the gravel road. I whistled softly. The figure faded, leaving me puzzled. Had I imagined the whole thing?

"I'm late, but I was delayed back in the village."

I swung around and there stood a boy looking down at me.

I rose, feeling cramped. "It's all right." And as I said it, I wondered how I could have found the time so long.

We crossed the road in single file and then made our way over the fields. The snow showed up in white patches under the trees, but otherwise the ground was hard with frost and now and then my ski boots made a ringing sound when their iron supports struck a frozen rut. Everything was very quiet and the men behind me didn't talk. Only one whistled softly through his teeth—a tuneless sound. I don't think the guide, marching ahead, could hear us, so

I didn't say anything because I knew it was the wounded man.

Presently the boy stopped and motioned us down. That was easy, for we were standing on the edge of a ditch, and we all stumbled into it and sat hunched up, the wounded man on my right, the guide on my left. Suddenly I saw the guide turn his head irritably and I knew we were making too much noise. I whispered a sharp "Shut up!" A few seconds passed. Then came the tramp of feet sounding at first far away and then very close. The boots made the same noise as mine, only doubled in volume. The guide leaned over and whispered in my ear: "The patrol. We're in good time. The road is just above us. Beyond are the wires."

"How often do they pass?"

"At this hour, every ten minutes."

Something flopped against my chest. It was the head of the wounded man. He's passed out, I thought, and at that moment the patrol went by.

We had quite a job getting him to his feet while he groaned and mumbled, sometimes loudly, at others uttering small, pitiful sounds. We were rough with him, almost dragging him over the road into the blessed obscurity of the opposite ditch. Once there we dropped him to stare up at the wires only yards ahead, and the guide, who had been carrying my rucksack, handed it to me. I drew out my flask from one of the side pockets, spilled some aspirins into the palm of my hand, and forced the pills and the burning liquid down his throat.

Then we waited while he gasped and struggled with his pain and fever and I stared at the wires, feeling my watch ticking away the precious minutes.

"I'll wait here for you tomorrow night at two A.M.," the guide whispered. "Try to get over then. They're cold and sleepy at that hour. If you're caught by the Swiss or the others, get rid of this map," and he handed me a small piece of paper, which I pushed into my glove. Then the two of us crawled up to the wires and between us held two strands as far apart as possible while the men went through one by one. The last was the wounded man, whom we dragged by his good leg. He didn't protest, but he was breathing hard.

"Follow the white fence until you come to the wood. Afterward there's a path. The barn is the first building you will see. The door is unlocked and there's food hidden under the hay."

I ducked between the strands of wire and felt a barb wrench my stocking. It made me swear because I remembered I had only one pair left. Behind me the wires looked immensely tall and lonely, and in the distance I heard the returning patrol.

The men were joyous at being in Switzerland and started talking until I told them there were camps here too and that being interned in a neutral country was no fun. At first they wouldn't believe me.

"Listen," I finally snarled, "I've been in one, so I ought to know."

After that I had no more trouble, but I kept a tight hold on the wounded man. Somehow his weakness gave me strength. Tomorrow I still had to get to Geneva. My Swiss permit was in order, but one never knew. And I would have to leave my aviators in the barn by themselves while I tried to establish contact with the man whose truck was supposed to pick us up. The thought was not reassuring.

It was a long walk across the fields—longer than on the other side. The wounded man was carried by his two comrades, hands linked. It was a good idea because it prevented them from talking.

I was walking ahead when I saw the barn, a dark silhouette against the lighter sky. What a relief! Retracing my steps, I made the men lie low while I went ahead to inspect. Inside, it was very dark and stuffy and I couldn't see anything. The smell of hay was overpowering. I had just had time to stifle a sneeze into my handkerchief when I felt a snuffling just above my head. With a scream I fled.

Outside, I crouched against the barn. Should I go back? Or should I go and fetch one of the men? Finally I took out my flashlight and crept back, sliding cautiously around the door. In my beam I saw a gray horse looking at me over the top of a stall. Next to it was a pile of hay.

When we were all safely inside, we found the food our guide had promised and, with the food, a storm lantern. When we lit it, I was able to see the wounded man. It gave me a shock. His face was blotched, his eyes hazy, and his mouth quivered. "Jesus!" his Australian pal whispered, going down beside him, rolling up his trouser. I noticed how gentle his hands were. I didn't want to see the wound. I guessed what it would look like—all puckered up and smelling of pus or something worse. Tomorrow seemed suddenly a long way off.

"Look, Miss. . . . " The voice was alarmed. "We can't leave him like this."

I continued to uncork the bottle of wine. I won't look. I won't. . . .

"If there's a farm nearby, we—"

"Nothing of the sort. You're none of you to move from here." And then I saw it. My stomach turned over. Hot saliva shot up into my mouth. Somehow the loaf of white bread, the ham and the butter didn't look good any more.

"There's a bucket of water over there. Probably belongs to the horse. We could clean his leg with that and then empty some of the spirit from the flask over it afterward," one of the men suggested.

While they held him down, I cleaned him. He fainted when I poured the brandy. It was just as well, because he was starting to whimper.

Afterward the three of us sat for a long time staring at the food without touching it while he lay between us—conscious and in pain. Presently we began to eat, but I couldn't get the smell of pus out of my nostrils.

He watched us for a while, then tumbled off into a sleep of sorts, and when we bunked down for the night, we covered him with some hay while the horse stared at us sadly.

It was still dark when I awoke at six-thirty. I had five kilometers to walk and then a bus to catch. If all went well, I could be in Geneva before eleven. I tidied myself as best I could and, as nothing attracted more attention than dirty shoes, I laid my ski boots aside and replaced them with a pair of ordinary shoes.

One of the men brushed me down so that when I left I felt

clean and neat. I didn't look at the wounded man. He seemed to be asleep.

I didn't start to worry about anything until I reached the bus. Then I began to fret about the men. Would they do as I had told them—not move from the barn?

At the bus station everyone was muzzy from sleep and nobody noticed me. But as the day lengthened, a hum of conversation started and at each stop broad-beamed farmers' wives climbed in, looking healthy and well fed. No one jostled or shouted. Everything was a little slow, which made me sleepy, and I was about to doze off when suddenly I felt someone staring at me.

Oh, I was very casual about waking up. It took me quite a few minutes. First I stretched, yawned, opened an eye and then reached in my bag for my powder compact. Yes, I made every movement as unhurried as possible. Finally when I thought I could peep, I saw him sitting across the gangway in a seat parallel to mine. He wore a beret, but this headgear only served to bring out the bullet-shaped head, the hard face beneath it. He was dressed in a brown duffel coat with a fur lining. His legs were crossed, and although the crease of his trousers was impeccable, his black shoes were mud-stained. On his lap was a package wrapped in newspaper. When I glanced at his face, his eyes crossed mine. They were hard and very blue.

I shifted in my seat and closed my eyes. Geneva was getting very close. The first outskirts were already sliding past. I knew there would be a police check-up at the terminus. There always was when a bus came from the direction of the French border. People began to gather their things. I stood up and, with my empty rucksack rolled beneath my arm, pushed my way toward the entrance.

When the bus stopped I was the second one off, but he was only three places behind, and I could feel he was bent on keeping up with me.

The Swiss barely glanced at my papers. In a second I was free, heading down the clean, wind-swept streets toward the station. There were few people on the sidewalks and I made good time.

Once I dodged into a tobacco shop and bought a package of cigarettes with my precious Swiss money. When I came out, my pursuer was there, staring vaguely into space. When he saw me an inexplicable expression flitted over his face and without a word he began to follow me, walking some ten meters behind. His performance annoyed me. It also left me puzzled. He didn't look the kind of person who followed women. Could he be a Frenchman, lost after crossing the border, who suspected I knew more about things than he did? Whatever he was, I made up my mind to have nothing to do with him.

In Geneva some apartment houses have two entrances. Coming to one, I turned in just in time to see a woman getting into the elevator. Slipping behind the elevator, I crouched down in a dark corner. Soon I heard the man, and from my hiding place I could just see his legs. I knew he was counting the floors. My heart was thumping hard against my ribs. In a little while the elevator slid down. Without a moment's hesitation he opened the gates and disappeared upward. I crept out and dodged through the courtyard into a side street. A tram went by. I raced after it.

It was well past eleven when I reached the address Blanc had given me, having deliberately changed direction several times. The man to whom I gave the password didn't know me, but I recognized him from a photo Blanc had shown me. At first he was suspicious. Finally he consented to contact Bridget's boss at the British Cousulate, Mr. X, and when I saw the green Ford with the CD plates come sliding down the street, an immense feeling of relief shot through me. So much so that when X came into the room with his old familiar smile, there were tears in my eyes.

They said I would have to wait until nightfall before starting back, and I told them about the man who had followed me. Perhaps it was because of this that we started off earlier—leaving me time only for a bath and a short sleep. Meanwhile X went shopping, coming back with the soap and oranges I had promised Blanc's wife and some Nescafé, chocolate and cigarettes for me.

X remained with me until a few minutes before I left with his agent. He told me he was going to England on a month's leave, but when I asked him to take me along he shook his head. "Wish

I could, but the Swiss are getting sticky. The long road over the Pyrenees for you. Be patient. Spring will soon be here. We'll see then. My regards to Blanc." I envied him as he drove his car down the street, free in the only free country left in Europe.

The road back didn't take long. The agent spoke only once and what he said wasn't encouraging: "Tell Blanc he'll have to keep the rest of the boys for a few weeks more. We're having trouble with the Swiss police. We'll have to lay low for a while. I'll let him know when it's all right."

It was dusk when I saw the barn. We went beyond it into a small copse where the van couldn't be seen, and I almost ran to the door, I was so excited at seeing my men again. They were asleep, sprawled out untidily, and for a second I was almost disappointed at the anti-climax. The wounded man saw me first and raised his hand in greeting. He seemed better; we carried him to the van and then they all drove off. It was done so quickly that the barn was lonely when I returned to it. Even the horse thought so, for he nuzzled my sleeve, neighing softly, and I buried my face in his thick old mane.

The return journey went quickly. That night I slept in the house of a blacksmith, and shortly before noon the next day I once more climbed the steep path toward Blanc's house. Somehow I couldn't get the thought of X flying to England out of my mind, and as I looked around the bleak countryside, I envied him. While his plane would be winging its way to England, far back down the line Blanc would send his message: "Keep the men. No passage to Switzerland for the moment." Then I began to think of the long road over the Pyrenees. There again lay danger. How many guides had been arrested these last months as they escorted escaping aviators and agents? I was so engrossed in my thoughts that when I came to the house I didn't bother to hide—as I was supposed to. Instead I pushed open the door and walked straight in.

A policeman was sitting at the table. Opposite him was Blanc, whose eyes opened in alarm when he saw me. I turned back, my hand on the door.

"Don't go, Mademoiselle," the gendarme snapped.

I paused and then saw the gun. It was pointed at me. I could see the small, neat hole at the end of its barrel. I also knew what people looked like when a slug went sliding down it. A flame of rage shot up within me.

"Come over here. Take your rucksack off."

I obeyed slowly. By the stove in the far corner of the room I saw Blanc's wife.

"And how was Geneva?" the gendarme said.

I didn't reply.

"I have an order for your arrest. It comes from Lyon. It's been passed on to us because there are no occupying forces here."

"Well, you could always say you couldn't find me," I suggested.

Blanc grinned. I thought he must be feeling better.

There was a short silence.

"What have you got in the rucksack?" And probably because he didn't trust me, he opened it himself.

The oranges spilled out all over the place. They looked very colorful rolling about the dirty floor. We all looked at them. I knew Blanc's wife stirred because I heard the sharp sound of a cover being put on a pot.

The gendarme stooped and picked them up. I wondered if X would eat oranges in England. Suddenly all my anger vanished, to be replaced by despair. Time was standing still. Time had forgotten about our war.

"Get out of this district before the end of the week. I'll report I couldn't find you. Meanwhile I'll take the oranges," he snapped.

His words left me stubbornly ungrateful.

We watched him put on his kepi, fasten down the buckle of his holster and tap it affectionately with the palm of his hand. Afterward we heard him whistling down the road.

Finally Blanc's wife came out of her corner. In her hand she held some shriveled apples. She spilled them into a glass dish on the table.

7

Although I really became a member of the household after that, it was only for a short time. To disregard the gendarme's order would have been folly. I had to leave.

This time my destination was Annecy, a charming city I had known in prewar days, and I was accompanied by a still shaky and yellow Clément. Boarding a bus—a wood-burning contraption—in Frangy, we arrived as evening was falling. After ambling aimlessly through the streets looking at the shops faked up to give an illusion of plenty, we loafed away from the main street and, after a short walk, found ourselves in front of a large apartment building. It was opulent after Les Daines and so was everything in the apartment of the people destined to shelter me for the next few weeks. Their kindness proved incredible. Nothing seemed too good for me. And, frankly, I don't know which was best, the food or the hot baths.

My host was a successful building contractor who had succeeded through perseverance and hard work. Unfortunately, the war had caught up with him before he was able to enjoy the fruits of his labor. Partly to spare his workmen from being called up by the Germans for work in Germany and partly to hide his other activities, he was working for the Todt organization, building—with other French contractors—the Atlantic Wall, that concrete defense perimeter stretching from Belgium to the Spanish frontier which was intended to repulse the Allied invasion when it came.

Since money was no problem in this household, his wife ran their home in the prewar manner, buying all their food on the black market. It was doled out liberally, not only to her own family but to some of her husband's workmen as well. I arrived skinny and I left fatter and restored.

There was a constant coming and going in the household, sometimes connected with my host's business, at other times involving black-market deliveries. These suppliers employed the most extraordinary subterfuges to slip by the concierge, and one even turned up dressed like a fireman, complete with brass helmet —an incident which sent the cook, who had been talking to the mistress of the house, running to her huge kitchen stove. But there were other matters afoot, and if my host hadn't been connected with the Germans, I am sure neither the bribes he paid nor the disguises would have prevented his being raided by the Vichy police.

For my part, I kept to my room, coming out only in the evening to play bridge with a few intimate friends of the house. My cover story was that I was a niece of my hostess.

For several weeks I saw nothing of Blanc. Then one day he showed up very sprucely dressed in the uniform of the Vichy Youth Movement. This organization had been created by Marshal Pétain himself, with the approval of the Germans, who saw in it a means of keeping track of young Frenchmen.

I stared at him in surprise.

"It's very useful," Blanc said. "It gives me the chance to fake the boys' ages so that they keep on being too young to be shipped off to work in Germany. But it's getting difficult because the Germans are drafting even unskilled workmen."

"They must be short of manpower. When do I leave?"

"I want you to meet some people—ex-officers."

I stared at him, amazed. "Whatever for?"

"Don't you understand?"

I shook my head.

"The boys we keep out of the German draft are going into

camps—youth camps. And then they disappear into the mountains, the forests. In other words, they take to the Maquis."

"The what!" I had never heard the word before.

"The underbrush. It's the Corsican word for taking to the hills."

I remembered the farmer's wife who had been so annoyed with me because she had been wakened by Boldo's barking. That's what her son had meant when he had talked about going into the mountains. "Surely it's still a little cold to be perched on a mountaintop!"

"Smart rich girl!"

I flushed angrily.

"They're not perched," Clément continued. "They're up in the high valleys. Keeping them going requires a lot of stuff. That's what the officers want to talk to you about."

"Me! But what can *I* do?"

"You'd think this war was your individual effort to prove yourself!" Clément said mildly, helping himself to a handful of the cigarettes on my nightstand.

"You might ask," I protested. "You know I have no money and they're given to me."

"When you reach Spain you'll be in touch with the Americans, the British. You are to memorize and report every word of your conversation with these men you're going to meet here."

"In other words, you want me to be a parrot! All right, but give me back my cigarettes."

He grinned, revealing gums from which the teeth had rotted away. There were times when I positively hated him. "I have some others for you—German ones. They taste like the American kind. I don't like them and you don't really like Gauloises, so it's a fair swap."

"But I know nothing about this Maquis business."

"You will." And with that he left me.

My individual war! Blast him! On the other hand, I preferred him this way. I hadn't enjoyed seeing him sick.

A few days later Blanc returned with three companions. Two were dressed in the uniform of the Vichy Youth Movement.

Another—an older man—wore civilian clothes, with a cluster of ribbons in the lapel of his tweed jacket. I guessed he was a retired high-grader because, after kissing my hand, he did most of the talking; the others spoke only when questioned. Blanc sat in a corner of the room, silently smoking. I could feel his blue, gimlet eyes watching me.

"Your journey is a long one, Madame. We're sure you'll get through. We need you to plead our cause."

"But I'm nothing," I protested.

"You're an American."

I don't know why, but this made me feel as if I was some strange creature from another planet.

"The invasion will come. When it does, the young men who didn't go to Germany must be ready."

I had no idea of what he was leading up to and I kept silent.

"We must have arms so that our boys can be trained. Arms, ammunition, medicine, clothes, blankets, everything necessary for guerrilla war."

"And I'm to tell this to the Americans and British! What makes you think they'll listen to me?"

"You can try. Now for the details." And with that he plunged into an explanation of how he intended to set up the camps. I noticed he gave me no indication as to where they would be.

"But how will this equipment reach you?" I stammered when he was through. The whole thing was a very large-sized order.

"By parachute in containers. But if it works . . ."

My God, it just might, I thought, feeling a surge of excitement. "But if it works and the Americans agree, you can't just drop equipment like that any old place. The Germans would be on to you right away."

"Naturally. Therefore, the most important factor is a French-speaking radio operator trained in England. That would simplify matters because he'll have to move around a lot. You realize that yourself, Madame," and they laughed.

I smiled back dutifully, glancing at Blanc. But he wasn't interested. Instead he was riffling through the pages of a book I'd been reading aloud to myself to correct my accent. I knew he was aware of my efforts in that direction because I had done the same thing at Les Daines with the few books there, mostly texts on sheep-farming and mountain-climbing.

"I'll do my best," I said a little lamely, but still feeling very excited. "If I get through, how will I contact you?"

"Blanc will see to that. Plead our case well, Madame."

"I will. But if the Americans in Spain are like someone I met in Switzerland, I haven't much hope."

"The gentleman from Berne doesn't believe in this sort of thing, but then he doesn't know our mountains nor does he believe in the fighting spirit of our young men."

"So you've met him?"

"Many times, but on other matters. From now on, your code name will be Tarte aux Pommes. I'm told it's your favorite dessert."

I stared at him, feeling like a fly caught in a spider's web.

A week later Blanc and I left for Carcassonne after a tearful and affectionate farewell from my hosts.

I wondered why we were going to the famous walled city. It wasn't near the Spanish border. But when I asked Blanc, he said curtly: "For security reasons," a phrase that was destined never to leave me from then on. I learned to hate it because it seemed to eliminate so much of the spirit of adventure. Of course I was wrong. Keeping one step ahead of the Germans was no light-hearted matter. It involved too many people.

I don't know why, but Blanc seemed nervous during our journey, which involved many changes and long waits listening to the sighs of midnight trains in empty stations. This nervousness showed in his failure to tease me and in his long, appraising stares. Somehow his attitude reminded me of a horse dealer dubiously sizing up a possible purchase.

Some twenty kilometers from the Pyrenees the Germans had created a forbidden zone similar to the zone that skirted the Channel coast. This area, which stretched to the foot of the mountains, was a natural hiding place for everyone trying to escape into Spain. Most of the people living in its isolated farms were smugglers before they were farmers, and had plied that trade long before the Germans invaded France. In fact, they were a race apart, part Catalan, part Basque, who lived in a world of their own. The Germans decided to control that world, and to do so they instituted a census and issued a pass to each inhabitant. This act, which "allowed" those fiercely independent people to travel in their own territory, was so galling to them that they decided to go in for smuggling in a really big way—smuggling human beings to freedom. Knowing every path of their hills, every pass through the highest snowbound mountains, they guided into Spain Allied aviators who had been shot down, Allied agents, Jews and young men eager to join the Free French. Alas, many of them were betrayed, some by their own people, others by Frenchmen who infiltrated the various escape organizations.

Trying to establish contact with these people was a difficult business, requiring the right introductions, which in turn was always a complicated and dangerous affair because when the links were forged in one place, the chain might already have been broken elsewhere. The Gestapo and its spies weren't asleep. And this was what was worrying Blanc and taking us to Carcassonne. He wanted the all-clear before we turned up in Perpignan. He also wanted to be sure I would be accepted. Recently a great many escape lines had been broken, with the arrests of men who, under torture, divulged the names of others who, in turn, under the same treatment, supplied more information.

Our rendezvous in Carcassonne-le-Nouveau was a small bistro that we reached just before curfew. I stayed in back, in the darkest part of the café, while Blanc talked with the owner, a fat, blowsy woman ready to heave us out. Finally, when we were the last clients in the place, she agreed to let us stay. We slept on long, wine-stained tables, flimsily covered with worn blankets.

The following morning, after a cup of wartime coffee sweetened with saccharin, we left on bicycles she lent us. I had no idea where we were going and I was so stiff and dirty I didn't care. I'd had only a summary wash in the yard behind the bistro, surrounded by curious hens and smelly rabbit hutches. How Blanc felt I don't know, but he pedaled energetically ahead of me, obviously following a road he already knew.

Soon we left the town and started to climb, not along a main road but on a dirt track bordered by vineyards. Somewhere over to my left the citadel raised its crenellated walls against the cold morning sky. It looked lovely, far more beautiful from a distance than close up. Viollet-le-Duc, the architect who had restored it, liked grandeur and his concept of grandeur was an overabundance of stone towers and turrets that time had not yet weathered. It had always looked to me like something made in Hollywood.

At first we climbed furiously, standing up on our pedals and swaying our machines sideways like sprinters. The exercise helped take some of the cricks out of my back, but gradually we adopted a more leisurely pace and I was able to see the vineyards stretching for miles over the hills.

At a small farm we were greeted by a mother and daughter as alike as two peas in a pod. In their lilting, nasal accent they said He was over there. "Over there" implied a walk down a rough track, more climbing and finally the distant silhouette of a man working near a crumbling building set among the vines.

I was exhausted, or almost, and certainly hungry and thirsty when we finally reached him.

He didn't seem surprised to see us. He only nodded and continued to work, clearing away the winter debris from the gnarled trunks of the vines.

Finally he joined us and then I saw he was quite young and had a long scar down the side of his face. It didn't look new, but it didn't look old either. He was handsome in his Basque beret, even distinguished-looking, with a high-bridged nose and a Red Indian complexion.

He stared at me and I knew that his small eyes didn't miss a detail of my person as they swept over me. Then he moved off with Blanc to talk out of earshot.

I leaned back, bracing my back against a rock that had once been part of the ruined building behind us. The sun was pleasantly warm. In fact, after a moment I could feel my face tingling. No wonder the scarred man had such a tan. I stared at the vines. They looked so gnarled and stunted I wondered if they would ever be green, ever bear dangling clusters of fruit.

For the moment they were just black and gray sticks. And then I saw it—a tiny, timid spot of green sprouting shyly from between two V-shaped sticks. I stared unbelievingly. It was a bud—a tiny, brave one. Spring. The miracle of the season! The miracle of continuity. I touched the bud gently, trying to borrow some of its courage! Maybe this year the harvest would be one of peace. Maybe . . .

A sudden shadow made me turn. The man with the scar was staring down at me.

"C'est le printemps! Regardez!" I said.

"I know. It means work—much work—and I am alone now. But spring comes slowly. Come." And, holding out his hand, he helped me to my feet and drew me around to the back of the ruin. "Look at them! Aloof, cold and much too clear. They are like a décor de théâtre."

I gasped. Along the horizon stretched a jagged mass. With sawlike teeth, monstrous and beautiful, it reached high into the blue sky. The Pyrenees!

"They're not like the Alps," I whispered.

"No. They are sharper and just as dangerous. Is it the first time you've seen them?"

"No. But never like this."

I felt his musing stare and wondered if I should tell him. Fort Romeau . . . skiing! Another day, another age! God, but they were beautiful!

Shrugging, he turned away, and I was relieved. I hadn't really wanted to tell him that I had seen them from a luxurious winter-sports resort.

"Here you can dream of spring, but over there it's still winter. This morning they're on their best behavior. But this afternoon the clouds will return. She says they're not like the Alps," he said, turning to Blanc.

"To each his own! Here your sky is not the same blue."

"And I suppose the snow is another color, too! Our skies reflect the Mediterranean, the shores of Africa, the ruins of Carthage."

What a strange wine-grower!

I started to make some comment that might prompt him to say

something about himself, but he cut me short.

"You must be thirsty and hungry. Come and sit in the lee of the wind. Soon someone will bring food."

The food was delicious—black homemade bread and a rabbit pâté tasting of wild thyme which we washed down with thick red wine. Afterward I left the two men. I wanted to see the mountains again.

They were gone. Wiped out like a chalk line on a blackboard. And yet the sky was still the same. Just as blue. It was uncanny. Suddenly, at my feet, small particles of earth started to twirl and I felt chilled.

"They're still there. Your legs will learn to feel them soon enough," my host said, joining me. "Bon voyage, Madame."

And that was that, except for Blanc's tuneless whistle all the way back. But at least it was downhill.

That evening in the train we were alone in our compartment. "Who was that man?" I asked.

"I don't know."

You damned liar! I felt like hissing.

"He was once in the Legion." And with that he shut his eyes and fell asleep.

The Legion! The Foreign Legion! That would account for the reference to Africa as well as the scar. But what about Carthage? I had never supposed the soldiers of the Legion were so well versed in the history of Roman conquests! But what did I know about them anyway? Not much, except that a good deal of glamour surrounded them—that they signed up under false names so as to lose their original identities—that the Foreign Legion became their raison d'être from the day they joined. I fell asleep thinking of my wine-grower and saw him with a kepi, a white handkerchief pinned to the back of it, striding over hills of sand surrounded by crumbling Roman ruins that sheltered stunted vines.

In Perpignan the mistral was blowing—a nasty, wailing wind sweeping down the streets into the tiniest corners, leaving a film of dust everywhere. But the sky was blue and just gazing at it made one think of spring. And my room, in a scruffy little hotel in a narrow street, had nothing scruffy about it. It was enormous; the furniture was old and the red-tiled floor was partly covered by a worn rug. The window looked out on a courtyard with faded laundry flapping on a clothesline. Across the courtyard was a furniture factory and shop, with a wrought-iron balcony running the length of its first floor. The balcony had something not quite French about it. This was the Midi, all right—and that section of it bordering the Spanish frontier that had a long, turbulent past. Yes, the Midi, with only those damn mountains to cross.

For days on end I was often alone, but I tried not to grumble because I guessed Blanc was trying to find a guide to get me over. "Guess" is right because he was totally uncommunicative. Once he asked me to run over the details of the conversation that had taken place in Annecy with the men from the Maquis.

"What is your code name?"

For a moment I stared at him blankly.

"Well, what is it?"

"Tarte aux Pommes." And I found myself wishing I could eat some and said so, but he only shrugged and left me alone again.

Sometimes I went to the movies. Most of the pictures were either Italian or German, and the newsreels showed horrendous scenes of the bombings of Rouen and the suburbs of Paris as well as pictures of Hitler posturing and yelling. I thought he looked older, which seemed to confirm rumors about his health, but I doubted if the population of Perpignan cared one way or another because they were too busy looking for food. If some of them had been undecided about the German occupation, they were slowly changing. Secret murmurs of resentment could be heard in cafés and on the interminable queues, but they were few and brief because the secret police were everywhere. Sometimes you could recognize them by their belted trench coats and the fact that they always moved in pairs. Other times it was more difficult because they were Frenchmen. In every aspect of life the Midi was learning what the stomp of boots meant—learning what the north had known since the Armistice of 1940.

I learned never to leave my hotel without a careful look around.

I also learned never to return to it by the same route. But even then I could not be sure I wouldn't one day feel a hand on my shoulder. In the end I gave up going out, and I think Blanc was relieved because he brought me books and writing paper—gray, flecked paper that blotted when I used it. One Sunday he took me out to Canet plage in a rickety tram, but we didn't stay long because the mistral was blowing huge waves up the beach and hordes of German soldiers were milling everywhere, making things even bleaker. The Mediterranean was as gray as the English Channel. Looking at it, I wondered how anyone could call it La Grande Bleue.

Shortly after this aborted excursion I woke up one morning with a high fever. How high I couldn't tell because thermometers were so scarce only doctors were allowed to buy them. Blanc didn't trust any of the doctors in Perpignan because they were all under surveillance, but he finally called one he knew from out of town.

The diagnosis was a cold—despite a swelling beneath my ear—and the doctor suggested I should put off my departure.

"You know that's impossible. Our passes have a date limit," Blanc protested.

"Well, bon voyage. I wish I were going with you. I'm sick of this hide-and-seek game—this split-personality racket. I'd rather be in North Africa. At least it's a clean death with no hole-in-the-corner business, no dodging and lying in ditches, imagining every sound to be a German with a gun."

After his departure there was a long silence.

"He wants to be a soldier," Blanc said lamely.

"Obviously. On the other hand, maybe he would rather just be a good doctor with enough medicine. Just a neutral."

"He no longer has any choice. He's needed up in those camps. He says he wants to be a soldier. Well, he *is* one, only without a uniform. There are hundreds like him and one day there will be thousands—an army of shadows the Germans will learn to fear wherever they go, wherever they sleep."

"I thought *I* was the one who had the temperature!"

"You have. Go to sleep. Tomorrow you must be fit to meet someone important. Get drunk." And with that he left me the aspirin and a bottle of brandy.

Perforce I followed his advice, and the following day I was better, with only a hangover and a slight ache beneath my right ear. Just as I was wondering if I should get up, there came a knock on the door—the same knock Blanc used.

"Entrez," I called and a French police officer stepped in.

Shocked, I slowly pulled my sheet up to my face (as if it could make me invisible). This was it! I was caught. All the dodging for nothing. I hadn't thought I would get through. But what of Blanc? God, I hoped they hadn't caught him too. I must forget. Forget everything I had memorized. Forget the man with the scar. I'd go back to my original story about being an American.

"Don't be alarmed, Madame. I only want to talk to you."

And then suddenly Blanc was in the room, carrying a basket covered by a red-checked napkin.

"I'm sorry. Very sorry. I should have told you," he said, and he sounded very contrite as he stared at me. "This is Commandant Puget."

"For shame, you cold-blooded northerner! And Madame or Mademoiselle has a temperature! Very foolish, mon ami. She might have screamed. I have brought something that will help cure your cold, Madame—an old bottle of Bordeaux that I picked up on the way through my cellar."

I began to wonder if I wasn't dreaming—a sort of comic nightmare that took into account the cobwebs on the policeman's sleeve. Policemen. No one liked them these days even when they were French. Doing their duty in obedience to German orders had made law-breakers out of most of the population.

I tried to smile at him.

"That's better," he said, patting me (he was old enough to be my father). "Now we'll have lunch. That's where I am supposed to be—yes, peacefully having lunch with my wife. No one knows the cellar of this hotel connects with mine. A very useful arrangement. If I were younger and this country at peace, I could have my wife on one floor and my mistress on another. But I'm no longer young and I love my wife." And, helped by Blanc, he began to unpack the basket—a basket filled with food that was still warm. A stew that made my nose tingle.

"My wife made it. It's rabbit—guaranteed not cat. Her sister raises them at her country place. A little wine, Madame or Mademoiselle . . . "

"Mademoiselle."

"Good. That's what's written on your pass. You're the daughter of a brother of mine who is married to a schoolteacher. They live in a small town that is literally at the foot of the mountains. It's the end of the line for everything but mule trails. It's on the border of the Pays-Catalan. These trails have never been used up to now, because it's hard to establish a connection with those people. That's why Mr. X, the man in Geneva, has been saving them as a last resort. But now we have to open a new escape route because we've had trouble—great trouble."

"I know. I was told."

"Switzerland is a bottleneck. Mr. X wants you to try this new route. I don't know the guide. He speaks no French. Only Spanish and Catalan. You will go high up—the passes will probably be covered with snow. Once you're over, you'll get a salvoconducto from Barcelona. Payment is your business—that is, you are to give the guide very little, but promise him a lot more if you're satisfied. In other words, you are an éclaireur, a scout."

So this was what Mr. X had meant when he'd said, "I'm afraid it's the long road over the Pyrenees for you." And it certainly looked as if everything had been planned in advance. I began to feel again like a fly caught in a spider web.

"You must not think," he continued in his clipped but smooth voice, "that life in Spain means freedom as we once knew it. All foreigners have to have a permit to travel. Sometimes even the Spaniards themselves require a salvoconducto, depending on how they stand with the authorities. Franco is a dictator in every sense of the word. There are concentration camps everywhere. Miranda is filled with young Frenchmen trying to join the Allies, aviators who've been shot down and Jews who were caught before they could reach a British or American Consulate. The French claim to be Canadians or members of the Fighting French Air Force, the RAF, or anything to get away from these stinkholes. As a woman and an American, you will be looked after by your Consulate in Barcelona. When your identity is solidly established, you must go to the British and ask to see Major Adrian, but please do not tell the Americans you intend to see him."

"Why?"

"Because you're working for the British, and if the Americans find out they'll drop you like a hot potato. You must play the whole thing by ear. Some more wine? It's a good bottle and Blanc tells me you've lived in France long enough to appreciate fine wine. Poor France! I never thought I would see her beneath the boot. During the last war I was a liaison officer with an American regiment."

I let him ramble along, only half listening. I knew I was working for the British, since X was an Englishman, but why the complications? We were allies. Maybe his police work had distorted everything.

"There's no need for me to play a double game. The Americans and the British are allies."

"Yes, but their secret services must never overlap one another except in the field. The American in Berne turned you down for some reason he alone knows. You went to the British. Mr. X has told Blanc the Americans will not like this. Your situation and the Americans' way of handling it shows they are amateurs in the game. Believe me, use your nationality only to get to Barcelona. After that, play it by ear. And I assure you it will be the British who will listen better. They have been playing this game for centuries. Perfide Albion, with American money, will run the line you are to open."

I sighed. It all seemed very complicated.

"Don't forget your countrymen are backing Giraud in North Africa while the British are behind General de Gaulle. General Giraud was a prisoner in Germany; he is a Johnny-come-lately. But General de Gaulle—" and I noticed he said the name almost reverently—"has been in England right from the start and it was his voice that told France she had lost a battle but not the war.

And the news we hear comes from London, and every Frenchman who listens in secret thinks it's his personal way of fighting against the occupation."

"I agree with you about that, but the rest sounds like politics."

"It is, and I wanted to warn you. But you'll be all right."

I lay back on my pillows and closed my eyes. The wine had made me sleepy. I dozed, lulled by the sound of the two voices.

Blanc shook me awake.

"I must go now, Mademoiselle," Puget said. "I have to return and finish the rest of my lunch with my wife. Often my German counterpart drops in. Today he is sure to do so because of the shooting. They are going to take hostages."

I knew what he was talking about. A German had been gunned down and one of his assailants had escaped, leaving a trail of blood. I was about to say something about it, but I saw Blanc, a finger to his lips, staring at me.

"Thank you, Monsieur le Commandant, I will do my best. Perhaps when all this is over I will be able to thank you and your wife adequately."

"Perhaps . . . " and to my amazement I saw a shadow pass over his bland features. "If I'm careful not to let the German see cobwebs on my uniform," he said, brushing his sleeve. "They are not as stupid as we think and my counterpart might wonder why I was in uniform down in my cellar during the luncheon hour. Goodbye." And he left.

The following day we too left, although I still wasn't feeling well. And at the station I stood in the background while Blanc was getting the tickets, trying to make myself as inconspicuous as possible.

Our train was late—very late. But one train was very much on time, a freight that came rattling down the tracks without an engine and stopped in a crash of wood against a bulkhead.

For a moment everything paused as if frozen. Even the Germans stopped pacing the platform to stare, amazed. When the dust drifted away, freight cars were lying lopsided across the tracks and oranges were spilling from them in all directions. In an instant everyone in the station had dashed across the tracks any old way to pick up as many as they could. Me too. It was pandemonium, with everybody yelling with delight.

The wayward train and its cargo must have been destined for the Germans, because they soon took control, driving people away with kicks, rifle butts and curses. Soon a company of soldiers commanded by a corporal started to load the fruit onto trucks. They reminded me of a swarm of green locusts.

"How many did you get?" Blanc asked.

"More than a dozen," I replied delightedly.

"Throw them back on the tracks."

I protested.

"You fool! If we're stopped and searched on the train, you'll have some explaining to do. Throw them away. Hurry! The Germans are beginning to search people. Throw them away!"

He was right, but I was suddenly very tired, almost close to tears. My ear ached and I could feel my temperature rising.

Blanc stared at me. "Take some more aspirin. I'll get you a glass of water." I sat huddled on a bench as he disappeared. Farther down the platform a Frenchman who had protested too vehemently was dragged away between two guards.

"The fool," Blanc said, holding out a tin cup of water. "The damn fool! He'll be one of the hostages. And all for an orange!"

As we chugged out of Perpignan, I caught a last glimpse of a young boy crawling between the platform and the track and picking up my oranges. It looked as though he had a chance of getting away with it, and I was glad.

I don't think we had many kilometers to cover, but the journey took hours because of the frequent stops. At the start our compartment was filled with farmers and their wives laden with nails, candles, anything they'd been able to barter for the food they raised. Gradually they all left, and the country began to change. The flat lowlands fell away as the train chugged uphill, sometimes between steep ravines and along swift streams that were bordered by fields sweeping upward to the farms that clung to spurs of rock. There were fewer and fewer roads; nothing but dirt trails with arched bridges over the streams. I fell asleep, my scarf wound tightly around the upper part of my sore neck, and I woke only when the train came to a jolting stop, banging my head against the window.

The door of the compartment was flung open and two Germans entered. My heart flipped and started to thud against my ribs. I also felt a little sick. I didn't dare look at Blanc opposite me.

They snapped a few words to each other which I didn't understand; then one disappeared, to return a few minutes later dragging a woman with him.

She was handcuffed and they sat her down between them, right next to me. She was older than I, very pale, and I judged from her disheveled clothes and dirty shoes that they must just have caught her. She was obviously in a state of shock because she sat as stiff as a ramrod and stared straight ahead. After a while one of the Germans pushed her—not unkindly—against the back of the seat and they began to talk together.

I leaned back in my seat and closed my eyes. I had trouble understanding them because they spoke a rough dialect, but one thing did get through to me. They were insensible to the woman's plight. They had been on patrol, seen her and asked for her papers. When she hadn't produced them and had tried to run away, they had arrested her. It was as simple as that. And in compliance with their orders they were right. It wasn't up to them to ask, much less to wonder why so many people were trying to cross the Pyrenees. I don't suppose the question even entered their minds.

But for the grace of God, I might have been in her shoes. Dear God, I prayed for myself and for her, and then muddled all my praying so that I was just repeating over and over: Dear God . . . Dear God . . .

Who was more important, the woman or me? Could I really continue to sit and do nothing, pretending to be asleep? Maybe she was an innocent farm woman who had wandered too far from home and panicked. Maybe? But deep down within me I knew this wasn't so—knew I was trying to turn aside from the truth. I loathed myself, my cowardice. Surely there was something Blanc and I could do? Knock out the man beside me, whose rifle was pressing against my leg. And then what? Jump off the moving train? It was going slowly enough, panting like an old horse on a warm day. But on one side of the track there was a wall of jagged rock and on my side a drop of more than a hundred meters. Even if I could get the message to Blanc, I knew he wouldn't play. He might even restrain me, considering his existence in our own chain of events more important than any foolhardy action. Yet he was a brave, humane man, however gruff. Maybe he too was having to stifle his feelings? Today and every day all scruples had to be stifled. For the moment, only one thing counted: getting me over the Pyrenees to deliver two different sets of messages that might not even be listened to. Damn! I would make those British listen if only for the sake of this unknown woman. I owed her that. And many others like her . . . herded behind bars and into dingy torture chambers before being dragged out and shot.

I opened my eyes and stared at the profile of the German next to me. He was a youngish chap with a ruddy, healthy complexion. I tried to picture him out of uniform and saw a country man or a construction worker with a wife and children to whom he wrote weekly letters, laboriously scrawling simple words on cheap paper. What devil's caldron had brewed this monstrous regime—dreamed up by perverts, pimps and freaks—that forced simple human beings down the path of degradation? They went like sheep, and one day their shepherd would lead them not into green pastures, but over a precipice. The doctor in Perpignan was right: fighting in North Africa was a clean death. If I made it, I would drive an ambulance in England or North Africa. If I got through . . . Perhaps . . . Maybe . . . And again I knew fear intermingled with pity, not for myself but for the woman they had caught. I would scream my messages: I would not forget anything I had been told. Perhaps, God willing, this new escape route would reduce the number of these incidents.

I looked across at Blanc as I fumbled with the scarf around my neck—and I saw relief in his eyes.

Suddenly the train came to a clattering halt. We were out of the ravine and puffing idly alongside a wooden platform and a hut over which floated an aggressive, gaudy swastika. The two guards rose and left, pushing the woman between them. Outside I heard shouts in German. The checkpoint!

A German officer appeared brusquely in the doorway. Behind him a soldier was talking to the guards from our compartment.

"Papiers!"

We handed them over, in that obsequious manner we all displayed. No wonder the Germans felt nothing but contempt for us. The officer glanced at them, handed them back, clicked his heels and, with a vague, arm-lifted "Heil," disappeared to bang his way toward the other compartments.

My newfound aunt and uncle were waiting for us when, minutes later, we reached the town that was the end of the line. Beyond it lay other towns, but civilians were not allowed to go farther. We were too close to the Spanish border—a no-man's-land lying along a twisting road that was edged by steep mountains.

I felt a chill in the air when I stepped down onto the platform and into the arms of my relatives. They fired questions at me—how were Tom and Dick?—for the benefit of the soldiers who were milling around. When we finally trooped out, after showing our papers again at another contrôle, I noticed Blanc hanging back as if he didn't know any of us.

Later, when I was lying on a bed in the little house beside a noisy stream on the outskirts of town, I asked him why.

"Because when I return I don't want anyone at the contrôle to suspect we were together. I'm going back alone, remember? Well, so far, so good. Tomorrow it's up to you. You behaved very well on the train. I know you were seething."

"Weren't you?"

"It serves no purpose."

"Have you no compassion?"

"Today we have to live without it—pretend to, anyway. Shove it away inside us, into our very bones, so the contempt we feel at our inadequacy gives us courage to carry on."

I was surprised at his words. In one sentence he had described everything I felt. I looked across at him with affection. We had traveled a long road together. I would miss him. After the war I would go back to Les Daines. After the war . . . Supposing there was no "after" for him? Suppose someone he trusted gossiped too loudly, or his false identity was discovered? (I knew he reserved his real one for his home.)

"I will miss you, Blanc," I said, thinking of the blood-spattered cellars.

"When you've done all you have to in Barcelona, what are your plans?"

"Drive an ambulance in England or North Africa."

"Other people can do that—are doing it already. You're a little late."

"I'll find something to do."

"Of course you're not a heroine, but, all things considered, you might have done worse. Too bad . . ."

"What's too bad?"

"That you won't follow things up."

"I haven't the slightest idea what you're talking about, and stop smoking all my cigarettes!"

"Your 'uncle' has plenty of Spanish ones. Yes. Too bad. You could be useful if you came back."

"Come back?" I shouted, grabbing at my sore neck. "After all I've done to get out? You're nuts!"

"You know France. You know the way things are—the stupid but important details of everyday life."

"Like what?"

"The ration cards, the latest jokes, prices on the black market . . . just living under the boot."

"I never want to hear the sound of the boot again."

"You will. Love and hatred are twins, and you'll miss hating when you're far away. Yes, you'll miss the sound of the boot. Of course, it's not an easy life. . . . Well—" and he shrugged his shoulders—"I wouldn't want to have your death on my conscience, but I'll miss you too, rich Tarte aux Pommes. . . . And now I think we'd better join your 'uncle' and 'aunt' and your baby 'cousin.' "

I didn't sleep much that night because of the pain in my neck and the return of my fever. But toward morning I dropped into sleep from which I was awakened by my "aunt" standing over me with a smile and carrying a tray.

Laying it on the bed, she said in her singsong southern voice: "You look better and the swelling has gone down. It's a lovely day, but chilly. Later my husband and Georges want to speak to you."

"Georges?"

She shook her head. "We only know him by that name."

Of course. How stupid of me. Would the time ever return when people used their real names? For the moment, I didn't even know the surnames of my newfound relatives!

Later the two men joined me, Blanc or "Georges" looking spruce and freshly shaved.

"I think you'd better tell her the plan now, she's looking better," he said.

"The Germans survey the road and the mountains with binoculars," my "uncle" informed me. "Come Sunday, they ease up. We've noticed it before. Maybe they think people don't try to escape on the Lord's day.

"This afternoon, after lunch, my wife, the baby in his pram, and you and I will go for a walk. 'Georges' will creep over the fields to a small bridge farther down the road. Once there, he'll hide under the arch until we come along. Then you'll change places with him so that any binocular-minded German will see three people go out and three people come back. Since it will be dusk they won't notice his clothes. I'll hide your rucksack in the pram under my son's mattress. Now I must go to church. 'Georges' will explain the rest." And he left us.

"When they've gone to church," Blanc said, "I'll fix a bath for you. There's no running water, but they've put two buckets on the stove. It will wash away the dregs of your fever. You had quite a high one during the night."

"How do you know?"

"You were so restless I heard you and came in. I don't think you even recognized me. I gave you some aspirin and your 'aunt' made some hot wine. You look much better."

It was true, and after I had bathed and dressed, I listened to Blanc with real excitement.

"Wait until dark before you cross the bridge. Incidentally, it's a tiny bridge—it's only used by mules and donkeys. You'll find two tracks on the other side. Take the right one up into the mountains. It's a steep climb and it brings you to a cluster of huts. You're right in the middle of the Pays-Catalan then. It's poor country and so isolated even the Germans rarely go into it. Knock on a nail-studded door. You can't miss it because a candle will be burning in one of the stone arches. An old woman will open the door, but she won't talk to you because she only speaks Catalan. She's the grandmother of your guide. She'll keep you there until he turns up. Don't offer any of them any money. They're proud people and they're doing this because they not only hate the Germans but Franco as well."

After a late lunch which I had trouble swallowing, my "uncle" wheeled in the pram. He put my rucksack under the mattress and then sat his son on top of it. It was a disaster. The poor child looked as if he were perched on the Eiffel Tower.

We burst out laughing, but seconds later I glumly watched the two men empty my rucksack, throwing my possessions pell-mell onto the dining-room table. Of course the first thing they cast aside was my gray flannel suit, then a book by Colette and a couple of sweaters.

I protested, my "aunt" commiserating with me.

"Sorry, Mademoiselle. But there are plenty of clothes in Spain. Why don't you wear your sweaters? It will be cold, you know. You're going up to the snow line. Even if you can't button your jacket, your raincoat will hide the bulge."

In the end, all that my rucksack contained were toilet articles, a blouse, some handkerchiefs, pajamas and a pair of shoes. Even so, the baby was sitting up abnormally high, and he began to cry. I would gladly have joined him.

"I'll keep your things for you," his mother said, rocking him in her arms.

I shook my head. "Keep them for yourself. You need them more."

She smiled, her dark eyes lighting up. Some of her joy must

have communicated itself to her son, because he stopped bawling and held out a hand to me.

Slowly we laid him back in the pram with his fingers still clutching one of mine and we started out. I felt like an advertisement for a Michelin tire. Even my shoulder bag had trouble finding its customary niche on my shoulder.

"I don't think you could get work as a model," Blanc quipped. "But you'll need all those sweaters. Goodbye. It will take me a good hour to crawl to the bridge. The guide will be our contact. You can write to me through him. We'll be waiting to hear the results of your talks with the British. We're counting on you." And putting his arms around me, he whispered: "I'll miss you."

Tears stung my eyes and I wanted to say something, but the words stuck in my throat. By the time I was able to speak he was gone, and I felt foolish standing in the middle of the room, the baby chortling in his carriage, his mother fingering my gray suit and her husband staring out the window.

Later, walking down the road between my "aunt" and "uncle" and casually chatting, I felt miserable and I couldn't understand why. I should have been happy—glad to be leaving everything. But I wasn't. In fact, I was thoroughly unhappy and I stared at my surroundings as if to lap them up like a thirsty puppy. I thought of Mother in the Vittel internment camp, friends, the good and the indifferent, my home in Brittany now occupied by the Germans, everything that was part of a life that would never be the same again. Of course, I knew people in England—knew them well—but their lives too had changed. What interest could I hold for them today?

Between the road and the noisy stream some stunted vines grew. Looking at them reminded me of the man with the scar and I wondered if he knew where I was. Or had our encounter been just a routine check-up? In any case, I was glad he couldn't see me today. With my swollen face I wasn't a pretty sight. But I would never forget him. His personality had captured my imagination, even though I could hardly have captured his. Only Mr. X would remember me. He had planned this whole expedition.

And I would not fail him. I owed it to him, to Blanc, the policeman in Perpignan, the couple walking next to me, the woman in the train, even to the man with the scar who had given the all-clear.

Dusk was falling when we reached the bridge—a lovely arch of time-worn stones that blended into the blue-and-gray twilight. My "uncle" gave me a light shove, nodded his head, and I turned down a footpath to meet Blanc on his way up.

"Well timed! Don't stir until it's dark. Keep in the shadow of the bridge," he said as he passed me.

I didn't have long to wait for darkness. The light didn't fade; it clamped down, and I knew Blanc would only be noticed as one of a group of three who had gone for a walk wheeling a baby carriage.

When I finally crept out, it was cold. Before reaching the footpath I hesitated, listening. But the only noise was the stream and even that had a lonely sound.

In the end, I made a dash around the buttress of the bridge and, head down, raced across it until I reached a clump of firs on the other side.

It took me more than half an hour to scramble up the steep path, dislodging pebbles in the process. In the still of the night they sounded like an avalanche. It was so dark that I probably would have missed the village entirely had it not been for the grunting of a pig followed by the mournful moo of a cow. But even then it was some time before I located a pinpoint of light flickering in a window niche. Next to it was a door.

I knocked and the old crone who opened pulled me inside. She left me standing in the dim light of a huge room filled with the smell of countless fires while she shuffled to the window to blow out the candle. Then she led me to a fire blazing in the far end of the room and sat me down on a bench while she stirred the contents of an iron pot simmering over the hot embers. Soon, still without a word, she ladled some soup into a wooden bowl and handed it to me. It was surprisingly good and, to my relief, I was able to swallow it without pain. Although I was still hungry, I didn't dare ask for more, but in her silent, slow way she must have understood. Something like a smile flitted over her face, causing it to crack into a million ripples like throwing a pebble in a pond, and she ladled some more into my bowl.

Afterward I dozed there, with a cat curled at my feet, while the old woman told the beads of her rosary, whispering endless Hail Marys in a language that was neither French nor Spanish but a little like both. I woke up when the cat stretched against my feet. Minutes later a man slipped in, a dog padding at his heels.

He stared at me and said something to the old woman. She thrust a branch into the fire and handed him the flaming torch, and he held it up between us so that we could take stock of one another. He was a huge chap with a hooked nose and thin lips, but because of the flare I couldn't make out the color of his eyes. He spoke to me, but I didn't understand, and then he pointed to my neck. I tapped my teeth because I was convinced by then that I had an infected wisdom tooth, and he nodded curtly and flung the branch back into the fire. Then, having unslung the goatskin gourd that hung from a strap across his chest and filled it from a barrel propped against the wall, he sat down next to me, cutting slices of sausage and bread with a long, bone-handled knife. The odor of wine drifted around us and mingled with the smell of the fire. It was as if I didn't exist, and I was relieved. It seemed to augur well for the journey. I had no desire to be raped in a snowbank.

As soon as he had finished his meal, he gestured to me that it was time to go. On the way out, I tried to convey my thanks to the old woman, but without much success. Outside it was black and cold, but at first the going was good. Soon, however, the goat track fizzled out in front of a drinking trough and we started to climb. We were moving up across pastureland, helped by a moon that played hide-and-seek with the clouds until we reached a pine forest. Once there, my guide proceeded to swing from tree to tree, looking like a bat when the moonlight caught his figure. I tried to imitate him, but I kept stumbling into the patches of snow that grew more and more frequent as we climbed. I was cold and hot at the same time, and I had a tearing stitch in my side. All too soon I collapsed against a tree and groggily watched the guide disappear. I was going to die—many had during this hellish crossing. And I didn't really care. It was as good a place as any. If only my neck wasn't so sore.

"Viens!" And the word, laconic and harsh in the cold silence, annoyed me. It had been so peaceful just to fade into oblivion.

Suddenly I was hauled to my feet and my rucksack and handbag were roughly torn from my shoulders. He is going to kill me, I thought, remembering his knife. And my body won't be found until summer.

"Viens!" he repeated, dragging me along.

I don't know how long we struggled on, but somehow I got my second wind and managed to keep up, even though the rough, frozen bark of the pines had by then worn through my gloves, hurting my hands. Pretty soon I knew I was about to collapse again. Mercifully, we stopped and I instantly flopped down into a shelter that was no more than a windbreak. Somehow I knew we were above the tree line and at the head of the pass.

It was very cold and we didn't stay long, barely time enough for me to catch my breath, but on the plateau the walking was easier because the snow was iced, indented with rivulets like a beach when the tide goes out, except that here they were carved by the ever whining wind. The moon was clear, lending everything a blue glare. Sometimes we walked abreast, and the guide helped me around obstacles or hollows which I took to be frozen ponds. Now and again I would stumble and once I went down on my knees, dislodging what seemed to be a piece of wood. There seemed to be a lot of wood around, and I wondered what it was doing so high above the tree line. When I tried unsuccessfully to drag one piece out, the guide took it from my frozen hands, scraped off the ice and showed it to me. It was a rifle butt. He threw it away and waved his arms as if to encompass the whole dreary plateau.

"The Republican Army!"

For a long moment I had no idea what he was talking about in his harsh, broken French. And then it dawned on me. This was the route the defeated Republican Army had taken in its flight from Franco into France. I remembered an American pilot I had met in the American Hospital in Paris when I was recovering from a skiing accident. He had been shot down while fighting on the Republican side—what my family and their friends called the Communists in those distant days. Of course, at that time—if I'd thought about it at all—I would probably have gone along with their attitude. And now I was sneaking into Franco's country—Franco, who had managed, despite all Hitler's pleas, to stay out of the war. Franco, who, by the grace of German armor, was the dictator of Spain.

We plodded on. Gradually I felt the ground sloping beneath my feet and I began to worry about having to go through the Tarzan act again. But my fears were groundless because when we reached the tree line the slope was leisurely and we followed a narrow path overgrown with stunted bushes. Compared with what we had gone through, it should have been pleasant, but my guide's behavior was strange. Until then he had been walking like a man at ease, but now he continually stopped and listened, taking shelter wherever he could. Naturally, I had to do the same, which was tiring, and sometimes I clumsily bumped into him. He cautioned me in a low voice, and once or twice swore at me in Catalan. I can't say I blamed him. He was the one who was in danger, for I had no doubt that the Spanish patrols we were dodging would be no more merciful to him than would their German counterparts. I was again the privileged American, whose country was not at war with Franco's Spain.

The country changed under the bright moonlight as we slowly made our way downward. The wind was still cold, but it didn't have the same bite. The mountains had changed too. I no longer had the feeling of ice-capped peaks, rocky crags. Instead the high hills were rounded. Once I thought I saw a light moving on my right, but I wasn't sure because, although the vegetation was sparse—mostly stunted, wind-blown pine and scrub—it was thick enough to block out the view. There was rarely any snow now and when we suddenly rounded a curve in the pebbly track there was none at all. It was then that the wind started to change. It was warmer and it carried the smell of wild thyme.

We sat down. The guide handed me his goatskin gourd, and I knew we were in Spain. I fell asleep for a little while.

When we moved next we went slowly, trying to avoid dislodging any stones. We finally reached a road I had noticed winding at our feet and there we stopped, lying down in the roadside ditch.

"Tais toi. Route de Puiserda. Patrouille Espagnol," the guide hissed.

We stayed there for quite a while. I wondered why, because the road was empty, the moonlight shining in speckled shadows on the macadam. Then, just as I was dozing off and rubbing my sore neck, I caught the gleam of headlights, twisting, disappearing until they were suddenly upon us. Oh, they had a very different sound—very different from the German cars or the chugging wood-burners!

As soon as they had passed, we quickly crossed the road and walked slowly onward. My feet were covered with blisters and I was very tired. Several times I stumbled into my guide's back and I knew that I had actually slept for a few seconds. We climbed a little, but not so high as before, and suddenly the guide pointed to a cluster of lights below us and told me they were our destination. I almost cried in relief until I realized that lights at night seem closer than they are.

Dawn started—a faint streak. With it the smell of wild thyme came again and rabbits sprang about in all directions. My feet were getting worse and I knew one of my heels was bleeding. The perspiration trickling down my face added to my misery.

It was early, golden daylight when we reached a noisy, chattering stream. The guide pointed to a house on the other side of it, long and ocher-colored, with a ray of sun slanting on its tiled roof. Incredibly, I had made it.

When I woke hours later I was lying half undressed on a bed; even my feet had been attended to and bandaged. Sitting up, I stared at them tentatively, pulling apart the dressing to sniff at the evil-smelling black salve.

"Bon—bon," a voice said from the doorway.

I looked up to meet the smile of a short woman whose black hair was drawn back in a tight bun. She wore a red-flowered apron over the black dress that hung down almost to her feet, and she reminded me immediately of an Austrian spinning top.

8

We continued to smile at each other, which was all we could do because "bon" seemed to be the extent of her French, and I got up and tottered into a room that was clearly a common-room, a replica of the one I had seen in France.

"Truita," the farm woman proposed.

I thought: My God! Trout! I nodded delightedly, and felt my neck. Surely I would be able to eat that. They probably fished them right out of the stream we had crossed how many hours ago? Eight hours, I saw when I looked down at my watch.

I was wrong about the truita. Wrong on two counts. First, it wasn't trout but an omelet and, secondly, the minute I tried to swallow, the swelling increased and the pain made me groan and shake my head. All I could do was sit in misery by the fire and nurse my swollen jaw with vinegar compresses while the kind woman clucked around me sympathetically. In the end, I went to bed with a cup of thin broth I was only just able to swallow.

The following day the guide reappeared, bringing with him another man, who agreed, after much palavering over money, to go the U.S. Consulate in Barcelona and obtain my salvoconducto. The guide and I made an appointment to meet on a specific bench on the Rambla in Barcelona in a month's time. Since I didn't know the city very well, he pointed out the spot on the map he gave me, and he also showed me the whereabouts of the

American Consulate. From the other man's deference as he listened to our broken conversation, I concluded belatedly that my guide must be some sort of a leader, but he himself gave no indication of his role before he left to return to France.

After three days the messenger returned from Barcelona with my salvoconducto, a cardboard pass with my description on it—the only genuine thing about it!—and although my feet were far from healed, we set out with a donkey at dawn the following morning to walk over the hills to the nearest railroad station. Naturally, I thought the animal was for me. But no such luck. The sturdy little beast was loaded with sacks of flour, among which was my rucksack.

Between my sore neck and equally sore feet it was a hell of a walk, but eventually we reached a small inn beside a main road. I took off my shoes, peeling off pieces of skin as I did so, and while I washed and tidied myself at an outside pump my companion went to fetch a taxi to take me to the station. It was like returning to the twentieth century from a journey into the Middle Ages. I waved goodbye not only to the donkey tethered to a tree but to one hell of a trip, and climbed happily into the taxi.

En route to the station we were stopped by two policemen wearing funny cardboard hats that reminded me of Napoleon, unless it was Nelson. My companion started to say something, but they ignored him and instead spoke to me. I mumbled a wordless reply which made them glance up from examining our papers, gasp in horror as they looked at me, thrust our papers hurriedly inside and slam the door, waving us on. Obviously, I was a much worse sight than I had imagined, which no doubt staved off any serious challenge once I was on the train to Barcelona.

My reception at the American Consulate in Barcelona was certainly better than it had been in Geneva, although I was inevitably eyed with suspicion. But, after much chit-chat interspersed with pity for my swollen face, sore feet and broken-down appearance, a younger member of the Consulate staff invited me to his home for lunch. There I luxuriated in a proper bath and also borrowed a shirt from my host. Then we were joined by an older man and the real questioning started. I told my story from the beginning—that is, from the moment of my first leaving Paris. When I mentioned my interview with Dulles, I saw their glances cross and I knew they were interested, but I couldn't decide if they were impressed.

"Why didn't you stay in Switzerland?"

"Because I wanted to do something either in England or North Africa. Drive an ambulance. Anything. Switzerland was a dead end. When Mr. Dulles gave me up, I decided to cross the Pyrenees."

"How did you obtain your contacts?" the older man asked sharply.

"Through the English girl with whom I crossed into Switzerland. She works with the British Consulate."

"Her name?"

I gave her name and her address as well, and the older man noted them down in a little black book. I was delighted. In a very short while Mr. X would know I had arrived safely.

My interview must have satisfied them, for that night I slept in a comfortable bed and they paid the man who had guided me from the Spanish farm to the Consulate. They even lent me some money and made an appointment with a dentist for the following day. As it turned out, the Spanish dentist spoke no French and only a little German, but in this way—with the help of a dictionary—I learned I had the mumps.

"Since you've come so far," he said after tapping all my teeth, "there's really not much I can do for you. Stay warm and eat unspiced food." And with a pat on my shoulder he dismissed me and the young consular official who had insisted on accompanying me.

I followed his advice for a week, and it worked, although I think my mumps disappeared sooner than the blisters on my feet. At the end of the week, summoned by the U.S. Consulate, I sallied forth into the street to be instantly shattered by the noisy trams and busses and the honking cars intermingled with horse-drawn carts. I was lost; I felt as though I had stepped out of time into another era. The fact that the traffic cops were all dressed like English bobbies added to my amazement. Before crossing the streets, I watched them, fascinated. When I finally reached the Consulate, I was utterly bewildered by the shops and milling crowds on the sidewalks. Even Geneva hadn't been like this.

"We've been in touch with Berne and decided to send you back to the States," the man with the little black book said.

Oh, no! Not again! "I don't want to go back. I'm over here and I think I'd be more useful in North Africa and England."

"The State Department will have to decide that. You get a good rest and as soon as we can we'll get you to Lisbon. You've had a rough time. You should never have stayed over here in the first place. The States is the place for you."

"Have you any news of my mother?"

"Only that she's in Vittel. Yes, we'll get you back to the States."

"At the risk of being torpedoed or shot down," I replied as calmly as I could.

"The risks of war. Surely you know that."

I felt like saying I preferred the Germans to a watery grave. But I was relieved by the decision because from now on I would have no qualms about contacting the British. If my own countrymen had no use for me, the English were all I had left and everything I had been told in France would go to them.

Sadly I left the Consulate—my Consulate—and wandered around the streets, finally coming to rest on a bench. It was then that I realized I was being watched. I moved on. The man in the drab coat did likewise. He looked Spanish, but then who was I to decide what he was? I knew only one thing for certain: he was trailing me. I walked on slowly until I came to a movie theatre where they were showing *Rebecca,* sauntered in and listened for a good hour to Daphne du Maurier's prose in Spanish (without understanding a word), slipped out and walked quickly to the British Consulate.

Once there, I had a long wait and a lot of explaining to do before I was introduced to an elderly man with a gray mustache and very shrewd, twinkling blue eyes.

"So you made it! Geneva told us to expect you. How was the trip?" he asked in a very matter-of-fact British way.

"Bloody awful! I don't think my feet will ever be the same. On top of it, I had the mumps."

"I know. . . . Oh, yes, we keep tabs on as many of you as possible. Your fellow countrymen have been very kind, so we left you in their hands. Your interview with them this afternoon was routine stuff. In due time you would have been passed on to us. But red tape must be allowed to follow its course. After all, you might have *wanted* to return to the States. Now tell me everything. I hope mumps hasn't affected your memory." He smiled as he pulled a bottle of whiskey and two glasses from a drawer in his desk.

It hadn't, and what was especially nice about talking to this man was the feeling he gave me that everything I said was important. He made me feel worthwhile, genuinely useful, and he confirmed that feeling when, a week later, the red tape having presumably been bypassed, I went to work in his office, translating French messages—most of them incomprehensible because of sentences like "Georges has seen Jules by the old mill but there were still no ducks!"

In the beginning the Major, as he was called, was with me most of the time, and when he wasn't his secretary was in the room. I got the idea, of course: I was not really under suspicion, but I had to be watched, evaluated. I didn't mind. It was natural. Wartime Spain was a nest of spies and I might unwittingly be associating with one. The only counter-argument was that I knew no one, and ambled home to my pension after work to try and talk to my hosts or read a book from the British library.

Then one day the Major said: "You've been cleared by the Americans and from now on you belong to us. We'll pay your pension and once a week you'll have some money."

"I won't have my passport taken away?" I asked, alarmed.

"No, but you'll have British papers for the duration. You're not the only American working for us. Meanwhile you're to stay here. When is your appointment with that guide chap?"

"Next Tuesday morning at eleven on the Rambla."

"Good. We're interested. Find out how much he wants for each parcel."

"Parcel?"

"Yes. Every airman or agent is a parcel. The going should be easier now that the snows have melted. They'll be screened on the other side before setting out, but we can't use your commandant from Perpignan. We'll have to make up the false papers."

"Why?"

He didn't answer, but stared at some papers on his desk before shoving one over to me.

"Poor Puget," I said. "The cobwebs on his sleeve must have caught up with him."

"Now," the Major said, "please go down to the central police station. Two men have been brought in by the Spanish police. They're Canadian Air Force chaps. The police won't release them—think they're French trying to join De Gaulle in London or Giraud in North Africa."

"But I can't speak Spanish. How could I get them released?"

He shook his head as if I was a fool. "You're not to. Just bring them food parcels. Antonio will go with you in the car. He'll do the talking, you the carrying."

The ground floor of the police station was dirty and smelled of choked drains. It was also filled with boys in their teens armed to the teeth, who fingered their weapons as if ready to shoot on sight. Although Antonio was wiry and tough, he had quite a time getting through this barrage of thugs. Eventually we were allowed to go upstairs and were ushered, with a comical military flourish, through a pair of big doors. I trailed behind, carrying the Red Cross parcels.

The room was a corner one overlooking a street and a tree-lined boulevard and it was light and airy, thanks to its windows. Off in a corner, four men stood facing a rotund chap in uniform who was seated at a long desk loaded with files and papers. Two of the men were uniformed policemen; the other two, handcuffed and dressed in ill-fitting clothes and marked by prison pallor, were obviously the prisoners. Everyone stopped talking to stare at us. Antonio, not in the least nonplused, tramped across the room, beckoning me to follow him.

"We've come from the British Consulate with food and clothes for the airmen," he said.

"Airmen! Bah!" the little man behind the desk sneered. "More Frenchmen trying to avoid work."

"That's not true. We're Canadians," one of the men protested, his handcuffs scraping the polished surface of the desk as he leaned over it.

"Lies! You're Frenchmen!" the little man shouted, springing to his feet and slapping the prisoner.

Shocked, I threw the boxes down on the table, where they landed with a wallop that scattered papers and knocked over an inkwell.

Silence. Even Antonio was startled. I wasn't. The boxes had been heavy.

"I've been told to deliver these parcels to the Canadian airmen and that's just what I'm doing. Sorry about spilling your ink, but they were heavy," I snapped in French.

"Mop it up," the man snarled at me.

"Yes, mop it up," I said, turning to one of the policemen. "It was an accident."

"I mean *you,*" the little man said, springing out from behind his desk. "Mop it up!"

My heart was pounding and I had to ram my hands into my pockets so that no one could see they were trembling.

Like hell I will, I thought, turning to one of the Canadians. In the end, it was Antonio who did the mopping.

"You'll soon be all right," I said. "The Consulate is looking after you. When did you get through?"

"Months ago. We've been in Miranda—mostly in the stockade because we tried to escape. Not that there's much difference between that and the camp. Something ought to be done. There—"

"Silence! Get out!"

"With pleasure! But you'll hear more about this," I said.

Once in the car, I burst into tears while Antonio clumsily patted me with ink-stained fingers.

From then on the days went by monotonously. I don't know if the police incident had any effects, good or bad, on the prisoners in the Miranda concentration camp, but from my point of view it enhanced my prestige with the Major. Antonio's account of my behavior at the police station must have been highly exaggerated, but suddenly I was no longer under observation and was given a cubby-hole of my own. I learned from the grapevine that the Canadians had been released and sent down to Gibraltar, and I envied them. But once again I started to feel cooped up and left out of the real action.

"Well, we seem to have a good man in that guide White found for you," the Major said a few days after my meeting on the bench on the Rambla.

"White?"

"Yes. Don't you know your French? The only trouble is the payment."

"Is he asking too much?"

"He's asking the death sentence for Franco and his henchmen. He wants to be paid in guns and ammunition. He too works for a liberation movement. It seems to be the fashion these days. At any rate, your message requesting a radio operator and matériel to be parachuted into the Haute-Savoie has been passed on to London, along with your code name, Apple Pie. Incidentally, when you're working here alone on those files, keep this at hand," and he tossed me a revolver.

I stared at the thing in alarm.

"Don't you know how to use it?"

I shook my head, not daring to touch the thing.

In seconds my desk was cleared and the Major was giving me my first lesson in handling a weapon. I was fascinated. It was a far cry from my English governess.

"What's so funny? This chap is a mean little bastard," he said, balancing the thing in the palm of his hand. "Small but mean."

"I was thinking of other things."

"Well, one day you'll be able to afford the past again. But we have to win this bloody war first."

I picked the thing up. It felt snug in my hand, but I hoped I'd never have use for it—that I could just look at it and know it was there.

In my free time I began to wander down to the port. I'd stare at the ships, wondering where they were going—wondering if I couldn't find passage on one sailing south or direct to North Africa. But the closest I got was a sickly-green tub destined for Málaga. Normally I wouldn't even have given it a glance, but its broken-down appearance made me think the captain might welcome a passenger for the extra money.

Before I could pursue my daydreams much further, I was called sharply to order by the Major storming into my cubby-hole.

"Don't go down to the port any more asking stupid questions! If you do, I'll wash my hands of you and you'll never get to England. Do you think you're the only person trying to reach my poor, benighted country? Why did you pick that green tub?"

"Because it was so shabby," I stammered.

"Are you some sort of a nut about ships? So far you've gotten away with nothing worse than mumps! Do you want to be raped by a drunken captain and most of his crew?"

"I didn't know," I mumbled stupidly.

"You fool! We sometimes use that bum to get our aviators out. But never a woman. The trouble with you is loneliness. I'll introduce you to the club. Do you play bridge?"

"Very badly," I murmured, still feeling ashamed of myself.

"Well, you'll learn. And remember, Rome wasn't built in a day. For God's sake, be patient. . . . You'll be leaving eventually, and I don't know if I'm going to be sorry or glad to see you go. You Americans are all alike. Always rearing like wild horses—wanting to get somewhere even before you leave where you are! Now finish what you're doing and I'll take you down to the club."

I didn't have much chance to master the intricacies of bridge before the Major announced my impending departure.

"Well, it's all set!" he said, beaming. "You leave tomorrow night. You're to escort nine men to Madrid and deliver them to the Embassy."

"But surely they can go on their own?"

"Don't argue. The salvoconductos are made out for ten people. Look after them. They've all had a rough time. One had frozen feet. Another is an important person who escaped from jail in France. There's no need for you to know which is which. See that they all arrive safely."

"They can't jump off the train."

"You'd be surprised what can happen on Spanish trains!"

And with that he marched out, leaving me to tidy my desk for the next person to take over.

I never did find out what could happen on a Spanish train other than breathing soft-coal dust and getting dirty. My nine men were introduced to me at the last moment by the Major, just as I was trying to thank him for his kindness.

"I wanted to say goodbye, to thank you for all you've done for me," I gabbled, holding a glass of whiskey and trying to immobilize him with my other hand.

He smiled. "I think I'll miss you. Good luck. You'll get through all right."

The nine men were very nice. The Consulate had been able to reserve only two seats on the crowded train, and they were firm about my sitting down all the way. Obviously, the Spanish were born travelers, like the French in occupied France, despite the red tape. We agreed that the second seat should be assigned to the young chap who had frozen feet and was still limping, and we insisted on this over his protests, even forcing Spanish brandy down him under the startled eyes of our fellow passengers.

I never found out which of the nine men was the important personage. There would have been no way of telling even if it had been written on his face, because long before our arrival in Madrid we were so dirty we looked like chimneysweeps—tired chimneysweeps who had been traveling for more than twelve hours.

When we turned up at the Embassy we precipitated a commotion, chiefly because our arrival coincided with the release of most of the prisoners from Miranda and the hotels in Madrid were jammed.

"If only you were a man," a harassed official wailed, as he looked down a long list of names and addresses. "If you had arrived last week, everything would have been easier. We had a party of women on their way to Gibraltar. We settled them very comfortably."

I decided the poor man sounded like a clerk in a travel bureau. I was tired, dirty and homesick for the nice little Consulate in Barcelona and my frugally furnished room in the pension. The Embassy seemed huge, filled with pompous stone staircases lined with statues, its tall French windows overlooking a garden. I wasn't impressed. Only a bath would have accomplished that.

Finally, after endless telephone calls, a room was found for me.

"It's not much," the official said, scratching his head with a confused smile. "I'll have a car drive you there. Sorry about all this. Give me a ring if things don't turn out as they should. If only you were a man!"

The small hotel was pinched between two cafés on a tree-lined square and from outside it looked nice enough. But I became suspicious when the driver from the Embassy—a very straitlaced chap—said: "I'll come with you, Miss."

It was a hotel, all right—a payment-by-the-hour sort of place, but it did have regular lodgers in some of the rooms. When the proprietor saw me, she threw up her arms in horror and burst into an avalanche of Spanish beyond my capacity to understand, but I did gather I would have to share the room with someone else. I leaned wearily against the desk, my rucksack wedged between my feet, resolved to let the driver solve the problem. Obviously, there was a mistake somewhere, and it was no doubt connected with the fact that I wasn't a man!

Finally a gaudy creature was marched out of the hotel between two policemen. As she passed, she swore at me. I can't say I blamed her. Everyone has a right to live.

My room turned out to be comfortable and surprisingly clean, and after washing in a corner masked by a lurid curtain I decided to return to the Embassy in search of news of my mother. I had learned in Barcelona that one of the girls on the Embassy staff had escaped from Vittel. Before leaving, I made friends with the little maid making up my bed—a joyful person with a penchant for singing songs that seemed always to end in a raucous "Olé!"

Watching her small frame struggling with the huge bed reminded me of a miniature bullfight and I decided her boyfriend was a toreador.

After wandering here, there and everywhere in the Embassy and thanking my still harassed "travel bureau" expert, I finally found the girl who had been in Vittel. To my amazement, we knew each other. She was from Dinard.

She invited me to lunch, and at a small sidewalk café I learned that Mother had been released from Vittel on grounds of ill-health and was living in Paris. On what, I wondered, since her income came from the States? Nonetheless, it was good news.

"How come the name Rochester?"

"Because it's my real one," I told her. "The other is my stepfather's. Passport regulations . . . going to school in England . . . it was supposedly simpler." Tactfully, she didn't insist. Rattling skeletons in the family cupboard was none of her business, and I was grateful.

"Have you any money?"

"A little from my salary in Barcelona. I hope I won't have to stay here long. Major Adrian gave me to understand I would be in transit. All my papers are in order. For the duration I am a British subject—but a British subject who won't be eating much if I'm not on my way to Gibraltar soon."

"Don't worry about that. I'm in the finance department and all the refugees on their way to Gib have a right to some money. Not much, mind you. Come and see me tomorrow at the Embassy. I'll see what your status is. I don't think you'll be here long, but the trains going south are very crowded. Tell me about your crossing, but don't mention any names. These days everything has to be compartmented. Terrible word. Sometimes I wonder if it's English!"

I should have been able to get a long night's sleep—at least beyond dawn—but I was wakened by shrill cries and then a pebble whistled through the open window and landed with a plop on my pillow. Springing out of bed, I looked down into the street and saw some children pitching stones at a terrified, half-grown cat that was trying to reach the highest limb of the nearby tree.

Now, I am not particularly fond of cats, but I certainly don't like to see them ill-treated. I threw on a jacket and rushed downstairs and by yelling in French, English and a little Spanish I drove the wretched children away. Once they were gone, however, I stood helpless, wondering what to do. Clearly, the beast was stuck and would have to be brought down.

"Do you usually wander around at this hour en petite tenue? The Spanish are very prudish about these things."

I swung around. It was the man with the scar.

"Do something! Those abominable children! It's stuck!"

Well, the long and the short of it was that the rescue was accomplished by a grumbling hotel porter equipped with a ladder. "Rescue" is a big word, for the terrified animal decided to commit suicide when it saw him and jumped, landing squarely in my arms, but not before connecting with my face, all claws out.

Later in my room, while the man with the scar dressed my scratch, I was embarrassed and said so.

"Don't be. Your scratch might have been worse. Now hold still while I clean it with alcohol—Spanish brandy. It's quite a heroic wound—a few centimeters lower and it would have been your eye, not your eyebrow. What a mess you are! But then these things do bleed a lot."

As he dabbed I looked at him.

His Red Indian features were more pronounced than ever and I wondered how he could look like an Indian and have such cool blue eyes.

"You're a little far from your vineyards," I said as I drew back, suddenly aware of my half-opened pajama jacket.

"They're growing nicely, thank you! Maybe one day you'll see them for yourself again. Who knows?"

"Don't say that. You remind me of a man I met in Perpignan—a Commandant. In Barcelona the Major wouldn't talk about him."

"And you talk too much. There! You'll do now and live to see some real wounds in England or elsewhere. Meanwhile go back to bed and I'll see if I can't find some breakfast and some milk for your wild beast. Incidentally, where is it?" and he went down on his knees and crawled around the room calling, "Kitty . . . kitty . . . puss, puss . . ."

I burst out laughing.

"You're as cruel as that hellcat! Laughing at a grown man crawling around a lady's room! For shame! Incidentally, it's under your bed."

"Do you think it will stay there?"

"Yes, if you don't attempt to dislodge it. You've earned your medal. Enough is enough. See you in a minute."

He made the minute a long one and I was sure it was in order to give me a chance to wash and dress. But then I wasn't so sure and suddenly felt like crying. My room was lonely with only a wild cat.

I was in tears when he did return, but he tactfully ignored them as he dumped on my bed a half-dozen small loaves, butter, jam, fruit and a jar of honey. Obviously, he had gone to the nearest market. He had everything but coffee and milk.

"I found the maid—the one you made friends with yesterday. She's bringing coffee and milk, but I brought honey because there's no sugar."

"How did you know about the maid?"

"Do you think your eviction of the glamour girl passed unnoticed?"

"But I had nothing to do with it," I protested.

"I had to spend half the night persuading one of her lovers of that fact!"

"The Embassy sent me here. Apparently, all the hotels in Madrid are full. Something to do with Miranda . . ."

"I know. And your arrival here was as unwanted as a vixen's in a chicken coop. . . . Ah! Here comes what we want."

It was a wonderful breakfast. Even the honey in the coffee tasted good. The only trouble was that afterward I fell asleep. But when I woke up an hour later, he was still sitting in the only chair by the window, reading a book.

"You sleep very quietly . . . très distinguée," he said, looking across at me and shutting the book with a snap. "How about a ride around town in a victoria?"

“Wonderful! But surely that’s very expensive?”

“That’s my worry and so is the lunch we’re going to have.”

Much later, in a smart restaurant on a terrace overlooking the city, surrounded by people dressed in the sort of clothes I’d thought no longer existed, I began to giggle with tears in my eyes.

“What’s the matter?”

“You make everything as marvelous as eating strawberries out of season. I’m embarrassed to be in such a smart place, but I don’t care. I once would have. I wonder why I don’t any more.”

“Maybe crossing the Pyrenees with the mumps made you grow up.”

I shook my head. “Do you know everything?”

“God, no! Otherwise I’d predict the end of this war.”

“But aren’t wars your specialty? Under burning sands, striding through the ruins of Carthage like a Roman legionary?”

He glared at me and I was delighted. I had caught him off guard.

“Touché! How did you learn that?”

“From Blanc, and even he wasn’t sure—said it was hearsay.”

“I suppose you’re going to ask me why I joined,” and he sounded disappointed, bored.

“Heavens, no! Of course I’m dying to, but I learned from a book called *Beau Geste* that the rule is never to ask. It sounded very romantic, but I have a feeling it was exaggerated.”

He looked so relieved I almost wondered if he’d been a thief or a murderer.

“I’m glad you stifled your curiosity. Not because I did anything bad, but because it shows you’re a little different from most women. I really don’t know why the word ‘Legionnaire’ has so much glamour attached to it. The Legion is a stinkhole, but I’m proud of having belonged to it. It either makes or breaks a man. Incidentally, my name is Marcel Duroc—phony, of course. Don’t tell me yours, I already know it. May I call you Dev?”

I gave up. There was nothing else for me to do.

“Are you really determined to go to England?” he asked later, when we were sitting on a bench outside the Prado after a tour of the museum.

"Well, after all I've been through and all the things people have done for me, it would hardly be fair not to. Besides, I want to be in at the kill. The British have been very good to me. Sometimes I wonder why. You know, Blanc once said I'd learn to miss the sound of the boot."

Marcel didn't answer, but I didn't feel squelched. Instead he tucked his arm through mine and led me to the hotel. "I've invited some of the boys to our luxurious palace for some drinks and sandwiches. The maid you befriended—incidentally, she thinks you're crazy to have rescued the cat—well, she's arranged everything."

"Do you think I'll be popular? My moving in has caused so many broken hearts."

"Broken hearts aren't worn so low down!" he answered with a lopsided grin.

The maid with the toreador technique had really done a wonderful job in the drab hotel room. There were flowers everywhere, next to ceramic platters loaded with sandwiches and bowls of black olives among red and green peppers stuffed with rice; there were also shrimp fried to a crisp with a sauce that later proved—to the dismay of my palate—as hot as Dutch love. Bottles of wine were everywhere: on the floor, in the lavabo. Of water or fruit juice, there was not a sign. I supposed the tapwater would have to do.

When Marcel and I came in, three men were already sitting on a couch borrowed for the occasion. They came to me, hands outstretched, while Marcel murmured introductions. An elderly man with a slight limp and a shock of white hair kissed my hand, murmuring: "Mes homages, Madame." The other two were younger, one of them barely twenty, and he was clearly shy, blushing when one of the others chided him about going to a café because "la serveuse" was a buxom wench! Trying to ignore his tormentor, he stuck close to Marcel. There was something appealing but weak about him, and I wondered how he had ever reached Madrid.

We were about ten in all; most of them were French and one was an Algerian, obviously a non-practicing Muslim, for he kept up with the others in their drinking. I was monopolized by the white-haired man.

"I hope you had a better crossing than I did, Madame," he said, pointing to one of his feet. "I fell into a snowdrift. The guide panicked and it's thanks to a couple of American fliers that I'm here. I knew Marcel in France. I acted as one of his couriers between Carcassonne and Perpignan. When that got blown, I had to leave. Very sad about the Commandant."

"What about him?"

"He was betrayed by his wife."

"But he loved his wife."

"Love can be one-sided, especially when a young SS officer is in the offing. We'll get him—and her too. Two of our men were shot in the hotel and the elderly women who owned it are in jail. If they survive the torture, they'll be deported to Germany."

I felt sick. Supposing Blanc had been caught in that round-up? Supposing he had been in the hotel when it had happened? I had to know. Would this man talk? I couldn't say Blanc's name. Georges . . . yes, maybe Georges.

"Was there a man called Georges mixed up in the affair? On our side, of course."

"Never heard of anyone by that name," and the white-haired gentleman eyed me curiously.

"When did it happen?"

My companion's eyes suddenly veiled and the lines around his mouth tightened. I had learned to recognize that expression in the Major, Blanc and, fleetingly, in Marcel. I was talking too much—asking too many questions.

"I stayed in that hotel," I hurried on. "The Commandant was the man who got us our passes."

"*Our* passes? Marcel told me you crossed alone, opening a new escape route, with messages from the Maquis in the Alps."

I sighed. God, how I hated this beating around the bush. "Georges accompanied me to the stepping-off point and was with me in Perpignan. That's why I asked about the tragedy and when it occurred."

"Not long ago. About a week or so."

Blanc was safe—yes, Blanc was safe. I had heard from him just two days before leaving Barcelona. The guide had brought a note from him, a crumpled-up scrap confirming some odds and ends to be settled. He must have just escaped, and should have been on a train rattling north. I closed my eyes, hearing again the sighs of those midnight trains in empty stations. The Allies were pushing into Tunis. We were gaining ground everywhere, but back in France the nightmare continued.

"Well, Dev, not drinking?" Marcel asked, leaning over me with a glass of wine and a plate. Suddenly I wanted to do just that. Drink . . . Many drinks.

As the party wore on, it became very gay. We danced and sang to the sound of a concertina played by the shy young man who appeared to be Marcel's protégé. Around midnight I left them, tired out by too many cigarettes, too much wine and a palate that felt as if it had had intimate relations with a volcano. The night was clear but far from calm. I sat on a bench on the farthest side of the square, opposite the two cafés, where life was still going on. Like the Italians, the Spaniards never seem to sleep. People were either playing cards or drinking and singing plaintive melodies accompanied by a guitar. From a distance it was all very soothing, especially as a small breeze whispered through the linden trees.

Yes, Blanc must have escaped. Or hadn't he? Doubt gnawed at me. Was that why Marcel and the Major had avoided my questions? But what of the note I'd gotten? True, it had been hastily scrawled, but then he had surely had other things to do. Other things like being on the run? It would be nothing new to him. . . . The guide hadn't said anything because he probably hadn't known anything, and his not knowing anything was probably the reason Blanc had been able to give him the note. Therefore Blanc must be all right. But supposing Blanc hadn't given him the . . . And those poor women who owned the hotel. I had seen them only once, fluttering down the corridor with their keys clicking as they walked, and they had seemed like two sweet old maids. I hadn't even known they were the proprietors. They would die. God was a German.

Suddenly a shadow glided up to me. It was Marcel. For a

moment I hated him. He could have told me. He must have known all along.

"Don't look so angry and shrink away from me. I wanted to tell you. Blanc is all right and since no one knows him he'll be all right for some time. He was the one who brought me the news. He watched the whole thing happen and when he saw nothing could be done he came straight to me. Lecoque, that young man I use as a courier, was with me and so I was able to alert everyone immediately. Brisse and I left for a safe house, where we waited until we could cross. Not your way. On the Atlantic side. Now my organization is blown to bits."

"With the vineyards growing by themselves."

He ignored my sarcasm and I was a little ashamed of it myself. The breaking up of his organization, the deaths, the betrayals must be hurting him terribly.

"Yes, but I don't think the women will be bothered—the ones up on the plateau. It was a good cover story. Only Brisse, Lecoque, Blanc and you knew about it. Not even the Commandant. His wife is a young bitch who married to get away from the farm. Had dreams of grandeur. Even her sister knows nothing. But she will soon."

And suddenly, putting his arm around me, he drew me toward him: "It's horrible, but it's the same everywhere in France."

For a while we stayed like that, quiet and even serene. Serene because the thought of Blanc's being safe gave me serenity.

"Brisse talks too much," I finally murmured. "Normally speaking—if I can use that phrase—I shouldn't have known anything."

"I know, and he won't be going back if I have my way. Besides, he's too old. A job in London at French headquarters will suit him. He has the 'grande manière.' We've gone beyond that stage." And leaning toward me, he kissed me, at first lightly and almost humorously but then harder. I was shaken by surprise and then by a warm and thrilling emotion and I found myself returning his kisses. When we finally drew away from each other, I ran my fingers gently down his scar.

"I didn't mean it to be quite so soon. I'm sorry."

"Oh, don't be. I have a confession to make."

"So soon?"

"Stop laughing at me. Ever since the day I saw you I've been thinking about you."

"Do you mean to say you rescued a mangy cat to see me again?"

"Naturally. I also managed to have the prisoners from Miranda released so the hotels would be jammed!"

There was little conversation after that and we strolled across the square hand in hand.

At the desk the night porter—the same disgruntled one who had produced the ladder—gave us our keys, but Marcel came to my room instead of his.

The coming together of two lonely people can sometimes be a hideous disappointment, a sordid mess one would rather forget once the initial excitement wears off. But it wasn't like that for Marcel and me. I can't swear we were made for each other, but we suited one another and I think we would have remained friends all our lives. As it was, the week that followed was an interlude like the eye of the storm. We wandered the streets, eating in small cafés, now and again visiting a museum, behaving like what we were: lovers on a holiday. They were halcyon days, with even the weather in tune. And on every front the war was changing. Stalingrad had been the turning point; Montgomery had stopped Rommel at El Alamein, and the Allied troops were pushing along the Mareth Line to Tunisia. Would the invasion come this year? We speculated about it constantly, and even the Spaniards no longer glanced over their shoulders in fear.

One morning in bed Marcel reverted to the conversation we'd had on the bench in front of the Prado. Just like that. As if nothing had happened between us—as if we weren't lying in bed with the dawn creeping through the windows. "So you think the British have been good to you . . ."

"Of course. If it hadn't been for them, I'd still be kicking my heels in Geneva. Of all the dumps!"

"Do you miss the sound of the boot?"

"I don't know. I don't think so, after what happened in Perpignan. But I did when I was in Barcelona. Working on all those mysterious messages made things seem very close. Here it's different and you're with me."

He burst out laughing—one of those wonderful laughs that seemed to shake his whole torso, as if it summed up all the good things in life. Taking me in his arms, he said: "Darling, it's the first time my charms have had to compete with the German boot! You are distressingly naïve as well as aggravating."

"I think that calls for an explanation," I said, throwing a pillow at him.

"I don't owe you one, chérie. Only a heart full of thanks." He tossed the pillow back and started to dress. "Do you know what panache means?"

"Not quite. Glorification or something. Kings charging into battle with white plumes on their helmets. I don't know . . . Why? Where are you going? It's still early."

"I'm off to get breakfast and find a home for your mangy cat."

And with that he slammed out of the room, which was very uncharacteristic, because he was usually quiet in his movements.

"Happy, darling?" he asked later, when we were lunching in the restaurant he had taken me to that first day. "Your blouse looks lovely."

"The top part of me is fine, but the shoes are shabby. You know what snobs the personnel of these places are. I once knew a man who went to Maxim's and ordered a soft-boiled egg with prune juice. No one said anything. He was a millionaire. Can you imagine it?"

Marcel smiled a restrained smile. I thought he looked tired and wondered where he had been all morning. I wanted to ask, but didn't. Instead I chatted about everything and nothing until the dessert arrived.

"Fraises des bois!" and I looked down at my plate as if they were rubies.

"We had only two portions, Madame. It was the German gentleman over there who gave up his."

I turned. A tall, immaculately dressed man in tweeds was bowing to me. With him was a dark lady, waving.

"It's the German military attaché," Marcel hissed. "Wave back. Perhaps he'll join us for coffee."

But he didn't. They left before we did, and it was only then that Marcel slid an envelope over toward me.

It was a third-class ticket for Algeciras, the town just opposite Gibraltar.

"The Embassy gave it to me yesterday. Since then I've been trying to get a place in first class or the wagons-lits. No luck. The Spanish are putting on as few cars as possible in order to discourage travel. I'm sorry."

"Don't be, darling. Will you see me off?"

"I don't know. I have a meeting. Everything always comes at once. I've been expecting it for days. Now it's set for five thirty. Your train leaves at seven. I'll try to make it."

"If you don't, when will I see you again?" I asked, looking down.

"I don't know," he replied as he paid. "Let's go home."

The station was crowded, and with my rucksack slung over my back I shouldered my way through my crowded compartment to a seat by the window. I was grateful for that. Seated opposite me was a young man in uniform, his arm in a sling. On his upper right sleeve he wore the Spanish Foreign Brigade insignia, the insignia of the Spanish fighting with the Germans in Russia. He glared at me and I looked at his arm, his weary, pain-racked face. I knew he had gangrene. I could smell it. And then I forgot everything. Marcel was down on the platform handing up a paper bag.

"A bientôt—à bientôt," he kept calling as he followed the moving train. "A bientôt," and then he was gone, swept away by the crowds and the increasing speed of the train.

For a long time I sat there, seeing nothing and feeling a bar of loneliness in the pit of my stomach.

In the end, I opened the bag. They were oranges.

9

I rediscovered London through the busses lumbering down its streets. They reminded me of a fat Victorian housewife returning from a shopping spree, arms loaded with Ovaltine, Rose's lime juice, Players Senior Service, with "Guinness Is Good for You" stuck obscenely to her buttocks. Uniforms were everywhere, Australian, American, Polish, Dutch, Czech, French, Norwegian, making the rare civilian conspicuous. The city wasn't gay nor was it sad. Everyone and everything seemed to have a purpose—even the partly cleared, dirty, gutted buildings along the streets and squares. If no nightingale sang in Berkeley Square, wild flowers bloomed among the rubble, while near the anti-aircraft guns in Hyde Park manned by women of the Army Territorial Service (ATS), gray balloons floated overhead. There were still Horse Guards at Buckingham Palace, but they were dressed in khaki drab, which made it not worthwhile to watch the Changing of the Guard. Sandbags in doorways, sandbags along the walls, with aggressive arrows posted everywhere pointing "TO THE SHELTERS."

After my first interview with the War Office, I was tired and slept almost all day in the stuffy room of the hotel near the Albert Hall, where they had lodged me. I felt lost, and another thing bothered me. I had been asked every sort of question by those immaculate colonels and majors, who put their inquiries as if they were skirting around the edge of something. Within me I knew what their proposition was going to be. I could see it in their eyes. I didn't know immediately, of couse. It sort of grew on me. How could it be otherwise? They were just too nice. Finally one of the colonels said—over lunch at a corner table at the Ritz, of all places —"Your French is pretty good and of course you know the conditions over there. Useful, that."

Maybe I was missing the sound of the boot after all, or perhaps I was being persuaded to. Certainly I had no intention of becoming a land worker, which was the only definite suggestion put to me so far. Somehow I couldn't picture myself milking cows or driving a straight furrow with a tractor. Farming is an honorable occupation, but I didn't think I was suitable for it. And so I tossed and slept, thinking of Blanc and Marcel and wishing they were with me. Marcel had said: "A bientôt." Had it only been a phrase? . . .

I decided to look up an old friend. Even if I couldn't tell her my problems, she was still a friend.

After a great deal of wandering from one ATS office to another, talking to people who had never heard of her, I finally turned up someone who had known her—before her marriage.

"Marriage!" I exclaimed to the girl in dungarees who was polishing a staff car, a cigarette stuck to her lower lip.

"Why, yes. She married a chap in the Eighth Army. We were in training together. Half a tick! I'll get her address before cleaning this carburetor. Stupid Captain, claims she's using too much petrol. Can't be true. I tuned it only last week, but he's always complaining. He's made that way. A regular old maid. Wait here. Be back in a jiffy!"

Betty married! Betty, too, tuning carburetors for fussy old maids? Betty, the belle of the county! No one had ever had a chance when she was around, but, strangely enough, no one had minded because she had that rare quality in a beautiful woman: spontaneous kindness with either sex, seeming to find happiness in helping everyone. I wondered what had happened to her family's lovely home, her sister and parents. I knew her father was dead —a nice but not too intelligent gentleman who used to tell me about his experiences in World War I. What *had* happened to that old house? Probably requisitioned, and the horses turned over to the Army. I was suddenly sad because I had loved the place. Loved the cheerful, noisy tennis parties, swimming in the local pool, singing in the evenings accompanied on an upright piano by a cadet from nearby Sandhurst. All you had to do was hum a tune (not me, I've always sung off key) and he'd improvise. Maybe Betty had married *him.* He was very keen on her, but then so were all the rest and on her sister too. Prewar England. The generation of those who had lost their fathers in the trenches of France. We had been a singing crowd while others goose-stepped and preferred guns to butter.

It was the year an aunt had given me a car, which I brought over on the *Europa,* traveling with my stepfather. It had been an eight-cylinder Oldsmobile roadster. A lavish, wonderful gift but far too expensive to run on my allowance. In fact, there were times when I had to content myself with looking at it. Betty said laughingly that it gave her home a showy look sitting in the courtyard next to her Morris Minor. But carefree though we were, we sometimes found time in the evening to pause and hear the church bells pealing across the village green, or sit silently listening to that old English garden going to sleep. I'm sure that then many of us wondered, asked deep down: "How long this peace? How long?"

And now I was to see Betty once more, hear news about the gang, learn of deaths. I was suddenly tired and decided to put it off until the following day. Somehow I couldn't face her in uniform. I who was not.

The next morning I stepped out of the tube closest to the address I had been given and climbed up the stairs to face a row of bombed-out houses looking like a batch of drunken sailors. I lost my bearings. I wasn't familiar with this part of Kensington and on top of that I had forgotten my map.

I walked on, asking directions, but no one seemed to know where I wanted to go. Not surprising, for wartime London was filled with strangers; even the Londoners themselves had changed homes, finding lodgment where they could when they were blitzed out.

As I walked, looking at the gutted houses, I noticed that the damage was more extensive than I had at first thought. A block of apartments had been hit and half toppled over, revealing the familiar vision of a bed dangling above empty space. Some of the less damaged houses were still occupied; they seemed to stand like palaces next to their neighbors' rubble. I was reminded of Rouen, especially when I saw a cart pulled by two middle-aged women, helped by a panting dog.

Suddenly, and as dramatically as a scene shift in a theatre, everything was normal. I would hardly have been surprised to see a nanny in stiff blue with white cuffs wheeling a perambulator. The only trouble was there were no children in London—at least, very few.

I started to wander through squares that all looked alike with their once-trim center gardens. By then I was completely lost and, to make matters worse, there was no one around to ask. Then, rounding a corner, I saw a detachment of ATS girls standing to attention while an officer read out orders in a clear, impersonal voice from the top step of a building that might once have been a private house. It was Betty. I recognized her voice before her face because that was masked by a peaked cap. Also her hair was shorter. Regulation cut, I thought, wanting to giggle and cry all at the same time.

When she finished, I stepped forward.

"My God! I thought you were dead! Where have you come from?"

"From France."

"How the hell did you make it? Nobody gets out of France these days."

"Well, I did."

Dazed, she shook her head, for a second losing her British composure. "Come into my office," she said finally.

We talked for hours between telephone calls and a constant stream of women in uniform.

Yes, some of the old crowd were gone. Even her mother was dead—not on a battlefield, at sea or in the air, but of cancer.

"She went just before Dunkirk. She never really wanted to live after Daddy died. The doctor said cancer, but I think it was a broken heart. Biddy is living with our old cook down at a place by the sea we bought after selling the big house. For a time she was on a gun site, but since her marriage and the baby, that's finished. I'm glad too. They were a tough lot. You look tired. Why don't you come down this weekend with me? The sea air will do you good."

And that's just what I did after getting the all-clear from one of the colonels. A cryptic all-clear: "Think over what I said to you the other day at lunch. Give me your answer on your return. Have a good weekend."

Waiting for Betty at Victoria Station the next day, I was once again struck by the shabbiness of everything, especially in that station where in prewar days the Blue Train had pulled out for Paris, Monte Carlo and other cities on the continent. Now part of the skylight was broken and patched with tar paper, and the platforms were dirty, while over everything hovered the sour smell of coal. Instead of porters wheeling their trolleys filled with smart luggage, golf clubs and tennis rackets, there were people milling aimlessly about looking for their trains. "Lost in transit" was a frequent experience, which made me wonder if that fact didn't explain the signs posted everywhere: "IS YOUR JOURNEY REALLY NECESSARY?" Seeing them gave me a guilty feeling until I saw Betty coming toward me, dressed in khaki slacks. They didn't suit her, but then they didn't suit a lot of people and everyone was wearing them.

We were the last to get into the half-filled compartment and I noticed people staring curiously at my rucksack. I wondered if it had a hole in it, which would have made me sorry because I had grown fond of the thing. We had been through a lot together. I started to say something to Betty, but I stopped when she gave a barely perceptible nod toward a sign with the words: "THE ENEMY HAS HIS EARS EVERYWHERE." A depressing thought, stuck as it was next to a grinning Tommy, fingers held up in a V for Victory. I turned away to look at the lush countryside, but signs of war were everywhere. Barrage balloons floated in the sky, while the villages seemed to huddle together like frightened sheep; huge iron stakes loomed in the surrounding fields. Invasion was in everyone's mind, but the idea didn't mean what it meant on the continent. It wouldn't promise liberation here.

I think that Betty, Biddy and their old cook, Nellie, thought I had changed. And so I had. All this long journey from France only to return? And if I was caught, this time there would be no reprieve. "Is your journey really necessary?" I kept on mumbling in my mind. In a way—a very little way—I was aware that my long talks with those intelligence chaps had confirmed what they already knew. Namely, that something had to be done for the Maquis. Oh, I was just a minor cog in a very big wheel. I couldn't see myself as anything else. But then everyone had a part to play —Betty, the ATS girl tinkering with the carburetor of a staff car, the old maid of a captain, women drivers on the London busses.

I was content to be a cog. But I had to find my place, the right spot in the giant mechanism. And because I couldn't say any of these things to my friends, I was quieter, more reserved than the American girl they remembered.

"Why don't you have a game of golf?" Betty suggested the following day. "The caddy master will lend you some clubs and you can borrow my bicycle to get there."

It was a horrible game I played by myself. A game of weary concentrating, trying not to think of anything but the peaceful green surroundings—blue where the sea shimmered on the horizon. A game of running away from a decision that was already made but that I wouldn't bring to the surface of my mind. It was like trying to steal from my right hand what my left hand already had. Of course I sliced all my shots, landing in bunkers and having to dig into the sand like a burrowing rabbit. In the end, I lost the only two balls I had in a huge crater filled with water. Standing on its rim, I wondered what it was.

"Wonderful job Jerry did!" the caddy master said behind me. "A few yards to the left and that would have been the end of the clubhouse. Not playing too well, are you, Miss? We all have our bad days."

"When did it happen?"

"A few months ago. Want me to fish out your balls?" And

without waiting for my reply, he rolled up his pants and unwound a seine net he'd been carrying over his shoulder.

"Usually I do this after the weekend, but the weather has been so bad I put it off. Been waiting for weeks for a chap to come and fence the thing in. Seems he's busy up at the American camp. A lady fell into it a few weeks ago. Had hysterics—claimed there were things swimming around her. Said she'd sue. I told her to take her complaint to Hermann, the fat swine!"

At first try he only brought up a pair of tired old boots.

"I always heave them back. They're my markers or good-luck charm!" he exclaimed, throwing them back into the water. "Keep them there to see if the crater isn't getting deeper. I think it is. Maybe one day we'll make a swimming pool out of it."

I began to wonder if he wasn't a little nutty until I realized his English sense of humor was coming to terms with a bomb crater on a golf course. "Ah, here are your balls! All nice and clean. Not had time to really sink. Now for the Americans!"

"Americans?"

"Yes, they play every weekend and never seem to miss this spot. Sometimes I think they do it on purpose, because some of them are pretty good. Well, it's all to my advantage. Waste not, want not. They're a happy-go-lucky crowd. Want to buy some balls, Miss?"

I shook my head, laughing.

"Ah, here's a beauty! Of course they're larger than ours. But then, in the mighty U.S.A. everything is larger. . . . "

On my way home a bus drove me into a ditch. It happened so quickly I hardly noticed it until I felt the bike on top of me and the sting of brambles on my backside.

Naturally, I cursed the driver as heartily as he cursed me, but when I climbed out I knew it had been my fault. I'd been riding on the wrong side. Dear England, with her left-hand driving! Maybe it was just as well I was leaving her again.

That evening after supper we made a fire and Betty and I sat on the floor in front of it with glasses and a bottle of whiskey while Biddy nursed her baby daughter on the couch.

"I think you ought to tell us how you got here. I don't suppose you swam," she said, staring down at me. I shook my head, thinking the war hadn't been kind to her. Her face, a sharper reproduction of her sister's, was worn and her blue eyes were paler than I remembered. She was also thinner, and as she had never been anything but slender, she was now skinny. There was also something taut and jerky—puppetlike—in her movements. All this saddened me because she had been a vivacious person and if she'd sometimes had a sharp tongue, her words had always ended in laughter. Now I didn't know how they would end.

I wondered if Betty had changed also. Certainly not physically. She was just as smooth and neat, her brown-flecked eyes, the windows of her soul, calmly observing the world around her, her creamy complexion a perfect advertisement for whatever soap she used. I remember someone calling her a glamour girl with a snub nose. Her voice was huskier, but then she had become a chain smoker. She was thinner, too, but, in contrast to her sister, it suited her. It was then that I realized she had indeed changed. She was remote. She was there and yet she wasn't.

I was so startled that the words I was about to say died away.

"Come on now, Dev, unless you want to give your statement to the press."

"God, no! Certainly not!"

"Pity," she sighed.

"Why?"

"It would be a refreshing change. Things are so drab."

"I haven't found it so. I think you're putting up a splendid fight. The whole world is breathless with admiration."

"What world?" Biddy hissed, laying her baby down beside her.

"Yes, what world? Is there still one?" Betty cut in as she splashed some whiskey into her glass.

"Switzerland," I mumbled lamely.

They burst out laughing, and so did I. "France, all the occupied countries. They look to you."

"Their looking comes a little late," Biddy snapped.

I gulped my drink, choking over it as if it was the English Channel.

"Don't mind us. We're just spilling some wartime blues. You

still haven't told us how you got here," Betty said.

"I walked over the Pyrenees with mumps."

"My God!" and Betty leaned over to touch my hand. "No wonder you look tired. How long ago was this?"

"Weeks ago. I stayed for a while in Barcelona working at the British Consulate."

"You—an American?" Biddy exclaimed, horrified.

"We're allies, you know," and as I said it I thought of the runaround I had received from Dulles.

"Yes, allies! Don't we know it! Your GI's are everywhere. Think they own the world, too. They've taken our girls, started a black market. I don't know why, because with their pay they could have anything."

"Oh, shut up, Biddy," her sister said sharply. "The black market isn't the sole prerogative of the Americans. Besides, it's a natural reaction."

"Natural reaction!"

"Please," I said. "Don't let's argue. You make me feel my countrymen aren't liked and it upsets me. They've come from so far, and for the second time. The black market is nothing here compared to elsewhere. Even in Switzerland and Spain there's a black market. It's created by the need for anything that's scarce. Here you have enough to eat, your ration cards are honored. Across the Channel, people are starving."

"Did *you* starve?"

"There were times when I was hungry," and I told them about Laurence Blanc and her shriveled apples, her thin cabbage soup with no meat in it, the blank stares of the children hungrily watching her every movement by the stove.

"What did you do wherever you were?"

"Once I escorted some fliers into Switzerland."

"How did you do that?"

"By crossing the frontier at night—slipping between German patrols."

"Wasn't it dangerous?"

"Yes, but then isn't it dangerous to be on a gun site, Biddy, or in London like you, Betty, dodging bombs? We all do our share."

I must have sounded very stuffy and righteous. In reality, I was annoyed by their lack of understanding. I shouldn't say "they" because I could feel a current of sympathy from Betty as she stared at me musingly.

"And the rest of the time what did you do?"

"I watched over the sheep of my host, who was keeping them to sell on the black market. He used the money to help Allied aviators who'd been shot down and young men going into hiding to escape forced labor in Germany."

After that there was a pause and I found myself staring at the flames, remembering the last time I had seen an open fire. Another time, another place, and this grate would never hold a pot of simmering soup!

"I must go and check on the blackout curtains," Biddy said, jerking to her feet. "Nellie has gone to bed. Jerry may be over if it's a clear night and I don't want to be machine-gunned again!"

"Machine-gunned?"

"Yes, we aren't heroes. We left the family car on blocks in the garden under green canvas. Jerry took it for a military target. He missed the car, but machine-gunned the house."

"Don't get angry, Dev," Betty said after she was gone. "She's been through a lot. She had a terrible time with the baby, and before that she was badly shot up on the gun site. Then she comes here and is practically pursued by a low-flying plane."

I thought of the refugees on the roads of France, but refrained from saying so. After all, we all had our private little hells. But I found it difficult to contain my annoyance at their attitude toward the American soldiers.

"That means nothing. It's only war nerves. We're tired, drawn tight as wire. Your countrymen are so fresh and healthy. They behave as if it was child's play. We were like that in the beginning. Not any longer. The patriotic balderdash has worn away. Now we're just carrying on."

"Everything seems all right and it's starting to rain," Biddy said as she came in. She lifted her baby from her sister's lap and it began to whimper softly. I was glad. It was such a quiet little thing that to hear it cry was a relief. I hobbled over on my knees to look at it, wiggling my fingers until it smiled.

"Mummy would so much have wanted to be a grandmother," Biddy said softly. It was the first time I had heard the real Biddy.

"What are you going to do now?" Betty asked, taking up her former position and lighting a cigarette.

"Join the land army," I lied.

They burst out laughing.

"Well, after all, I never thought to see one of you on a gun site or giving orders on a square in Kensington," I protested. Then, catching Betty's speculative look, I busied myself with another drink.

"You'll probably join the FANY's. We had two in our unit," Biddy said. "One was a Dutch girl. A captain appeared one day, complete with red tabs, interviewed her, and in a few hours she was gone. Weeks later someone ran into her in London. She was wearing a FANY uniform and didn't seem particularly pleased at being recognized. The other girl was Italian and it was the same thing. After that we called the unit the disappearing brigade."

And that's the way it was a week later. But I didn't feel as if I was vanishing when I donned my First Aid Nursing Yeomanry uniform, at least not until I was sent with six other girls in a military bus to a country estate known as the Psychological School. Here I began to wonder if the crazy tests I underwent weren't going to change me into a multi-colored athletic ghost.

The house was large and ugly; the grounds were spacious, filled with woods, with army huts sprawling all over the place. Our sleeping quarters were at the top of the house in what must once have been the servants' quarters. They'd made a dormitory by knocking down the partitions and walls and filled it with regular army cots. It wasn't uncomfortable because it was airy and the view from the dormer windows over the rolling countryside was pleasing.

We arrived in the late afternoon and shortly after dinner we were encouraged to go to bed by our escorting officer, a FANY who had joined us in London.

Reveille was at six, followed by a hearty breakfast for some. Not me (I've never been at my best in the morning and the thought of eating kippers or kidneys was exceedingly distasteful). Instead I concentrated on toast and marmalade. At nine a couple of Tommies herded us into a classroom that must once have been a living room. They kept on repeating: "It's going to be all right. Wish I could go to school again. No blinking 'ope."

As we filed in, some of us curiously, others sheepishly, we were greeted by a tall, ungainly man sporting a walrus mustache. In battle dress—like us—he surveyed us from a dais through dark horn-rimmed glasses. He spoke in a squeaky voice, and since I was sitting at a desk like a schoolgirl, I naturally wanted to throw paper balls at him. But since I had no paper but only a cloth-covered tray in front of me on the desk, I stared down at it instead.

"No peeping, please," Walrus squeaked, tapping a ruler. Several hands moved away from their trays and I felt better. I didn't want to be the only one caught out. Then we all smiled at one another, apparently affected by some current of mutual sympathy. Extraordinary what classroom surroundings can do to grown women!

"You are now going to play a game. The trays contain colored pieces of cardboard. Sort them out according to your taste and make them up into a square. Be quick, because you have only three minutes. I'll buy a beer in the mess tonight for the one who wins. Go!"

Getting into the spirit of this nutty exercise, I gave a yank to the cloth and the damn tray slid into my lap, the pieces of cardboard fluttering to the floor. The girl at the next desk giggled.

"Do it on the floor," Squeaky shrieked.

Needless to say, I was last and was left clutching a heap of lavender and mauve pieces. I wasn't especially amused when Squeaky said: "You get the booby prize. The drinks are on you."

"Hard luck!" one of the girls whispered in French. "I've always thought the British were nuts. Now I'm sure of it."

"No talking, ladies. Now, one by one, pick up your trays and go through that door and see the instructor. One at a time."

"But I did mine on the floor," I wailed.

"You're definitely an impulsive person," he said, coming toward me with another tray. "I'll give you one more chance."

I didn't know whether I was amused or annoyed as I did his crazy square while he stood over me looking at a timepiece. Yes, a timepiece. His great-grandfather must have worn it during the Napoleonic Wars.

"Well, that's not bad. A pity you missed the first time. Impulsive, that's what you are."

Without a word I picked up my tray and went through a low door into a sort of cubby-hole room, dark and smelling of stale fires.

"Come in, come in, Miss. Sit down over here." I swung around to face another individual in battle dress, only this one didn't have a squeaky voice; only glasses and a nice smile. His smile disappeared when he examined my tray. It was a turn-the-moon-on, turn-the-moon-off sort of thing!

"Very curious. Yes, very curious," he said, peering at my tray. I joined him and our heads were so close together I could smell his hair oil.

I couldn't see anything wrong with my color scheme and was about to say so when I saw the white of an eye peering at me through glasses. I jerked back.

"Don't you like mauve or lavender?" the pleasant voice asked soothingly. I wasn't taken in. I couldn't forget that eye.

"Not particularly," I replied, remembering the evacuation of the lunatic asylum in Rouen.

"Can you tell me why?"

"No."

"Just one of those things?"

"That's right."

"Oh, well, we all have our quirks."

Like hell we have, I thought, sitting back and longing for a cigarette.

"You can smoke if you wish. I'd like to see how you smoke. Have one of mine."

Of course that squelched my desire, but I didn't dare refuse his offer. He didn't light it for me, which I thought was rude, but instead he sat back and watched me, and I found myself trying not to fumble the process.

"Now take a few drags and put it out in the ash tray and we'll get on to something else."

I was glad it was his cigarette—a lousy weed, the cheapest kind. Still it seemed like a waste.

"Now, how about doing some ink tests? Rather fun, really."

Suddenly I burst out laughing. I couldn't help it. He looked shocked and dismayed.

"You must take this seriously," he said reproachfully.

"But I do. You're rather awe-inspiring."

He looked across at me doubtfully. I began to get the creeps.

"I'm supposed to be," he replied, and I thought he meant it, but I couldn't be quite sure.

The ink tests were fascinating. I hadn't done anything like them since kindergarten. Once we almost came to words when he wanted me to see a bat where I saw a dragon. In the end, because I thought *he* was bats and because I felt sorry that such a young man should be a future patient in a mental institution, I gave in to him with my most winning smile.

"Of course, you give in with charm," he said, showing me to the door. "Incidentally, it *was* a dragon."

Outside I hardly had time to let out a sigh of relief when the escort officer sprang on me.

"Hurry! You'll find some gym things on your bed upstairs. Change into them and join us here. Too bad you missed morning coffee."

It was too cold outside for shorts, and I didn't like it, but my goose pimples quickly disappeared in the course of doing push-ups and then leaping and crawling over stone walls, barbed wire, through a stream . . . urged on by the bellowing voice of a sergeant bent on making Olympic champions of us. At the end, I was bleary-eyed. So were my companions—a meager consolation.

At lunch we ate ravenously. Afterward we were allowed some rest. I fell asleep listening to my neighbor, the French girl, muttering: "Ils sont fous—fous!"

Later we crawled down the stairs, once more in battle dress and cursing and groaning at our aches and pains. We must have looked like something out of *The Beggar's Opera* as we filed into the classroom once again. There, instead of Squeaky, was our burly sergeant. Some of us groaned and let out weary sighs. I was reduced to a frustrated silence.

"You may smoke, ladies," he said, turning to a huge blackboard covered with dashes and dots. I hadn't the slightest idea of what it was all about, and instead of listening I gingerly began to massage the knee I had hurt skiing.

"*You* there! . . . What's this?"

I almost leaped out of my skin. The usual giggles rippled through the room.

"Who, me?" I asked as plaintively as I could.

"Yes."

"You sound like a German."

"What do you know about them?"

"Plenty. If you lower your voice, I'll answer your question. It's a dash."

"Is your knee sore?"

"All our knees are sore."

He grinned, the big burly bastard, and because it was the first time I had seen anyone look normal, I liked him.

The stuff on the blackboard was the Morse code and there were keyboards in our desks which the Sergeant linked up to outlets under the desks.

Di-di-da, di-di-da, and I was hopeless at it. Not memorizing the code, but transmitting. Either my longs were too short or my shorts too long. But some of the girls caught on almost immediately, especially the French girl, who slowly tapped the first letters with hardly a mistake. The Sergeant was jubilant.

"She's a natural," he boomed, rubbing his hands.

I was miserable as I started through the code for the umpteenth time, and I wondered if there could be something wrong with my hearing.

"Don't worry, Miss. I was just like you in the beginning. That's enough now. See you tomorrow for another go at it."

But the next day was the same and I was depressed; only the obstacle course cheered me because I came in first despite a new graze, this time on my other knee.

For three days this went on . . . di-di-da, obstacle course, weaponry (this fascinated me), tennis, silent killing, swimming, riding. On the last day our program was changed. Instead of weaponry, each of us was told separately that we were to practice silent killing on a man disguised as a German sentry guarding an ammunition dump. Each of us was to go through this rigmarole in a separate part of the garden under the watchful eye of an instructor. My instructor was Squeaky and the spot chosen for me was a sunken road with a small cliff overhanging it.

"Go!"

"Where?"

"Read your map. It's marked with a cross. This is your knife," he squeaked, handing me a wooden spoon. I pored over my map and started off. Behind me trudged Squeaky, clutching a pad and pencil as if they were the keys to civilization. When we neared the objective, I signaled him to make less noise. I really wanted to carry this off and he sounded like an elephant.

When we were within a few meters of the cliff, I started to crawl as I had been taught on the obstacle course. Out of the corner of my eye I saw Squeaky reluctantly doing the same and I wondered if the dampness wouldn't affect his voice! Easing my way forward, I looked over the cliff edge and felt a quick shock of anger when I saw the German helmet and the long gray coat.

He was standing just right for what I wanted to do—at ease, his gun over his shoulder, peering warily toward the other side of the road where the trees were thicker and were growing almost to the top of the embankment. It reminded me of my crossing into Switzerland with the Jews.

I stood up slowly and, once I was sure of my equilibrium, I jumped.

The man went down like a log, but I had time to grab his rifle and ease his head to the ground so his helmet wouldn't clatter.

It was hard work trying to get him out of his coat, which I was supposed to bring back to the house, and while I was laboring at it he whispered: "You're heavy, Miss. You hurt my neck."

"All right," Squeaky said, coming toward us on the road.

I never found out if my exploit was a success, but that evening

I went into the men's mess to buy a drink for the soldier. Maybe I *had* roughed him up a bit.

Of course none of us was told the results of our tests, but I suppose the word "impulsive" was written in letters of red across my sheet. I didn't care. I was given leave and four pounds pay—four and sixpence—which seemed to prove I had been accepted for something.

It was during my leave, when I was coming into Prunier's one evening with a young Fleet Air Arm pilot, that I saw Marcel sitting three tables away and talking to a British colonel wearing parachute flashes. For a second I didn't recognize him, perhaps because he was in battle dress and also because of a piece of adhesive tape marring one side of his face. An accident? No! . . . Plastic surgery! The phrase ran through my mind like the mean wind stirring grains of dust in his vineyard. So he was going back too.

I willed him with all my heart to look at me.

"You must help me, Dev," my host said, handing me the menu. "I was never much good at French. And this place is really *the* French restaurant in London. Look at the crowd. I'm probably the only Englishman here."

"Not quite, but probably the only one fished out of the drink yesterday." God, why won't he look? I'm not as bad as all that in uniform. Or am I?

"We'll have champagne to celebrate."

I shook my head. After all, I hardly knew this boy with his china-blue eyes and straw-colored hair. I didn't want him spending a lot of money, at least not on me, even if he probably had only six more months to live. Six months. I stared across at him. God, and he's only twenty-one!

"No, John," I said, but with little conviction. "Hock is good enough."

"Eh bien, that's why I couldn't reach you at your hotel!" a familiar voice said, driving all my remonstrances to the wind.

"I wondered when you were going to notice me."

I was indeed noticed and not quite in the way I would have

wished. Hand-kissing is viewed in certain circles in England as affected and foreign.

I pulled my hand away gently. But Marcel continued to tease me with his eyes even while I was making introductions.

"John is celebrating his rescue from the drink yesterday."

"Well, I expect you'll find wine less salty than the Channel! Tell me about it," and he pulled up a chair and sat down, but not before calling the wine steward and ordering champagne.

"But, Sir, you shouldn't," my host protested, looking in awe at the ribbons on Marcel's chest.

"I was once lost in the desert, and when I was brought back to camp by some nomads, I was delighted to be given drinks. It will be my pleasure to do the same for you."

And so we drank, toasting our host and laughing at his description of his icy bath. I laughed with Marcel and the British colonel, who had joined us, but all the time I heard someone saying: "Fleet Air Arm! Their life expectancy is six months!"

Of course, at first I was embarrassed for the boy. Maybe he would rather have been alone with me and talking to me about modern art—a subject I knew nothing about but which he was obsessed by. But I soon stopped worrying because he seemed perfectly happy to be talking planes and parachutes. In fact, I began to wonder if I wasn't de trop. Men are all alike, especially soldiers. At least, that's what I thought until I caught Marcel staring quizzically at my uniform. I returned his scrutiny by sliding my finger along his decorations, of which I recognized only two—the Légion d'Honeur and the Croix de Guerre.

"How was your trip?" he asked.

"Fine. I enjoyed Gibraltar. If it hadn't been for the jeeps, I would have thought it very old-fashioned. Rather like a war camp from another age, with all the men putting themselves out because I was a woman. Living on that rock must be monotonous."

"You're right, Miss. I've just come back. I was there only a week, but I was glad to leave," the Colonel said. "It's really a dreadful place."

"It means a lot to people who have been trying for months to reach it," Marcel said.

"Well, it can't be worse than Malta. Know some chaps who've just come back. They say it's hell. Things have calmed down now, but it's still being bombed by Jerry." John solemnly poured the last of the champagne. I knew from his flushed face that he was feeling no pain.

Nor was I. We had drunk three bottles . . . each of the warriors buying one. Only my dinner had been a skimpy affair—not because of my host but because Prunier's in wartime London was the meeting place of the French who could afford it and had small appetites.

"Are you all right, chérie?" Marcel whispered.

"Yes, but I'm hungry."

"You host is a tired but happy man. I think we can slip away. The Colonel will look after him."

It seemed rude. On the other hand, John was drunk, and I didn't fancy the idea of playing wet nurse to him. So slip away is just what we did, creeping out of the half-empty restaurant into the London blackout. We were kissing when the air-raid siren wailed.

"Come on, you two! There'll be time for that in the shelters," a voice said out of the darkness. "Off you go! Follow the arrows. Hurry! Jerry hasn't been over for a long time. He may make a night of it."

Suddenly the sky was lit by a stabbing beam which blotted out the stars and made the heavens look like a curved dome of indigo. From far off, dull thuds sounded. "Hurry!" the air-raid warden shouted, pushing us.

It was a very leisurely affair walking down the stairs and along the corridors of the tube station that served as a shelter. People either stumbled along in sleepy silence or talked as if loath to interrupt their conversation for such a thing as an air raid. Except for Marcel and me, everyone seemed to be carrying something. Pillows, blankets, mattresses. One man even had a typewriter and a satchel of books tied with a canvas strap of garish purple.

When we came to the foyer near the ticket booths, we heard

an accordion. It was being played by a French sailor, and a GI was accompanying him on a mouth organ. Near them, a couple of WAC officers were sitting on a piece of canvas, beating time, and not far away, near a staircase marked "SERVICE ONLY," was a wheeled cart, its shafts propped up on two wooden cases. In the cart were two caldrons steaming over alcohol burners; bottles of soda pop dangled along the spokes of the cartwheels. As we neared this contraption, I smelled tea—very strong tea.

"Like a cup, Miss?" a woman asked, bouncing out from behind a wheel, a helmet clamped over her straggling red hair. I shook my head, still feeling full of champagne.

"Oh, well, you will later on, tall girl, especially if the bloody Hun keeps us here all night. Everyone ends up at Ruth-the-Red's. Hello, Michael, my pet! Still writing your fairytales?" This to the man with the typewriter. "It's good to nurse a fantasy these days. It's like a wild rose growing on a heap of rubble. . . . How are you, Mr. Blyke! . . . Changed shelter? Never seen you here before. Caught napping! There's a bridge game on the platform. Maybe they'll let you cut in. . . . How about a dance tune, French maestro? Why don't you open the ball, tall girl? It will break the ice." And this extraordinary woman prattled on, shoving me into Marcel's arms.

Obviously, there wasn't much ice to break because in minutes Marcel and I felt as if we were on a nightclub floor. As we swayed, able to take only a shuffling step now and then, I stared at our hostess, as I had instantly come to think of her. Standing on one of the cases, red hair tumbling with perspiration, mouth wide open, she was singing. Funny part about it was she had a deep contralto that was not at all unpleasant.

"They're extraordinary," Marcel said. "She's dirty, vulgar, but it's the best of wartime London. Awhile back I went down to stay for a weekend in a smaller version of a stately home. There I found my hostess dressed in corduroy and working for a ball-bearing factory."

"You get around," I said.

"Not really. My host was once in the Legion—never found out why and never tried. We used to share the same corvées. I had no idea he would one day be a peer of the realm. If I had, I don't think I would have phoned him. Chérie, let's sit somewhere. The noise is awful and I want to hear your voice. Let's go to the platforms. Maybe it's quieter there. My God, what's that?"

Coming down the stairs to join us was a kilted figure, sporran swinging, bagpipes wailing. Conversation ceased and couples parted while with a whirl and a drone the piper marched over to Ruth.

She flung her arms around him. "I knew you'd come! I knew you'd come! It's a grand night for a reel! Anyone know how? Or are you all a lot of stuffy English?"

Two girls in ATS uniforms stepped forward. "We're from over the border," they cried, taking up positions on the spot where we had been dancing.

"Have you seen a little dog? I've lost her. I had to bring her down. She's frightened," a lady said to Marcel.

"No, I'm sorry. Where did you see her last?" Marcel asked and then, in a whisper: "You Anglo-Saxons! I hope she's not as vicious as your cat."

"I was on the platform and she was asleep. I came to get some tea and when I returned she was gone. Oh, my poor Flossie!" and the unhappy woman started to cry, huge tears running down her cheeks.

"Maybe Ruth saw her. Let me go and ask," I said, breaking away from Marcel, who had his arm around me.

It took a few minutes to divert the red-haired woman's attention from the Highland reel.

"No, can't say I have, tall girl."

Suddenly there was a scream. For a moment I thought it was the bagpipes. But no. It was an elderly woman. My God, what kind of animal has she lost? I wondered.

"My grandson, my grandson—a little boy of five. He was in transit. Just one night he had to spend in the city and Jerry has to come over! Oh, where can he be? What will I tell my daughter!"

In the calm that followed the woman's wail I heard a low, solid thump. I knew what it was and so did everyone else.

"I knew Jerry was going to make a night of it," the man with the typewriter said.

"Help me! Oh, please help me! If they put the power back on, he'll be killed."

"No bloody fear of that for some time, lady. We'll find him. He can't be far."

"Yes, love, it's going to be all right. We'll organize a search party," Ruth said, climbing onto her crate and clapping her hands for silence. "Everyone start looking—in groups of three."

"Maybe the bridge party saw him."

"Bah! All they see are cards. They've probably forgotten they're in an air-raid shelter."

"Flossie . . . Flossie . . . My Flossie . . . "

"Let's get out of this," Marcel said. "Too many cooks spoil the broth. The platforms are quieter."

Suddenly there was another thud—louder this time—followed by screams as everyone stared at a crack forming over a pay booth.

Marcel grabbed me and, instead of heading for the platform, yanked me along the corridor and up the stairs until we were outside, standing behind a wall of sandbags.

I filled my lungs with fresh air. Yes, it's better to die outside, I thought, remembering what a bomb had done to people in a shelter in Paris. It had been an Allied bomb, but death had been just as cruel.

"We can't go out," I whispered to Marcel as if an air-raid warden was on the prowl. "We'd be picked up immediately."

"I know. My poor darling. What a reunion! We'll crouch here. Can you see the searchlights? They're beautiful, but I don't think they've spotted any Germans."

The all-clear came an hour later, just as we had decided to risk walking to Marcel's apartment because we were cold.

"You're lucky to have an apartment. It's a luxury."

"I know. A friend of mine who is in Washington lent it to me. Come on, darling. A warm bath and a whiskey will do us good."

Hours later, sitting in the kitchen over a belated breakfast, I asked: "Have you been here long?"

"Nearly three weeks. I'm afraid this toast will never taste like our rolls in Madrid," and to prove it he jerked onto a plate some very burnt pieces of bread.

"Let me try." But my effort was even less successful, and we resigned ourselves to eating slabs of the indigestible stuff smeared with margarine and jam.

"You've lost some of your suntan and I miss your scar."

"So will the Germans. It was my identity card. They did a good job. I wasn't allowed to get in touch with you before it healed."

"So you're going back?"

He nodded, his blue eyes meeting mine: "Aren't you?"

"I suppose so, but I don't know how. I have to go into training, but what the training is I wouldn't know. Last week I went through a lot of tests in a psychological school—a bunch of nuts."

"Your training will teach you how to dangle in space at the end of a parachute."

For seconds I stared at him, slowly paling.

"Marcel, you can't mean it!"

He nodded and took me in his arms. "Do you still like the British? Did you really think they would go to all the trouble they have and then let you do some useless war work that others can do just as well?"

"Oh, what a fool I've been!" I cried. "But no one said anything about parachuting."

"Darling, they thought you realized it on your own. How did you expect to return?"

"By fishing boat or walking over the Pyrenees again."

He shook his head.

I buried my face in his shoulder, crying: "I'm scared! Scared!"

"Don't be. It's not as bad as you think."

But to me it didn't matter what he said. I didn't like planes, and the thought of jumping out of one terrified me. It even spoiled my love-making in spite of all Marcel's tenderness. Finally he slapped my buttocks and said, "Nothing wild about you now, my love. Never thought a parachute would have this effect on you. Let's dress and go to the organization. I promised to meet Lecoque at the mess."

"The organization?"

"Yes, we're in the same racket, but I doubt if our paths will cross when we go back."

"Have you jumped?"

"Yes. It's not half as bad as it sounds. In the end, I enjoyed it. Once the chute opens, it's a peaceful sensation."

"The chute opens?" I wailed, turning away from him and burying my head in a pillow.

"Look! . . . See these flashes? You feel good when you receive them," and he took the piece of cloth with the damn wings on it out of his duffel and made me swivel my head to stare at them. The sight only made me cry harder.

He became quite angry, and because I had never heard his voice so sharp, I dried my tears.

"There, that's better. Want a drink?"

I shook my head. "Why don't you wear them?"

"Not allowed to. We're not in a parachute brigade. We're just hush-hush people. It will be the same for you."

Some of my joy at finding Marcel seemed to have disappeared because of those flashes, at least until we went to the mews off Portland Place. There excitement caught hold of me once more. It couldn't be otherwise when you stepped into that mess. Wartime London vanished in a babble of French voices. Listening to each one was like having a map of the country spread before you. Here a Marseillais was telling a story that mostly made one laugh because his speech conjured up the smell of wild thyme and the sound of cicadas chirping beside sun-drenched gray stones while "La Grande Bleue" shimmered on the horizon. There was also the dragging voice of someone from Lyon, reflecting in its hoarseness the dampness which bathes that gloomy city between its rivers, and from somewhere in the background came the clipped voice of a Parisian talking to a man from the north who slurred his words.

"Salut, Marcel!" someone shouted, probably the Marseillais. "How was the air raid?"

"Bloody nuisance!" a very English voice sang out from behind a makeshift bar composed of packing cases onto which empty packages of cigarettes were glued. The bar was a good idea because it prevented one's staring at the "porte des adieux" next to it. Marked by a skull and crossbones and surmounted by a German helmet, this door seemed to glare disapprovingly at our boisterousness, as if saying: "Once through my portals, London will no longer see you and your laughter may become a scream in a torture chamber."

"Eh, te, was I scared!" the Marseillais said. "I think I'd rather be bombed by the Allies. They at least make an effort to hit the factories."

And so it went over pints of beer, but just as I was beginning to enjoy watching some clever card tricks, I was called away to another part of the mews by the man we had nicknamed Master Ill-fit. This poor chap bore the brunt of much teasing because he was our tailor, outfitting us in the hideous fashions of occupied France. There were those who claimed they could always recognize a member of the organization by the ungainly pleat just below the back of the jacket collar.

"I would like to take your measurements," he said in English, flipping his tape measure off his neck.

I was surprised until I remembered someone telling me his mother was English and in an internment camp.

"Do you ever get any news from France?" I asked, thinking of my own mother.

"No. Nothing but Red Cross cards and not many of those. Why?"

"I heard your mother was interned. So was mine."

He nodded, his watery eyes staring at me. "We're not supposed to talk about it."

"I can't think why."

"We're hush-hush people and the less we talk about ourselves, the better."

"It can't prevent us from talking among ourselves."

"And trying to recognize the telltale pleat," he quipped.

I had to smile. "I'll think of you when I wear your clothes."

He shrugged. "Please stand still, Miss. You have one tailored suit and a dress coming to you, as well as some shoes, sweaters and stockings."

"But I haven't done my training yet."

"It doesn't matter. If you don't get through, I can always give your quota of material to someone else. By ordering now I'm sure to have it when you come back. How about a nice tweed for the suit and jersey for the dress?"

While Ill-fit fussed about me, puffing and blowing, I chose my material. I must say he had quite a collection.

"May I take a sample?" I asked, wanting to show it to Marcel and Betty.

"Oh, no, Miss. No one outside the organization must know. You see, this material is prewar, requisitioned especially for our people. We like our agents to have the best when they go into the field."

He was right. The material was the best. What a pity he was the tailor! My dress shoes, as he called them, were awful-looking —wooden clogs with platform heels. I shook my head.

"Can't help it, Miss. That's what they're wearing. You must know that."

"How do you know I do?"

"You've been over there. Cheer up. I've got a pair of ankle boots for you with crepe soles. You'll like those. They're nice."

He was right and I wished I had had them when I walked over the Pyrenees.

"You'll need a mac. I'll give you some coupons so you can buy it yourself. Don't forget to save the bill so you can be reimbursed."

And so it went until I wondered if he wasn't going to fit me for underclothes. When we had finished, I had ordered a complete wardrobe.

Back in the mess, most of the gang had left, including my card sharper. I was sorry about that because Marcel was deep in conversation with Lecoque. I decided to play darts.

"How about lunch?" Marcel asked when he finally came over to me. "Will you join us, Lecoque?"

"Mes homages, Mademoiselle," the boy said, bowing over my hand.

Please, dear God, make him say no. Why don't I like Lecoque? He seems devoted to Marcel. And he's good-looking in a fresh, clean way. Nothing seems wrong. Why don't I like him?

We all did have lunch together in a French restaurant and, contrary to what I'd expected, I enjoyed myself because I found out why I didn't like Lecoque. He was a snob.

Oh, not because he held his little finger at a right angle when he drank or because he indulged in name-dropping. No, name-dropping wasn't for him yet. He was still in the collecting stage, noting names down in a little black book as Marcel pointed people out. And there were many people to point out in that restaurant. It seemed to be serving half the Free French forces. The other half—the richer ones—went to Prunier's, no doubt.

"What are you writing? Your memoirs?" I asked Lecoque maliciously when Marcel excused himself to speak to a small, vivacious, dark woman sitting with a young French officer.

"Oh, no. I like to remember the names of the people the Commandant points out to me. Maybe one day I'll write a book. You see that big man over there talking to the proprietor? His name is Remy. He's hush-hush, too."

Something like a Kodak shutter clicked in my mind. "I don't think it's wise to talk about these things," I snapped, remembering Ill-fit's words.

After that we had no more conversation because Marcel brought back to our table the vivacious woman and her companion, who turned out to be her son. Talking and laughing with him, I made up my mind I would speak to Marcel about his protégé and his black book.

The following day I saw my chance.

"There's something I want to say to you, but I don't know how to go about it."

"That's a sure sign it's something unpleasant, chérie."

"Well, it may be and it may not be."

Marcel flashed me a smile and made a rude gesture with a finger up against his buttresslike nose. "You're being very devious. You'll soon be the perfect spy."

"I doubt it. And I'm not being devious, but I'm wondering if someone else isn't. Oh, no . . . That's wrong too," I said.

"Well, what is it?"

"It's the black book."

He stared at me sharply. I stumbled on. It was all I could do. "I don't like the way Lecoque jots down the names of all the people you point out to him."

Marcel leaned back in the chair, swiveling the drink I had just given him. His face suddenly wore the same expression I had seen the first time I met him in the vineyards facing the Pyrenees.

"He's very young. He says he wants to write a book once this is all over."

"He said the same to me." And I was sad because I felt Marcel was annoyed with me.

"Well, then?"

"Darling, maybe you know too many people," I stammered.

Suddenly he leaned over and drew me toward him.

"It's an innocent pastime. What are you afraid of? He says writing things down helps him remember."

And that was the end of it. But during our last days together Marcel seemed thoughtful.

Three days later I was in the compartment of a northbound train. I've never acquired the capacity of my fellow Americans for following directions that run "Drive three miles, then turn east" on a foggy day, but I knew our direction because the weather was fine for once and I saw the sunset reflected through the windows of the corridor.

10

The two girls and four men who were to be my companions for the next six weeks were distributed between two compartments. Our escort officer was an FANY, but she wasn't the one from the psychological school. There was also a well-muscled sergeant wearing parachute flashes, which I stared at with dismay and admiration.

We were crowded despite the two compartments because everyone was rather big and we had a lot of luggage. But eventually my compartment was cleared and I climbed up into the luggage rack and dropped off to sleep, to the sound of a mouth organ played by a boy named Bernard.

When I woke hours later, daylight was scratching at the window, a faint bar across a muggy sky. Everyone was asleep, including the FANY officer, her head pillowed on Bernard's lap. Two of the girls were sleeping below me, feet covered by a blanket. On the floor a man was snoring. I suppose the rest were in the other compartment. I decided I had chosen the best place in spite of a cramp in one leg.

The next time I woke, everyone was stirring, yawning and stretching. It was very fuggy and someone suggested opening the window. It seemed like a good idea, but I regretted it a few minutes later when the chill air blew over me. The cold finally made me climb down, and I wondered where we could be.

The Sergeant came in, carrying two picnic baskets and a box

filled with cups and thermos bottles. He looked as fresh as a daisy, shaved and spruced. Not at all like us.

"All the comforts of home," someone said to the FANY officer, who was handing out sandwiches while the Sergeant filled the cups with black tea.

"That's right. Eat up. Hurry. We're almost there."

"Already there!" Bernard said, staring at the lines of bleak red houses flitting by the window.

And hurry we did, hurrying even faster once we were down on the platform. "Don't worry," the escorting officer said, "the Sergeant will see to your luggage." And she led us down platforms, up steps and corridors, through gates marked "ENTRANCE FORBIDDEN" until we came to an open track on which sat an old-fashioned railroad car with wooden doors and highly polished copper fittings. A real antique! Getting everything into it was a feat because there were crates and barrels to transport in addition to our personal things. While the men were loading it all, an officer and a soldier came by.

"Good job!" the officer said, looking up at the female members of this commando unit, who were helping by word of mouth to get the stuff in. "Had a good journey? I don't think you've been seen. Give them a hand, Macloud."

I was puzzled. Did he mean we were hoping to swindle the railway company? But I had no time to pursue the thought because, seconds later, I heard our car being coupled to another and we were all aboard it. I peered out through an open window and saw ahead of us a perfectly normal train with sleek modern coaches. I decided it was all very strange and also that it was going to be a fine day. And then I saw it: a monstrous spur of rock crowned by a weather-beaten castle.

"Eh!" I shouted. "We're in Edinburgh!"

"Shut up, you fool! And come away from that window!"

I turned to face the escorting officer, who was glaring at me.

"But . . . but . . ." I protested weakly.

"Never mind. Just shut up!" she said, pulling the shades down on all the windows.

And that was all I saw of the capital of Scotland. The shades weren't pulled up until we were well on our way, by which time I was dozing, draped in my offended dignity for having dared to recognize a city I had known before the war.

All morning we chugged along, somehow aware that somewhere along the way we had parted company with our modern train. We were on our own as we slowly meandered and puffed through nameless stations. Even the crossroads we passed had no signposts but only wooden stubs where signposts had been. Another precaution in the event of invasion. It was all very weird and, in a way, alarming and it was obvious that my companions thought so too. One doesn't recognize every place in the course of a train journey, but ordinarily one spots a signpost or the name of a station. Here there was nothing. It wasn't quite like a journey into a barren land because there were cars and people on bicycles traveling the narrow roads and once I saw a bus. There were also cows grazing in the fields, short-horned, stocky and fawn-colored. But gradually the farms disappeared. In their place the rolling countryside turned bleak and only sheep were grazing. The weather changed too. Instead of blue skies there were clouds and driving rain. Something in the contour of the land seemed familiar to me, but I wasn't sure until I saw standing on the crest of a hill . . . Glen Eagles. This time I made no comment. Instead I caught the escort officer's eye. She gave me a faint smile, which I returned. I knew at least where we were going: to the Highlands.

Sandwiches and tea were again produced and three of the boys started a card game, using one of the barrels as a table. The Sergeant played with them while the two girls watched.

"Do you know this part of the world well?" the FANY officer asked me.

"Not as well as I would have liked. But I once spent two summers staying with a school friend near Loch Awe. It's wonderful country."

"I'm sure you're going to recognize much more. Don't mention it. You see, we're doing our best to keep this part of Scotland a military secret. That's why I rushed you through the station in Edinburgh."

"It's hard to believe we're at war when you stare over those beautiful glens. And yet Scotland has a bloody past."

"Are you interested in Scottish history?"

"I'm always interested in history, especially 'la petite histoire.' "

"Have you studied Scottish history?"

"No more than most people, but the brooding quiet of these hills has always fascinated me."

"Well, we'll soon be coming to a part of the country I'm sure you don't know. You won't be doing much sightseeing in the next few weeks, but if we have fine weather it's beautiful. And please, no more comments when you see something you recognize. Incidentally, Dev, please call me Margot."

From then on I saw plenty that I recognized, but after Fort William I saw no more. We climbed into a military vehicle and drove under a canvas top for what could just as well have been an hour as two.

When we stopped, it was past four. We were at the head of a loch and so was a small cruiser, moored to a pier, filled with crates and fully manned. Real Navy. The air was mild, smelling of heather and pine. The blue sheen of mountains and hills was reflected in the quiet water. It was very peaceful, very quiet—a sort of pensive hush. Nowhere in the world is the light so beautiful as in the Highlands, especially during the long summer twilight. I was sitting up forward apart from my companions and I drank it all in as we chugged along. To the west the sun was blurred and I knew it would soon rain . . . that thin, silent drizzle that makes you damp and clammy but never really wet. And of course it did and of course we put on our macs. I didn't mind because the few moments of sunshine were stored in the mirror of my mind. The beautiful Highlands!

My home for the next six weeks was an ugly, sprawling turn-of-the-century hunting lodge with the women's quarters set apart from the main building. I think it had probably once housed the beaters during the shooting season. My room was sparely furnished with an army cot, a nightstand, a cupboard and a washstand holding a chipped jug. It overlooked a chattering stream, the same one we had followed up from the landing pier after our hour's journey down the loch.

"The bathroom is next door. The john is separate," Margot called, tapping on the wall. "Unpack quickly. The Colonel is waiting for us."

I don't know if we kept the Colonel waiting, but if so he didn't show it in his greeting, which was hearty, with tankards of beer and himself in kilt and sporran. His officers were in battle dress. He was a commanding pepper-and-salt man with gray eyes that snapped and a humorous mouth curving upward beneath a thin mustache. An imposing row of ribbons adorned his battle-dress jacket.

"Welcome! Welcome! This is Major Hyatt, Captain Duran and of course Sergeant Devere, who came up from London with you. They're your instructors and not as stupid as they look. Well, you're not too bedraggled. Sorry about the rain and your having to walk, but we needed the trucks for the stores. Besides, you'll get used to it—the rain, I mean. Too bad you weren't here last week. Regular Riviera weather. Too hot, really. Have another beer. It's on the house. You're Dev, aren't you?"

"Yes, Sir."

"Know Scotland too, don't you?"

"A little."

He smiled frostily. "Keep it that way."

I had no choice during the next six weeks I spent in those glens and hills learning to be a commando.

Reveille to the sound of a trumpet was at six, after which, rain or shine, we did exercises, dressed in shorts and gym shoes. The push-ups were the worst because my behind always remained higher than my neighbor's until it was smartly smacked by a corporal. He must have dreamed nights of a chorus line of bottoms.

"Le derrière, Dev! Le derrière!" was the singsong of my companions.

Some mornings, rain or shine, we ran a mile up the road to a loch, into which we then plunged "to get the cobwebs off our eyelashes," we were told. Did we run back? Yes. And I was always last.

Needless to say, breakfast was a hearty meal. I even learned to like porridge.

"Now, this is dynamite! A cutting explosive," Captain Duran said, tapping a gray-white block on the table in front of him, while I wished I hadn't taken the first row in the classroom. "If kept relatively damp, it's not dangerous. Now, this piece—" and he pointed to a flaking lump—"is a nasty bugger. It could go off at any time."

I started to squirm on my chair. So did my closest neighbor.

"Now, this is gelignite. You can mold it, do anything you want with it. Only use gloves," he said, pulling on a pair before modeling the stuff in his hands. "It's also a cutting explosive. But handling it causes a headache. Corporal, open the window and take this away.

"Now, you say, 'How am I supposed to blow up a train if these explosives are so tricky?' Plastic explosive is the answer. It's really the tops, even though it isn't a cutting explosive. You can do anything with it. Even use it for putty to hold a window. . . . Incidentally, that's a good way of hiding it. It won't explode and it keeps indefinitely. But it's not cutting and it has to be for steel girders. So we make it cutting by tamping it. Tamping for rails and for buildings like electric-circuit houses. Tamping for practically everything but booby-traps and trip wires."

And he went on with the varied roles of detonators, primers, time pencils and detonating cord. Everything was carefully explained and chalked up on a blackboard so that we could take notes, make diagrams. Just like preparing for an exam. It was fascinating.

But not all of it. We had classes in map-reading. Captain Duran taught us to pinpoint a spot on a map and convert it into a compass reading, and vice versa. And the maps weren't Michelin road maps, either. They were ordnance maps filled with contours, squiggles and circles. And there was instruction in camouflage—how to use it most effectively without looking like a tree crossing a plowed field.

Of course our favorite subject was weaponry. Perhaps because our instructor was the Sergeant who had come from London with us and we didn't stand so much in awe of him.

"Oh, Sarge, this is lovely!" exclaimed the Swiss girl, Vivien, holding a small pistol with a mother-of-pearl handle. "Now I can play the jealous mistress!"

"And I the faithless lover. . . . 'My darling, you've shot an innocent man,' " Serge, the dark boy, sobbed. He was always clowning, claiming to our doubtful merriment that his father was a Russian grand duke. "My love shot me. My most vital part lost and gone forever!"

"Now, ladies, now, gentlemen! That will do. What would the Colonel say?" the Sergeant said.

"That you're making a bloody noise!" this gentleman yelled from an adjoining room. "The Adjutant and I can't hear ourselves think. Serge, Serge . . . You young fool, I don't care a damn about your parts. Learn the parts of a Sten gun."

Unfortunately, we didn't have the Sergeant every day. Oh, no. Di-di-di-da also had its place in the curriculum. And I was still hopeless, to the disgust of the instructor, who was none other than the derrière-smacking corporal. I had one consolation: Bernard the athlete was scarcely better.

We spent the afternoons putting into practice what we had learned.

"Now, Dev," the Colonel said when it was my turn, "here's a compass reading. Locate it on the map. Get to it without being seen. Deliver this message and return. You have an hour. Beware of surprises." And he handed me an envelope and a slip of paper. I thought he looked immensely pleased with himself.

Outside I met the Sergeant. He looped a rope over my shoulders, gave me a compass, a pair of binoculars, checked my watch with his and, with a "Good luck, Miss," sent me on my way.

I plunged into the clump of pine trees opposite the house until I found some underbrush. Here I consulted my compass readings. Then, drawing a bead on my map, I located a hill across the stream. I was relieved because I had thought for a moment that my mission would entail climbing the cliffs and ravines behind the house.

I knew I couldn't be seen as long as I was in the pine grove, so I quickly moved as close to the noisy stream as I could get before the trees thinned out.

The stream was swift-running and, as nearly as I could see through my binoculars, not deep. There looked to be plenty of rocks to cling to. On my side the embankment sloped down easily; on the other it was steep, and I knew that while I climbed it I'd be in full view of anyone watching. Of course there was a small bridge. But trying to cross that would be no good either; the only thing would be to go under it and wade over. Trouble was I suspected the water was deep right there and there wouldn't be many rocks. But I decided to check and started toward it in a crouch. Suddenly I was brought up short by a pine branch lying on the ground. That's funny, I thought. There's been no wind. I crawled around it gingerly, feeling in the turf, and soon found what I suspected. It wasn't buried very deep, and feeling gently along the wire, I located the charges. Just plain noisy firecrackers. Only the bastards had set them on both sides of the branch. The hardest part was untangling the wire they had looped to the branch, but I needed that branch for camouflage. I wasn't going to go over or under the bridge, only pretend to.

Unslinging my rope, I placed it under the branch and played it out until it dangled down between the bridge and the embankment. Then I slowly withdrew it, retiring as I did so to the shelter of the trees. Seeing something move between the green and purple bracken, they would think I had gone under the bridge and be surveying the other side. At least, that's what I hoped.

Back in the pine grove, I ran upstream parallel to the water to a point where I had spotted pines growing down both banks almost to the water's edge. They were few and far between, but crawling slowly with my branch strapped to my back should cover me. All this was damned uncomfortable, so that I was tired when I reached the water's edge and dropped down onto a small rocky beach below an overhang.

Twenty minutes! Damn that trip wire!

Crossing the stream was a wet business, but I was sure I couldn't be seen until I reached the opposite bank. The branch strapped to my back made me clumsy and I fell once, startling some fish in a pool. I wondered if they were trout. Trout. Salmon. I'll bet there were a lot beneath the bridge. It would be nice to eat some fish. The food so far had been monotonous and starchy.

I didn't stop crawling until I was around the base of the hill and beside the small platform where my objective must be.

Half an hour! I needed to rest, but first I wanted to take a look over the rim. Good. No problem. The Guinness bottle was propped up between two stones only a few yards from the edge. I thought I could roll it over toward me with my branch. But slowly, slowly. They'd be watching now.

Resolved to sit awhile, I turned. Staring up at me was a small boy with a lot of freckles and red hair.

"Hello! Who are you?"

"Jamie, Miss. You're very wet. I didn't think there would be any field work today. Otherwise I wouldn't have brought the worms."

"Worms?"

"Yes, for Ian, down at the big loch. I dig and hide them here. It's for fishing."

"But why here?"

"His father sends him to look after the sheep and this is a good spot. They don't come this far. The sheep, I mean."

"Are you telling me that Guinness bottle is full of worms?"

"Yes, Miss."

"It's government property."

"The worms are too, in a way."

"I'm supposed to put an envelope in that bottle. I can't do that if it's full of worms. Ugh!"

"Well, I suppose I could get some more. But these are lovely ones."

I had to laugh.

"Give me your branch, Miss. I'll roll the bottle over without being seen."

"How do you know I'm not supposed to be seen?"

"Training to be a commando. You'll be jumping soon. Funny thing for a woman to do. My mother doesn't really believe you're women. Ah! Look! Aren't they beautiful?"

I drew back, staring at the disgusting creatures. "They're as big as baby snakes!" I exclaimed, pushing them away from my feet, where they seemed bent on burrowing into my boots.

"They're government property too—from the refuse heap behind the house."

"Ugh! Disgusting! More so now I know where they come from."

"Aren't you going to write something on the envelope?"

"I suppose so," I said, drawing out a pencil and printing a few lines with damp fingers.

"Are you going back the same way you came, Miss?"

"Yes. I'd better tie my branch back on. I hope I haven't been seen."

"I know a better way and you won't have to crawl."

Nothing had been said about my return, and as long as I wasn't seen, it seemed a fine idea.

"All right. But how long will it take? I only have twenty minutes."

"You'll be there. Do you want your branch?"

I nodded. It had served me well.

Instead of heading down toward the stream, we cut straight ahead and then turned left, passing some grazing black-nosed sheep on the way.

"Ian's father's," Jamie said, shoving one away that came bleating toward us. "Now we cross the burn. It's well above the house, so no one will be looking."

Three minutes later we walked in the back of the house and I left Jamie.

"Thanks. I'm sorry about the worms. Don't say you saw me."

His face broke into a broad grin, which gave him a sort of golden look because all his freckles seemed to meet.

"Damn it! Where can she be? Maybe the fool has fallen into the stream under the bridge," the Colonel was exclaiming.

"It's deep there." I recognized Duran's voice.

"The Sergeant is waving. Looks as if she delivered the envelope."

Duran spoke again. "Wherever she is, she isn't going to make it."

"Oh, I think you're wrong. I still have a minute to go," I said, strolling up to them.

"Damn it! Good show! I thought you were drowned," the Colonel said later as he handed me a whisky. "Drink it. You're soaked. I'm going to have to change the location of this excercise. Camouflage seems to have gone a long way with you. Fooled us, eh, Sergeant?"

"Certainly did! There's something written on the envelope, Sir."

"Literature, Dev? Wait till I put my specs on. Wretched things! Make me feel old. . . . 'We seek him here, we seek him there, that damned elusive Pimpernel!' "

Everyone was very pleasant, but I was glad to leave them, craving one thing only—a hot bath.

Increasingly, our days were spent in outdoor practice. In the end, only the di-di-di-da took place indoors, and there wasn't much of that because those classmates who were destined for radio work were to go elsewhere for more advanced training. But even strenuous exercise couldn't prevent me from thinking—between mortar and target practice, grenade-throwing, silent killing, night commando work in cork-smeared faces—of what awaited me once this was all finished. I was tough and lean, all right, but nothing had changed in my mind concerning the joys of jumping out of an airplane!

Of course we talked about it among ourselves, but since none of the staff—not even our nice Sergeant—would say anything, it remained in the domain of the great unknown.

Then came the day of our departure, after a riotous farewell dinner during which Bernard and Serge stole the Colonel's sporran and served it up on a silver platter.

The journey back took us through Glasgow and landed us somewhere near Manchester, in barracks despairingly grim and void of personality. Gray and khaki, with hardly any color to brighten the bleak countryside. We huddled together over our high tea, enclosed in our memories of the past six weeks, and kept as aloof as possible from the others, a noisy, hearty crowd.

Reveille was the same, only the bugle no longer dispelled the quiet of the glens. It was one noise among others.

Our first exercise was learning to land rolling over, head tucked beneath shoulders, forearms over face, legs and feet together. We practiced this for hours, jumping off higher and higher parapets each time. In the afternoon we were introduced to a funnel-like contraption set up on a high scaffold.

"Now, this is what you'll have to jump out of. An exact reproduction. Very simple, really, but if you don't go out stiff and straight you'll break your nose," a red-faced soldier told us in an impersonal voice. I think he was bored. After all, he had trained so many and he had been doing it for so long.

And so we jumped through the thing, rolling like circus performers. It wasn't very exciting. Only the height was alarming.

"It's not much of a jolt, Miss, not half of what it really is. Hurry! Hurry! No hesitating. Don't miss your drop. The plane isn't going to come in a second time. Jump! Jump!"

In the evening we were taken up in a real plane and made to lie on our stomachs looking through the funnel. The speed, with the roaring wind and the void below, provided all the elements of parachuting except the actual jump. I don't know how my companions felt, but my stomach was in knots and my mouth dry.

Before we jumped, there was still one thing we had to learn. We were taken into a classroom, where a hearty man with a booming voice explained to us how to fold a parachute.

"Now, I don't expect you to do this," he said, opening the great silk thing on a long table. "Feel how soft it is."

We crowded around.

"What lovely blouses it would make," I suggested.

"Forget it. Bury it. The Germans would know it immediately. Now, I don't expect you to fold this. Experts do that."

I drew away, butterflies in my stomach again. Vivien muttered angrily: "I should hope not!" We all agreed, coming together as one. The teamwork was still working. Even Margot, who followed us everywhere, was disgusted and shrugged her shoulders contemptuously. The man seemed slightly put out.

"The most important thing for you people is the rip cord. This . . ." and he held up a wire coil with a clamp on the end of it. "Once you have your chute on, never let go. Now we'll go outside to the mock-up. Hurry, please."

I followed the others, still trying to concentrate on what a lovely blouse that piece of silk would make.

The mock-up was the fuselage of a plane that was pockmarked with holes. Anti-aircraft, I supposed. With chutes strapped to our backs, helmets, ankle and chin straps, one by one we shuffled forward, each holding our ripcord. The chute was surprisingly heavy and, strapped as it was to our legs, it gave us all a crablike walk.

We went to our allotted places in the fuselage and since we were seven (Margot stayed outside, making thumbs-up signs to us) we formed a complete stick.

"Sticks are in lots of seven or five. Sometimes more when it's paratroopers. It all depends on the equipment." We moved forward, one on one side of the trap, the next one on the other. "When your turn comes and the light flashes green, swing your feet down, hands on the rim. Keep your head up. Never look down through the hole. Go out stiff. Watch the dispatcher. He's your man. You shove off when his hand goes down and he says GO. Now hurry. Hurry."

These words were always at our backs. By the end of my stay in that factorylike atmosphere I was dreaming of them. GO HURRY GO HURRY But maybe that was what kept us going.

We practiced all morning until each movement was automatic.

"Well, you're not too stuffy a lot. Keep your helmet and straps. See you after lunch for the real thing. I'm your dispatcher. Don't eat too much."

I didn't, but I was sick anyway.

There was no breeze, which was a relief, because being dragged by a billowing chute is no fun for either your face or your backside.

HURRY! HURRY! And we were in the plane holding the rip cords that represented our last chance of finishing life peacefully in bed. The dispatcher moved grimly around us, silently verifying each one's hook-up to the larger cable.

A bar of fear across my stomach. Bernard ahead of me. He looks enormous. I suppose we all do.

Christ! What a racket! Maybe the plane is crashing.

My turn. Swing down. Stay stiff. Oh, God, the noise!

GO!

A roar. Buffeting. Keep stiff. The slipstream and then a jerk wrenching my shoulders. The feeling of being a puppet. Something is wrong. God, what a way to die! What peace! It's open. I'm floating free. Oh, the silence. Wonderful silence.

I open my eyes and am immediately sick. The sky is at my feet and then swinging over to the left. Yes, I'm sick, but it doesn't matter. Surely a bird must feel like this. I reach up for my rigging lines and draw them around to steady the chute. I look at it above me. What a graceful thing it is. Oh, she's beautiful and I love her.

I begin to enjoy myself. If only I could get the mess off my front. I look down through my feet. God, the earth is coming up fast. Oh, there's Margot. She should have jumped. Everyone should. I'm euphoric.

"Dev, pull your rigging lines. To the left. You're drifting toward the woods. Pull! Pull! Good! Good! You're coming down fine." Someone is bellowing through a megaphone. He looks quite tiny. . . . My God! No! Legs bent! Forearms over face! Head down! Shoulders hunched! Roll! . . .

It wasn't long after that first jump when our training was over and I had my wings, even though I did refuse one later jump when I was the last to go. I had looked down and, no longer hearing the clatter of the other rip cords, had broken the momentum. We dispersed. The Englishman we called Jean sans Français became an instructor. The other one, so anodyne I hardly knew his name, became a demolition expert. Serge, Bernard and the two girls went overseas. One of the girls, who had almost been blown up by a faulty charge during training, was captured and deported to Ravensbruck. I don't know if she returned. Someone told me she was hanged on a butcher's hook. Of Vivien I know nothing. I heard that Serge was killed during the liberation of Paris; Bernard disappeared in the flotsam of the occupation and I don't know what happened to him.

Over coffee in the army hut I looked at my Colonel. I had met him only twice and neither liked nor disliked him. A handsome, burly chap with steel-blue eyes and a tight-lipped mouth that rarely smiled. I wished I could fall in love with him without hoping for a response. It would somehow eliminate the awe he inspired.

Our radio operator was an American. Later I learned he was the brother of the woman who had sheltered Bridget and me in Paris on our way to Switzerland, but he still had an accent despite his years in France. He was debonair, slender, with a slow, gangly walk and laughing eyes, and at the end of five minutes he was teasing me. His code name was Paul.

"I suppose you're glad not to be jumping, Elizabeth," said the English officer who had accompanied us down from London.

It took me a minute to remember that my code name was Elizabeth. Then I nodded.

"It's cold. You'd get chilblains," Paul laughed.

"But if you have to jump, would you?" the officer asked.

"Yes."

"Good girl. But I hope you won't have to. There's a lot of equipment going over in your plane and only some of it is in containers."

"Our plane?"

"Yes. For the first time we'll be putting two planes down on the same field. The Colonel is going in the first. I hope the cover party is adequate. A message came through before we left London. They're standing by. 'The apple pie sends love' went out two days ago. Well," the English officer said, "good luck to you. I think you'd better be on your way."

We stood up and shook hands solemnly. I gathered up my rucksack. It had been repaired but patched so that it still looked worn. I also had a suit case filled with Ill-fit's creations. Well, I thought, I'm going back with more than I came over with.

Paul and I were led over the dark tarmac to a lumbering plane with a gun turret sticking up in back. Swinging myself aboard, I couldn't make out if it was a Lancaster or a Wellington. Inside, the first thing I noticed were bicycle tires. They brought the occupation back. Very vividly.

It was a beautiful night. Never had the sky looked clearer.

"Are you comfortable, Miss?" the dispatcher asked.

"No," I replied, trying to fit my fanny between two packing cases while Paul, perched above me on what looked like a gun crate, was swinging his feet almost in my face.

"I'm sorry. I'll get some blankets. Meanwhile stretch your legs. The drink is coming up. Our escort planes are riding nice and easy. They leave us at the French coast. Afterward we'll fly beneath the ack-ack to our rendezvous."

I went toward the tail, lingering for a second in front of the bicycle tires and staring at the closed parachute trap. I found the john and on my way out saw the gun turret with the gunner's feet dangling from it.

I poked my head and shoulders inside the turret. For a second the gunner looked startled. Then, "Lovely night," he said. "Jerry is quiet these days. Come and look at the drink. It looks like silver."

And that is the way I reached France, squeezed on a gunner's knee. It was a wonderful sight. Blue, black, silver, white where clouds circled the moon. I knew I would never forget it.

"The coast is coming up. We'll have flak. Maybe a Jerry on the prowl. Better go now."

Yes, we had flak over the Atlantic Wall. But somehow everyone was so casual about it I thought it was only turbulence, until I saw through a porthole something darker than the sky, something that could have held a flash in it. And then we were over and everything was back to normal.

I looked at my watch. Twelve fifteen. Way past curfew. I saw a river and wondered if it was the Loire. France, dear France.

We flew for an hour or more over the dark and tranquil countryside, the shadow of our plane gliding along to keep us company. Then, when the dispatcher came and took our mugs of coffee, I knew we were almost there.

The pilots who flew these missions, whether in big planes or in tiny Lysanders, were the crack airmen of the RAF. They had to be because setting down their machines in fields lit only by flare paths cast by flashlights or bonfires required the most extraordinary skill. This time, perhaps because the other plane had already landed ahead of us and was taking off as we approached, our pilot missed his landing. Instead we hit a church belfry. The shock was tremendous, sending cases falling all over the place. What it did to the belfry I don't know. Monsieur le Curé would certainly have a lot of explaining to do.

"You'll have to jump. I think my landing gear is jammed." The impersonal voice came over the long-com.

Suddenly the dispatcher was there, fitting a parachute harness on Paul while the plane veered. I started to feel sick as I drew my rucksack toward me, preparatory to having it strapped to one of my legs. The suitcase would follow later. God only knew when.

Christ! All the Germans in the sector must be on the alert!

"It's all right! She's out! Stand by for landing. Hurry! Hurry!"

And hurry we did. So much so that I sprawled on my face in the mud of France.

Just as well. My mac was too clean, anyway.

I returned to France by the moon of October. There was a nip in the air and the sky was studded with stars. It was not a winter sky nor yet a summer one. A farewell-and-hello one, disputing the mellowness of summer, heralding the sharpness of winter.

11

I knew something was wrong when Blanc greeted me on the road like a long-lost friend: "Hello! How are you? It's been a long time!"

It was these words that settled it. I had seen him only yesterday.

I began to walk, matching my stride to his.

"It won't work," he said casually. "Stephen was caught last night on his return from Lyon. I heard about it from the bus driver. He was picked up in the station at Annecy."

My heart missed a beat and I was ashamed of my fear. Stephen was a good man even if I hadn't liked him. With his blond hair and fallen-eyebrow mustache and too well-cut clothes he was out of place in the France of 1943. I was just as conspicuous, but in another way. For a woman I was too tall to be French. Before the war Stephen was the sort of Frenchman who spoke French with a languid English drawl. It was a form of snobbishness which passed in Paris but not among the rustics of Haute-Savoie. If I had a drawl, it was because I couldn't help it. Still, the thought of having a comrade arrested was heartbreaking.

"I don't know how you'll manage, but the patron is set on having it done," Blanc murmured.

We began to leave the town behind us. The road skirting the border of the lake was rippled by a cold wind with gusts smelling of snow. I looked up at the mountains to the south by Thones and saw the Alps wrapped in clouds.

"It will be impossible without Stephen. It's quite a job. Besides, I think it's going to snow."

"Probably. But it must be done. The locomotives bring in troops. Every day makes the attack on the Maquis more likely."

"But even if we blow up the machines we can't block the roads," I objected. Somehow I hated to see those engines sabotaged right in my back yard as it were. My hideaway was in Annecy and it went against my principles to do violence so close to where I lived.

"When it's done you can go to Megeve for some skiing. You'll deserve it." And Blanc grinned, showing his yellow teeth.

I started to protest, but he suddenly laid his hand on my arm. I looked up. Two soldiers on bicycles were coming toward us. As they pulled abreast of us, I heard, in a daze, Blanc telling me about his farm.

"Papiers . . ."

We handed over our identity cards. While one man scrutinized them, the other examined my bicycle bags. Finding nothing of importance, he decided to ignore Blanc's hideous green ones.

His pleasant, boyish face was ruddy from the cold. I tried to think of everything except my papers. I could never get accustomed to the immense lie they told.

Finally the Germans grinned and waved us on. I smiled too, feeling no hatred but only a great weariness. We heard them get on their bikes and the squelch of their tires on the macadam road. We didn't even bother to notice when we were alone again. Somehow we just knew.

We went on, but now the road started to climb, curving inland away from the lake. In a half-hour we would reach the chalet I had rented. It was only the third in the last four months. Moving was essential to security.

"I suppose you'll want me to contact the boys so you can brief them?" Blanc said.

"You don't really think *I'm* going to do it?"

"Why not? That's what you were trained for in England. If you can teach *them* how to do it, you can do it yourself."

"But . . . but . . ." And I stopped, afraid Blanc might think I was scared. I was breathing fast, but not because I was pushing the bike. I began to think, sorting out in my mind the information Stephen had received concerning the station yard, the positions of the guards, the shed where the machines were kept. I thought the cover party was efficient. At least, I hoped they were because I had trained them. Stephen had used them several times and had never complained. In fact, he was quite proud of them. I had the plastic explosives, the primers, time pencils. I don't think I spoke until we reached the chalet.

"When will you do it?" Blanc asked, leaning against the gate with a tattered Gauloise sticking out of his mouth.

"Tomorrow. Tell the boys to come here tonight. Stephen left the suitcase with the guns down in the cellar. I'll make up the charges now."

"OK, Capitaine." And turning away, he made a small gesture with his hand somewhat like a Roman salute. It infuriated me because I felt he was laughing at me. But before he vanished I suddenly remembered something and ran after him.

"Please find out all you can about Stephen. If they haven't taken him to Lyon, maybe the Maquis could do something."

Blanc shrugged. I knew he had little hope. Suddenly I was afraid. Stephen would be tortured. They would make him talk before killing him.

I felt sick when I turned away. I would have to move again.

Back at the house, I clattered down the steps of the cellar, my ski boots ringing against the stones. Behind a heap of empty bottles I found the suitcase. From a separate cardboard box I took the detonators and time pencils, carefully wrapped in cotton. Laying everything out on a board stretched across two barrels, I began to make up my charges, not noticing I hadn't any waterproofing until the primer was wedged in the plastic explosive. Although there was no necessity for the charges to be waterproof, I needed a dark material to wrap them because, once they were clinched by magnets, they would show up lighter against the locomotives. I remembered a navy-blue scarf I had. It would be just right.

I went upstairs to my bedroom. It was then that I saw the old man who chopped the wood coming up the pathway, his shoulders hunched against the wind. It was lucky that I did see him, for it was down in the cellar that he kept his saw and hatchet. With my charges spread all over the place, I didn't think anyone could be dumb enough to ignore their purpose. I ran out to meet him, clutching the scarf in my hand.

In his younger days old Jean had been a sailor and now owned a cottage over the brow of the hill. He liked to chat if he could do most of the talking himself. Hiding my annoyance, I drew him toward the kitchen, with the idea of giving him a drink so that he would forget about chopping wood.

"I thought you might need some wood," he wheezed.

"That's good of you, Monsieur Jean, but I still have plenty in the kitchen."

"Humph! I suppose you've been away again. Can't you ever stay in one place?"

I smiled without answering. He could have no idea how much I wanted to stay in one place, at peace with the world and the world at peace with me! I began to steer him away from the cellar steps, but he jerked his arm away and, to my astonishment, went down on his knees in the mud.

"Look!" he exclaimed.

I stared. At first I couldn't see anything except his gnarled hands brown and hard as the earth. Then I saw it: frail, pale blue wavering uncertainly in the cold air. A violet! I knelt down and stared at it. Of course it would die. It was born too soon. But the fact that it was there was a pledge of blue skies, and blue skies might mean the end of this interminable war. It might mean invasion.

Old Jean took out his knife and carefully cut a square around it.

"What are you doing?" I asked.

"I'll plant it. You can put it in a plate," he said, laying the anemic-looking thing in the palm of my hand. "Take it. I'm going to fetch some moss. I'll be back right away."

I watched him trudge off down the hill, his back sturdy and

determined. If there was any moss left in Haute-Savoie, he would surely find it!

In the kitchen I laid the flower down on the table and rushed back to the cellar. Ten minutes later, when old Jean returned, the charges were packed away in the suitcase and hidden upstairs under my bed. I would see to the guns later.

Darkness was falling when old Jean finished with the violet. With him everything took a lot of time. Probably because he had lots to spare. Then he came and sat beside me and started a desultory conversation. After my protestations I didn't dare suggest he chop wood. I didn't want to talk either. He launched into a long story about a spell he had once laid in Haiti and seemed so engrossed in his story that I was surprised when he raised his head to listen.

"What is it?"

"Nothing. I thought I heard something."

"It's probably the wind. Well, did your charm work?"

"No, the wretched woman ran off with the butcher boy and the last I heard of her she was working in Marseille." And he giggled meaningfully.

Because of the wind, the chalet was starting to creak, the boards cracking one after the other, and it sounded as if someone was running across the attic floor on bare feet. Old Jean cocked his head sideways. His gesture annoyed me. After all, most wooden houses creaked.

"Things always happen when I start talking about Haiti. The last time—"

His words were drowned by an enormous crash. I started up.

Crash . . . Bang . . . Crash. Then silence. It was like waiting for someone to fire a gun. I was puzzled. It seemed to come from the back of the house, somewhere near my bedroom. Suddenly the wind broke loose again. It blew so hard I could feel the house lean backward. Crash . . . Bang . . . Crash . . . Then a slow creak. I knew then what it was. I went into the bedroom, where an icy blast met me. Back in the kitchen it caused the paraffin lamp, suspended over the table, to waver uncertainly so that long shadows sprang up, licking the whitewashed walls like flames. I groped my way to the window and caught hold of the shutter before it slammed shut again. Then I closed the window, jamming down the handle.

When I returned, old Jean was standing by the door, his beret pulled down over his head, the collar of his shabby Canadienne pulled up around his ears.

"Are you going already?" I asked, not knowing whether I was relieved or annoyed.

"The storm is getting worse. There'll be snow before morning. I'd better get back. I'll come tomorrow to chop your wood." And before I could say anything he pulled open the door and disappeared.

Peering through the window, I watched his stolid figure plod down the path while the wind blew the clouds free and the moon rode out, its wavering beam traveling over the yard like the dart from a lighthouse. When it faded, darkness clamped down and all I saw was the tortured silhouette of a bush struggling like a wild thing against the sky.

"There'll be snow before morning. . . ." Maybe not. Maybe the wind would blow it away. The cold affected the time pencils. Sometimes they went off at the given time; at others they didn't detonate at all. I wondered if I shouldn't use detonating cord. No, that wasn't possible—we wouldn't have time to get away.

As I turned from the window, my eyes fell on the violet. It seemed to be bearing up bravely in its bed of dirt and moss. I was glad we had brought it in. If it snowed . . . Yes, if it snowed? . . . Well, we would leave tracks in the station yard. . . . Oh, Lord, what shall I do? Put it off? Why isn't Stephen here?

I must have stayed by the window for quite a while. I couldn't make up my mind. Doing a sabotage job in a snowstorm struck me as the height of folly. Yet I knew that the longer we delayed, the less use the whole thing would be. Around me the house continued to creak and groan, somehow making my problem seem more difficult.

Suddenly a window in the attic swung loose, tapping spasmodically along the façade of the house. I knew I would have to go up and close it; otherwise the snow would blow in and I would burn a ton of wood in the kitchen stove. Drawing out the ladder from behind the door, I hooked it along the trap. It was then that I heard steps. Tap—tap—tap—a pause and then tap—tap—tap. I stared upward, one foot on the ladder. I was scared. Finally I took a carving knife out of the kitchen drawer. Tap—tap—tap—

Slowly I went up the ladder.

When I pushed the trap open, the wind hit me. But apart from the swinging window everything seemed normal. I moved over to it and it was then that I heard the steps again. I swung around. Over in a corner a shadow moved. I screamed at the round eyes fixed upon me in an unblinking stare. Whoo—hoo—tap—tap—Then I giggled and, when I was quite sure of what it was, decided not to shut the window but to wedge it slightly open. That was when I saw it was snowing. I cursed the soft white flakes drifting down. The yard was already beginning to glow. For a long time I sat hunched there, staring at the snowflakes and barely conscious of the cold, while behind me the owl hooted mournfully.

Much later the four boys turned up, and when they filed in, brushing off the snow and blowing on their chapped hands, I knew I was committed. The thing had to be done.

I drew out Stephen's plans and briefed them step by step. Then I opened the suitcase and handed out the Sten guns. For myself I kept nothing. I was carrying the charges; that was enough.

The next day it snowed until eleven. Afterward the sun came out and everything was crisp and fresh-looking. As I went down the hill, the lake was like a sheet of blue. I had planned the operation for nine, intending to wait in the house of a friend until then. When I hit the road and started toward Annecy, one of the boys tagged along behind. I was precious now. I was carrying the charges.

I left ten minutes before the rendezvous. Everything was quiet in the streets—the dimmed-out lamps casting long shadows on the snow. Only my footsteps made a ringing noise on the frozen sidewalk.

I turned off the secluded street into a busy thoroughfare and a shadow stepped out behind me. In front of the station it and

I turned into a dark, narrow alley. I was to meet the others in an abandoned warehouse, and as I walked through the cavernous building, I could hear the scraping of rats. Once the shadow behind me whispered: "Careful, Mademoiselle! The flooring is bad."

Through the dirty, broken windows came a glow from the snow-covered station yard. Vaguely I also made out the darker shape of the terminus, where the locomotives were. To my left, out of sight, was the station, where I knew people would be milling about, waiting for the night train to Lyon. In between these innocent French would be Germans or their French counterparts, the hated Milice. If our reports were correct, the locomotives would be unguarded because the Germans had decided the Resistance would never dare destroy them before the curfew at eleven.

I found the others grouped around a charcoal stove in a tiny room. They looked at ease, rather satisfied. I could almost hear them thinking: "At last something to do after all the talk!" We checked our watches. I had timed the whole operation to last twelve minutes, secretly keeping a margin. Seventeen minutes, time pencils half an hour, count forty because of the cold. In roughly fifty-seven minutes all hell should break loose in that terminus. I wondered if the blast would break the skylight. If so, I hoped no one would be beneath it.

When the cover party went off, they had four minutes to reach their appointed places between the station and the terminus. Once there, they were to post themselves at staggered intervals and use whistles to indicate caution or danger. My shadow was to guard the terminus while I placed the explosives.

He and I watched them go, their footsteps sinking in the soft snow. They moved quietly and I realized why Stephen had been proud of them. It was very cold while I clocked off the minutes. Near me a spider's web swayed in the draft. My face was hot from leaning over the charcoal-burner, but my feet were frozen.

Finally the time came for us to move. My guard went first. I followed some paces behind. As I left the shelter of the warehouse, my back felt nakedly exposed. We walked slowly, stopping only once—when we reached the tracks. I watched the shadow ahead of me. A wave and I followed, walking twenty yards or so down unsheltered tracks until I reached the reassuring shade of the terminus. We slipped in and paused while I guessed at the whereabouts of the locomotives. I located them almost immediately because they were blacker than the darkness.

It took only a few minutes to clamp the first charge onto the bearing rod. The second one was equally easy, but, walking around to the third, I stumbled against a steel girder. The noise was frightful and, to my horror, a sudden flare of light shot up just beyond the snub nose of the locomotive. I stood petrified while behind me my guard slid up and I felt the hard barrel of his Sten straining against my thigh. It didn't reassure me at all. There was a slow creak followed by a pinprick of light. A man was standing silhouetted in a doorway.

"Il y a quelqu'un?" he shouted.

"I'm going to call him around. Stay in the shadow, and when he comes, hold him up. He can't stay here with the charges. It's probably one of the drivers."

I called out that I had lost my dog and had stumbled, hurting myself. At first he hesitated, but I think the fact that I was a woman reassured him. He came out slowly while I crouched down as if hurt. When he saw me, he came toward me at once and at that moment my guard stepped out from behind the nose of the locomotive.

When the man felt the gun in the small of his back, I think he knew what was up. Taking the torch, I flashed it on the charges just over my head.

"The others are like that too. Are you going to come quietly or do you want us to leave you here?" my guard snarled.

The man shrugged. "I don't want any part of it. I'll come."

And he did, walking as quietly as we, except that I was in front this time and he was behind with the guard tailing him, the Sten on the ready. I hoped the damn thing wouldn't go off. They had a way of doing that when you least expected it. Down the track we went, with me almost missing the spot where we were to turn off. It was just as well, because I ran into the first man from our cover party and signaled him to recall the others.

Back in the warehouse, I made the boys dismantle their Stens and stow them away in a rucksack. They were feeling so pleased with themselves I think they would have walked through the streets of Annecy with the things on the ready just for the heck of it. The whole operation had taken fifteen minutes. The driver watched us with his eyes popping out of his head. Once he shook his head unbelievingly when I spoke sharply to one of the boys about making a noise. He had a nice, middle-aged face all wrinkled and black from years of living with coal dust. His hair under his beret was pepper-and-salt.

"What are you doing in that back room?" I asked.

"Sorting out cigarettes I brought from Switzerland this morning. I sell them." And he shrugged.

We left in driblets. Two of the boys went off with the rucksack. Another was detailed to see the driver to his home. I started off alone, but on the main street my guard caught up with me as if by accident. I was suddenly very cold, so that when we passed a café I didn't oppose the longing glance he cast in its direction. We went in and over a glass of hot wine I glanced down at my watch for the first time.

Twenty-six minutes since I had laid the charges. I began to worry. Supposing someone came before they went off. I didn't want anything to happen to a Frenchman. Oh God, I prayed, let everything be all right. I must have been scowling, because my companion laid a hand on my arm and, when I looked up, smiled confidently. Finally he paid and we went out.

Ten more minutes gone, I thought, as we turned our steps toward the lake. The night was clear and pitted with stars. I wondered how I could have missed looking at those lovely pinpoints of twinkling silver. Usually I noticed such things. Then I heard the slap-slap of the water hitting against the quay where in peacetime a fleet of small boats were moored.

"I'll leave you now, Mademoiselle. If I accompany you all the way, I won't have time to get back before the curfew."

I nodded and we shook hands. Long after his departure I stood there listening. Once I heard the whistle of a train, sounding as lonely as I was. Awhile later some Germans went singing their way to their barracks north of the town. Finally I pulled down the edge of my glove to glance at my watch. The luminous hands read a few minutes after ten. Still almost half an hour to go. I began to walk very fast. It was like trying to run away from myself.

I think I made the chalet in record time that night. I know I was puffing when I leaned against the gate. The air was now so clear I could see down to the lake. I tried to think of anything, anything but three charges wrapped in dark material clamped to a bearing rod. Maybe I'd forgotten to crimp them. It sometimes happened in the excitement of the moment. But no, I'd done it before placing them in the primer. I was close to tears when I thought of my instructors back in England. A hell of a life for an American who happened to have been brought up in France. I should have let the Germans intern me. Time now, I snarled between my teeth, gripping my watch. Yes, time, ladies and gentlemen. Time . . . A vision of beer in pewter mugs and hot, happy faces in a pub. Time . . . It must be. . . .

Bang . . . It was sharp and clear and sweet music on the cold air.

Grinning, I opened the gate and trudged across the yard. I had my hand on the door when the second charge went off. Almost immediately after, the third exploded. For once I didn't swear when I fumbled with the matches to light the paraffin lamp; later, when I added a few drops of water to the violet, I was very happy.

12

I was arrested on the twentieth of March, 1944, in Paris, as I was about to start for the convent which was my safe house. A safe house in which I was to hide until the twenty-ninth, waiting for a man from our organization to return me to England.

There were three of them and had they come ten minutes later to the apartment of the Swiss friend sheltering me, they would have found me gone.

Two were Germans. The third, who jabbed a gun in my stomach, was a French militia punk aged about twenty. I hope he's long since disappeared and is roasting somewhere in a special hell reserved exclusively for his kind. I and many others of the Resistance had decided long ago that the Milice, formed by Vichy and trained by the Gestapo, were a bunch of sadistic guttersnipes; some of us even prayed to fall into German hands rather than theirs.

This particular example was roughly told to go into the bathroom with my friend and lock the door.

The two Germans were not at all alike. One was a stocky chap with a ruddy complexion, a frontal baldness and small, round eyes like marbles that made him look like a pig. He grunted his sentences in atrocious French. His companion was just the opposite. He was a handsome, dark man with a pale complexion, dressed in a well-tailored pinstripe suit—unlike his colleague, who wore his clothes any-old-how and hadn't even bothered to replace his jackboots with a pair of shoes.

Of course I was panic-stricken. No matter what they looked like, they meant business.

"Sit down," Piggy grunted, pushing me roughly into a chair. "Your name?"

I tried to reach for my bag, but my hands were trembling, so I fumbled. It was finally snatched from me.

"False! False!" he shouted, waving the red cardboard. "Your name is Reynolds and you're a spy—an American spy."

Naturally, I denied it, but I don't think I was very convincing even though I was telling the truth. Reynolds had never been my real name; it was simply my stepfather's.

"Don't persist," the dark man said in English. "We know the truth."

"Well, if you know," I stammered, suddenly thinking this could be my defense. "Yes, it's true. I am an American."

What did they know and how did they know? Paris was not my sector. I had always passed through it only to change stations, hurrying through the Métro corridors head down in case I should meet someone I knew. Once I had stopped over to deliver a verbal message to the concierge of a school on the Left Bank, a message which I had no doubt would be passed on to someone else before it finally reached the person it concerned. Afterward, because I had been traveling for ten days without lying down, I had slept a few hours fully dressed on a cot in the loge of this elderly couple. Had I been betrayed by them? No. They didn't know my name, false or otherwise. No. It had to be someone who knew me. A friend! God, and what a friend! Judas more like it.

"Where did you get this card? How long have you had it?"

"May I smoke?" I asked, playing for time, fully prepared to be turned down. "My cigarettes are in my Canadienne on the bed." I had some others in my case, but it was in my bag and I didn't dare ask for it.

As there was no negative reaction, I pushed out of the chair and walked toward the divan-bed, expecting to be pulled back. Nothing happened and this gave me time to think. I had realized, with sad horror, who had denounced me. Someone whom I had imagined to be brave and unflinching in these troubled times. Someone I had always thought I could turn to for advice and help. Apart from my hostess, only she had known I was in Paris, and that was because I had phoned her from a public callbox in order to retrieve the bicycle I had left in her keeping when I had fled the capital in 1942. Of course, I should not have contacted her, especially since I knew she was friendly with a woman who had an Austrian brother-in-law. It was a shocking breach of security, and because of it my Swiss friend would go to jail, and at this stage of the war the Germans were in no mood to respect neutrals.

Still, so far they weren't behaving too badly. No doubt they were reserving it for later, unless I managed to make my story stick about being an American who had refused to be interned.

I wondered who the dressed-up man was as I lifted his black-and-white pin-dotted coat from the bed. My God—the brother-in-law . . . Yes, that's it! But why? Why? Neither of us had ever done anything to his sister-in-law or to him, for that matter, unless it was to hate him from a distance because he was occupying France—out of uniform, which was probably worse and more dangerous. Connected with one of the finest families in France, he was easily able to slip into every salon in Paris . . . and not all of them housed collaborators. I had no doubt any indiscretion he picked up over a glass of champagne would be relayed through the proper channels.

Slowly I moved the coats, the fine one and the drab duffel. In this last I felt a dead weight. With one hand I fingered around it while with my other I groped for the package of cigarettes I had bought from the concierge only an hour ago. Why hadn't I left then—taken advantage of his son's bicycle with its flimsy carriage, the only kind of taxi Paris now knew? Instead I was caught and so was my hospitable friend, while downstairs the concierge must be cursing me, the Germans, everything, as he tried to hide his stock of black-market goodies.

I groped a little more and felt the smooth butt of a revolver in Piggy's duffel.

I wasn't the only one to make mistakes. Could I take advantage of it? Yes, but I must be quick and aim true and pray it was a gun I was familiar with.

I turned. No, it was no good. The two men were watching me. In fact, for a split second I saw a sort of angry fear on Piggy's face. Furthermore, my friend was in the bathroom guarded by the punk and he had jammed a submachine gun at me when I had opened the door. Very proud he had been of it too.

I returned to my chair ostentatiously fingering my package of cigarettes. From the look on my captors' faces, I knew they had been afraid. Now they were once more in control and it was again my turn to be frightened.

"Where did you get this card?" Piggy snarled, waving it in my face.

"I bought the blank in a Tabac." I knew they wouldn't dispute this. They couldn't, because that's where you found them.

"And what about the seal? From Amiens, it says. I suppose you bought that too!" the Austrian sneered.

"No, I made it with a potato. You can try it yourself."

But I didn't get a chance to watch them because a chromium standing lamp was smashed down on my head by the Austrian. It knocked me for a loop!

"You fool!" he shouted in English, and after that there wasn't much I could do except stick to my story while I dabbed at my nosebleed, whining that I had fled from being interned and lived by selling my jewelry. To prove it, I showed them my dressing case —an elaborate gold-plated affair.

"It's all I have left," I wailed, tears running down my face, my handkerchief streaking blood on my cheeks. "I didn't want to be interned."

"Where did you get your card?"

"When I escaped in '42. It was given to me by Madame de C. . . ." And through my tears I peeped at the Austrian. The woman was his sister-in-law. He frowned, and his colleague stared at him suspiciously, which was a good thing because the thought of making trouble for this man who had just smashed a chromium tube on my head was highly gratifying.

"I suppose you'll send me to Vittel now?"

"That's for the Gestapo to decide. They have some questions to ask concerning your time since 1942."

My heart fell and I began to cry, which made my nose bleed even more.

It was still bleeding when my friend and I were taken in the inevitable black Citroën to Gestapo headquarters in the Rue des Saussaies. In peacetime this was where the office of the Surveillance du Territoire was housed. Now it was one of the principal Gestapo headquarters in Paris.

Driving through the guarded porte-cochère into the courtyard, I had a glimpse of a room filled with straw on which people were lying, men and women alike. It made me think of the French Revolution with tumbrels waiting instead of paddy wagons.

We tramped up four flights of carpeted stairs, escorted by a soldier. Here the Austrian left us—the punk had been abandoned uptown, his machine gun snatched away from him by Piggy when he had climbed into the car.

"I'm Swiss. I demand to see my Consul. I'm neutral," my friend protested. Since she had been saying this for some time, and rightly so, it had become monotonous, not least because her voice had developed a whine. In any case, no one paid any attention to her.

The door in the corridor where we were standing opened suddenly and a plainclothesman strode out. Grabbing my arm, he shoved me up a narrow flight of dingy stairs past a broom closet that gave out a faint whiff of floor wax. Apart from that, everything smelled of bad drains. Somewhere behind me trudged Piggy and my friend, still protesting. I would have liked to admire her persistence, which had a bulldozer quality about it, but the repetitiousness was aggravating. I could still feel the bump on my head, and my nose hadn't quite stopped bleeding. I hoped my captors wouldn't turn nasty. They could easily, without anyone knowing or caring, because we were obviously going up to the rooms beneath the eaves—the rooms where the first tortures were known to begin.

"Keep quiet," I said over my shoulder. "Save it for later."

Upstairs was a narrow corridor lined with doors. I was pushed through one of these, the key rasping in the lock as it turned. I assumed my friend must have received the same treatment, for I heard another door slam.

The room was bare, with only a rickety chair and a barred window. As my rucksack and elaborate dressing case had been taken away from me—probably to be searched—I had no way of cleaning my face, which felt as though it was covered with blood. Finally I found a spare handkerchief and, licking it, did what I could. After that I was left with nothing to do but think, and I didn't want to do that. What a criminal fool I had been! I deserved to be tortured. But would I resist? And my poor friend? What would happen to her?

I began to examine the lock on the door, the old-fashioned kind held by four screws. Riffling through my handbag, I found my cigarette case and, using the thin silver clasp as a screwdriver, I unscrewed the lock. In a few minutes the door was open and I was peering down the corridor. Then I heard footsteps. Cautiously I drew back, but their owner passed without noticing the slight crack of the opened door.

I could escape. The tricky part would be the door at the bottom of the staircase. I had a feeling they kept a guard there. Then I remembered the cupboard where among the brooms I had seen a dirty white apron hanging on a nail.

Still, something held me back—something prevented me from stepping out into that corridor and slipping down the stairs dressed as a cleaning woman.

I knew what it was. I couldn't leave my friend to face this mess alone. Alone, she would have no chance of ever being released.

So I screwed the lock back on. Then, standing bleakly at the window, I stared at the big drops of rain driving miniature canals down the dirty surface of the pane. The gray sky chilled me and I put on my Canadienne, absently going through the pockets. I was always very careful about this and I wished I had used the same care in regard to friends. God, what a lonely life it had been! Now it was ended. No more looking over my shoulder, stopping to let the people behind me get by. Changing trains on darkened platforms, waiting huddled in sordid waiting rooms for cold dawns to break so as to be the first out at the lifting of the curfew. No more of that. I was caught. But before they broke me, these evil, godless creatures, I would beat them at one game. I would sleep. Sleep soundly. Sink into oblivion, knowing that nothing could catch me any more. No longer would I have to make do with catnaps, the half-awake dozing, head lolling, legs cramped, sitting huddled over a suitcase in a crowded train corridor. Yes, sleep . . .

Suddenly I froze. Instead of paper, my fingers closed over a piece of cardboard.

Drawing it out, I gagged, saliva filling my mouth. It was a book of matches with the Allied flags centered like a fan on a white background. Beneath the flags the words: "With the compliments of the RAF."

Where had it come from? I had never seen anything like it before. The RAF indulging in such propaganda! It was ridiculous. Impossible. They had even stopped dropping leaflets, having decided that their airborne tracts fluttering to earth did more harm than good: if they were found on anyone, it might not mean his death but would certainly mean a prison sentence or even deportation to a labor camp in Germany.

I tore the thing into small bits and stuffed the pieces into my mouth, wondering what effect sulfur would have on my digestive tract.

But it wasn't until I found the sixpence that I knew I had been framed. Wedged down into the lining of a pocket! Yes, I had been framed. My Canadienne had been bought in France *after* my return from England. But why? And when? This morning, by one of the men? Who had gone over to the couch? Piggy or the brother-in-law of De C? For the life of me, I couldn't remember. Framed, I snarled, looking for a place to hide the coin because, small as it was, I didn't feel like swallowing it. In the end, I dropped it behind the wainscoting.

Framed! But why? Surely if they knew so much about me they didn't have to resort to such tricks? It was puzzling, horrifying. But it reassured me. Perhaps after all they knew very little and had no other recourse but planting evidence. If so, I knew what my story was going to be: the spoiled American brat living from day to day to avoid internment.

I was chewing the last of the matches when I heard the key in the lock. I picked up my handbag, slung it over my shoulder, took on a stupid look. Please God, help me pretend!

For quite a while they fiddled with that door—in fact, they took so long that my stupid expression wore thin and was becoming a smile as I listened to them curse. In the end, they went away, and I managed quietly to ease the lock into place. When they stomped back, I heard the rattle of metal and guessed they had a locksmith with them.

The poor, terrified little man didn't know what to make of it when the door flew open and he saw me staring at him, wide-eyed.

Piggy burst in, glaring everywhere. Even the soldier accompanying him was startled. He took the workman's arm and hauled him away. I'm sure that innocent locksmith must have had a lot to tell his wife that evening. And this is just the prologue, I thought!

I dutifully marched off with Piggy. The room into which I was taken was much the same as the one I had just left except that it was furnished like an office and was cleaner. My rucksack was on the floor, but the dressing case was on a chair.

There were two desks—one of wood, which Piggy sat down to, hauling out a portable typewriter. The other, a metal desk, was placed near the window with a rather nice-looking, neat blonde seated at it. She looked so little the kind of person who would work for the Gestapo that I was surprised. But maybe she had no choice, and appearances could be deceptive. Perhaps Piggy was a lovable husband and father! Whatever he was, he wasn't the boss, I decided. It was the secretary's attitude that convinced me. She practically ignored him.

For the moment, while he slipped a piece of paper into the machine, he was in a tearing rage against anything French, especially French locks. The secretary listened to him for a while with an ambiguous expression and then turned away and started to file her nails.

When he finally calmed down after a tug at a brandy flask, he started to question me. The muscles of my stomach tensed. I was dreading this. But I need not have—it was only an identification check.

American. Born New York 1917 of American parents.

Education. England, France, Austria. This last got more of a rise out of Piggy than my British education, making me wonder if he wasn't Austrian. But when I told him the name of the two schools I had been to—the Elizabeth Duncan School of Dancing in Salzburg and the Convent of the Sacred Heart near Vienna—he glared at me and I thought he was going to spit, he looked so disgusted. I decided then he was an atheist with no appreciation for revived Greek dancing! On this last point I agreed with him and wondered if I should tell him so, but on second thought I let it pass. I didn't think he would be amused by my description of the school, to which my mother had sent me in one of her less inspired moments!

"Elizabeth Duncan! Another spy—a spy school in the heart of the Fatherland!"

"Elizabeth Duncan was the sister of Isadora Duncan, the famous dancer." I felt like adding something about his use of the word Fatherland when applied to Austria, but again I didn't dare.

"Dancing! Bah! The can-can! *Folies-Bergères!*"

When the sense of this ridiculous statement penetrated, I almost burst out laughing.

"No. Greek dancing. Barefooted in a peplum."

"Pep . . . what's that?"

It was the secretary who answered, even spelling the word for him. "Ach, so!" he murmured with a shake of his head, staring curiously at me, his red pig eyes glinting behind his metal glasses. The secretary shrugged and returned to her typewriter or nail file, but not before looking at my elaborate dressing case; she even opened it and stared inside in amazement.

Piggy began questioning me again in his atrocious French, waiting with stubby fingers uplifted to jab down my replies.

"Yes, I traveled a lot. With my mother, sister, aunt, governess. We once went to India by the Cape, you know. We returned by the Canal."

"Canal! Ah, sabotage."

"I was only eleven," I protested gently.

And so it went, and as the years narrowed down I began to worry. But to my amazement he stopped at 1939, gathering the useless sheets of my useless life and stapling them together with a satisfied grunt.

After that he stared at me silently. It was disconcerting. I asked if I could smoke. He shrugged and tossed my dressing case over to me. I was startled. I hadn't expected this. It worried me too.

After a while the telephone rang. It was just as well, because the secretary and Piggy had been looking at their watches. It was the woman who answered, speaking in a deferential manner which probably meant her boss was on the line.

The long and the short of it was that I was told to slip into my rucksack harness, but was forbidden to take my dressing case. When I protested, Piggy scrawled out a receipt and stamped it with a black swastika. As I went out I said goodbye to the secretary on the theory that it didn't cost anything to be polite. She seemed surprised and I felt her staring after me musingly.

Downstairs Piggy handed me over to a soldier who shoved me into the straw-filled room off the courtyard. There I found my Swiss friend talking to a shoddy, dark woman with faded traces of makeup. They were sitting on the straw surrounded by other people, most of whom were dressed in shabby, wrinkled clothes. The men had no ties, shoelaces or belts and all were unshaven and pale.

"How did it go?" the strange woman asked, patting a place for me next to her. "You still have some blood on your cheek. Your friend told me they hit you."

Because I thought she sounded positively ghoulish and because she seemed much too friendly, I moved away before sitting down.

"This is the third time I've been here, but I've only been questioned once. They didn't do much harm, just beat me up like you. They made me undress. I didn't like that."

She was speaking in a hoarse, carrying whisper and I saw the others watching surreptitiously. No one warned me. No one would have dared. Stool pigeon, I thought! Well, let her go on with her false bonhomie. She would get nothing out of me.

Suddenly there was a shriek followed by hoarse shouts in German and a woman was thrown in. She sprawled on the straw like a sack, sobbing. Several people started over to her, intending to draw her into their circle, but the guard sprang at them, his rifle butt raised. They returned to their places humbly, some even cringing. The guard swung back toward the entrance, aiming a kick at the woman as he passed her. It was then I saw that she was pregnant.

I curled up and shut my eyes, feeling sick. I also wondered if my sickness wasn't caused by the bar of fear across my stomach. Probably it was a bit of both. Yes, and this was nothing but the prelude. I closed my eyes, but I couldn't shut my ears to the murmurs around me, especially those of the stool pigeon.

To my horror at what I imagined to be my lack of feeling, I started to feel sleepy and had to force my eyes to open. But I realized I wasn't the only one. All around me, men and women were dozing. The faces of some were so white, with bluish undertints, that they resembled corpses. One couple in handcuffs had propped their backs against the outer wall—the street wall. Between them was a suitcase. I imagined they were still, like me, at the prelude stage. Maybe they had been picked up in a raid or on a train. . . . Oh, God, what did it matter!

"Don't forget the greffe," someone next to me whispered.

I rolled over. A few meters away, a man I had thought was asleep was staring at me, holding his wrist. He was hollow-eyed and unshaven and, like the rest of the men, had no tie or laces to his shoes. I supposed he had no belt for his trousers either and I wondered how he was going to walk and nurse his wrist at the same time.

"The Fresnes wagons are starting to return. We'll soon be on our way. Quick! Give me the news!"

As I crawled closer, I noticed his smell. Oh, it wasn't so much the smell of dirt. It was something far more subtle, reminding me of a prisoner-of-war camp in 1940. Hunger!

I began to talk, trying not to think that I would soon have the same odor, and when I finished my news commentary, I added, rather lamely, something about the end being in sight, trying not to put too much fervor into it. After all, you never knew. Why not a male stool pigeon?

"Yes, it won't last much longer. But for many it will still be too late," he said, leaning forward to ease his sitting position. Horrified then, I saw he had a blue spot about the size of a large coin on the side of his head and that his hair was clotted with blood.

"You smell very good, Madame. I never thought I'd say this to a strange lady. Forgive me. We have water, but the soap . . ." and he smiled lopsidedly. "If you have a watch, hide it. Time is long. Sometimes I almost welcome these sessions. This time, however, they were rougher than usual. I think my little finger is broken."

"I have a scarf. Let me make you a sling," I said, getting to my knees and groping for it in one of the side pockets of my rucksack. "If only I could set it. Maybe it's a clean break."

He shook his head. "I am reserving my courage for the next time and the next time and then the end. The sling will help. It will also remind me of you, Madame. Lie down before they see you. It won't be much longer now. Remember about the greffe! They search you and confiscate all your things except underwear."

Fresnes to me had always been the name of a suburb of Paris. A place one rushed through on the way to Orléans, a dismal suburb filled with secondhand-car dealers of dubious honesty, surrounded by boxlike apartment buildings set next to abandoned lots overgrown with weeds and wild lilac. Until the occupation I didn't even know it housed one of the largest prisons in France. Why should I? Even less that it was supposed to be the most modern. Then, shortly after the occupation, the name would be mentioned—at first not everywhere—in a whisper, as though speaking of something unpleasant. Later the whispers stopped and it was spoken loudly and on a note of fear. Fresnes! . . . Jean went to Fresnes. . . . He was picked up in a raid. The things he heard! He was lucky. They released him, but Pierre is still there.

It was past five when we arrived at this place of misery, passing through huge gates set between high walls topped with broken glass. Of course the greffe was shut. In fact, everything involved in the administration of the place was shut, including the allocation of the prisoners to their cells. So that night my friend and I were thrown into a temporary cell on the ground floor and given two chunks of bread and two small slices of something that could have been almost anything. The woman guard was a big, heavy, blank-faced creature, her movements seemingly automatic. Later I heard her yelling down the corridor at someone entering a cell too slowly. She sounded like a bellowing bull. It was very impressive and not a little frightening. But worst was the grating sound the key made in the lock after the door was slammed. Evidently, no door was ever closed quietly in this place, nor did the guards walk otherwise than with a noisy tread. Every sound registers when you're locked away in a cell; each noise is magnified until it becomes a language of its own. In time I realized that striding steps echoing through the cement-and-iron building are a godsend when you're talking through the water pipes to your neighbor, but, unfortunately, there were times when that warning system didn't work because the woman guard who welcomed us when we arrived would sometimes wear slippers on purpose. Of course I only learned all this later. For the moment, my Swiss friend and I were two innocents locked away in a dark cell for the night.

We had been allowed to keep our things, and this was a benediction because we were able to put on all our warm clothes, one on top of the other. In a way, I was luckier than my friend. She had not had time to pack much of anything.

"I have a spare sweater. Do you want it?" I asked.

"No. I'll soon be out of here. That woman you were so rude to told me so, and she seems to know the ropes. I'm a neutral, and Switzerland is doing a lot for prisoners. After all, Dunant founded the Red Cross and he was Swiss. I'll be all right. I'll be released in twenty-four hours. That woman told me so."

"I bet she did!" and I didn't add, "How are you going to explain away your helping the citizen of a country at war with Germany?"

I did not say it. She did. "I intend to tell them you compelled me to take you in and that I did so because you were a friend.

I don't know anything else. Why should I?"

No, but I do. I know a lot. Too much. What a fool I've been! And this poor girl is convinced she'll be released in twenty-four hours! If she sticks to her story, I'll play along with it. It's the only way.

There was no bed or chair in the cell, only a slop pail with a spigot over it. I suppose running water in every cell was what gave Fresnes the reputation for being the most modern prison in France!

After our clothes session we sat down in a corner on the stone floor and huddled together under my Canadienne, chewing our bread and eating some chocolate she had had the forethought to bring from a Swiss parcel she had received the day before. It tasted delicious, and it reminded me of the shop in Geneva where I had met the Swiss agent, oh, so long ago. Remembering this caused my stomach muscles to flutter in panic. Forget . . . forget . . . It never existed.

In the end, my friend dozed while I wondered where I'd hide my watch from the greffe. Fortunately, it was not too large and fairly flat. If my rectum could take it, it seemed the best place, but even that was no guarantee. I would have liked to smile at the idea of a timepiece playing hookey in my ass, but I didn't. I was too worried about just keeping it in there.

Very soon what little light there was faded, and it was then I noticed that the darkness of the night outside was different from that in the cell. It seemed to lean up against the barred window and glow. This made me realize how shades of black vary. There's the sticky, clawing kind usually smelling of dampness, as was the case in the cell. Then there's the blackness with gray spots that cling, so that moving against it is like pushing through a curtain of evil. That kind always reminded me of a haunted house I had once lived in. Coming home at night was an ordeal because sometimes the clinging mass met you at the front door. Other times there was nothing, which meant a peaceful night without footsteps, shrieks, gongs or slamming doors. But on such occasions the relief was so enormous you became like doubting Thomas and crept to bed anyway. There's also a velvet darkness smelling faintly of spring, a blue-ink night singing with frost and sparkling stars. I imagined tonight would be a mixture of both because it was the first day of spring. Would I see another? Would I ever be free to walk and talk without doubt or suspicion dogging my steps or would I be floating in some nameless limbo? Would the Allies invade this year? It couldn't go on. This prison, one among many, was proof that the saturation point of cruelty was rapidly approaching. Too many men, women and children from all over Europe were being herded behind bars like cattle or sent screaming to their deaths to the sound of chattering machine guns. Liberation . . . Liberation . . . Had God turned his face from all but the pure Aryan German race? No. North Africa was ours. Italy had been invaded, and if the Allies were momentarily bogged down, the country was well on the way to being overrun. And the Resistance in other occupied countries was steadily growing stronger. The Maquis . . . No. No. I didn't know anything about that. I didn't know. . . . I didn't know. . . . And repeating this over and over, I fell asleep.

The next morning the greffe was crowded, not only by the prisoners from the night before but by a new batch. We were all hollow-eyed, but among us were newcomers, obviously just picked up. They stood apart from us, not yet having learned to shuffle and talk out of the corners of their mouths with blank faces. Only their eyes were like ours, filled with fear and anguish. Of course we were all frightened—I know I was—chiefly by the bellowing guards yanking at us to keep us in line. We were also suspicious of one another, darting furtive looks around us. I was no different from anyone except that intermingled with my anguish was the fear of losing my watch from my ass. Maybe my panties wouldn't hold it despite the fact that I had purposely put on a second pair.

As we shuffled down the line ten at a time, women on one side, men on the other, I managed to keep in the thick of the crowd, hoping in this way to reach the greffe when it was at its busiest. I don't know how I thought of this. I think I just played it by ear, unless playing something by ear signifies following the directives of one's guardian angel!

Yes, I surely had my guardian angel peeping over my shoulder that early, sad morning. It worked. They didn't search me. My watch was safe. I wished I could have found some telepathic way of letting the man with the tortured face and broken finger know of my victory. Because it was a victory—a victory over time becoming a vacuum.

They grabbed my rucksack and shook out its contents, then carefully labeled them, handing me back only some toilet articles and underwear. Nothing seemed to interest them but a book by Colette. They riffled through this, examining the pages as if they expected them to explode. As I knew Colette wasn't on the banned list (even our reading matter had to have the sanction of Dr. Goebbels), I guessed what they were looking for: pinpoints that could mean a code. In the end, it was slipped into an envelope and I was made to sign a receipt.

Clutching my belongings, I was shoved out of the line and ordered to stand with several other women who were being guarded by two women wardens. At first I didn't understand what the Germans were trying to do. Then, gradually, out of what seemed disorder—a disorder of shuffling women, suitcases and parcels—a method emerged. Our cells had been allotted. Suddenly I heard one of the guards yelling "Au secret!" as a woman was pushed into my line. Au secret! Someone had told me that in prison jargon this meant a cell to oneself! And only those presumed to be very guilty had a right to this privilege. "Au secret" also meant no parcels, no reading matter, just four walls, silence and much time to think. I was panic-stricken again and the story I was starting to construct suddenly seemed very flimsy. They must know something—know something that would tear it to pieces. But if so, why had I been framed? . . . I *had* been framed, hadn't I? Oh, God, even yesterday seemed far away.

"If I'm not here long, I'll take a message for you. Just your name and telephone number," a voice whispered.

Slowly I turned, watching the guard nearest me out of the corner of my eye as she sorted out some more "au secrets."

The woman was well dressed and so neat I guessed she had just been picked up. Older than I, she had a long, angular face that wore a haughty dignity most unexpected in these circumstances.

Oh, no, she wasn't at all like my friend's stool pigeon. And what did I risk? Nothing. After all, they had released my mother from internment on grounds of ill-health. If, therefore, I got a message to her, it would only corroborate my story. I quickly whispered the number, and it sounded so unfamiliar I wondered for a minute if I hadn't made a mistake. It had been so long—almost two years. Of my name, however, I had no doubt. Few people had it. "Silence! Ruhig! Taisez-vous!" the guard stormed, jabbing me in the ribs.

In my cell, I slept at first, but even when I awoke I was still in a sort of haze. Staring at the cell with its crude chair chained to a table that in turn was cemented to the wall seemed like looking down the wrong end of a telescope. But my mind must have been clear when I stared at the water spigot and basin because I used it. I was also aware of the single shelf holding my underwear, in which I had hidden my watch.

I wasn't thinking. My mind wouldn't allow it. It was resting, letting my subconscious prepare the slim defense I had. Lying on my iron cot on a mattress made of corn husks, I slept, dozed, dreamed, sometimes cried and then slept some more.

Between the shelf and the water spigot was the door. I was particularly conscious of this because three times a day it was unlocked. Even though I learned to expect this, the rasping sound always tore at my nerves. Later I learned to be grateful for its opening only three times a day because this meant no paddy wagon, no interrogation.

In the morning the door crashed open for a tepid brew of what passed as coffee, accompanied by a hunk of bread that had to last until the following day. Daily, when the door was closed again, I wound my watch. At midday the door opened for soup with stray pieces of vegetables and meat floating around in grease; at night the ration was a slice of sausage or cheese. At first I hadn't the courage to eat the soup out of the tin receptacle I could clean only with our weekly allotment of sand, but in the end I did because I was hungry.

Days and nights went by until I had my surfeit of sleep. By the way the peephole in my door was opened—I could hear the click

—I guessed the guards were . . . oh, not worried, but curious. I didn't care. They had caught me, but they couldn't prevent me from sleeping. Sleep was still free and that was a wonderful thought. In a sort of numb, animal way I think I was almost happy. Of course this sort of blank didn't last long—even the dullest mind pierces the blanket of sleep, creeps forth to face its physical surroundings, its anguish.

For some time I had been aware of noises not connected with the guards or the prison itself. Noises that were like whispers. They seemed to be all around and it took me quite some time to realize they came from over by the water spigot. In the end, I put my ear to it.

"Enfin!" a voice whispered. "I've been trying to get you for days. I have messages for you—from all around. Are you all right? What's your name? Mine is Rolande. Don't give me your real one. If no one has it on our block, you can keep it."

"Juliette," I said.

"Can't hear you. Don't talk—*whisper* down the pipe. But don't get caught."

The connection was made. Oh, not with the outside world, but with another human being—several human beings, because the cells above and below mine were served by the same pipeline. This did not apply to my neighbor. But sometimes at night when I was in bed, I heard tapping against the wall. I always replied. It was our neighborly goodnight.

Naturally, the first thing I asked for was news of my Swiss friend. The question was passed along the "telephone" from block to block to the top floor. No wonder the whole building seemed to be perpetually hissing.

"We'll try. Swiss, you say? It will take time because the line will have to be broken and the message given to one of the girls who handles the food trolleys. It's lucky they're all in the same block —some even in the same cell. They're very cooperative even if they're not political prisoners."

"Political prisoners?"

"Yes, they're black-marketeers, thieves, whores. All condemned to serve their time here."

The next evening she whispered that the message had gone out and added: "I haven't been called up for interrogation for a long time. Maybe they've forgotten me. Did you hear the news? The Russians are advancing. If only the Allies would invade."

Yes, I had heard the news. Its sameness was depressing.

Every evening after supper, during the lull that marked the changing of the guard to the night shift, a man's voice would yell out the news across the little square courtyards where once a week we took our walks, shuffling silently one behind the other while a bored guard watched, rifle on his shoulder. There were few of these yards and, as far as I could make out, they probably represented the length of six cells.

Every night the man who shouted was different. I suppose they must have established a rotation because there was a Marseillais among them. It was good to hear his voice because it reminded us of the sun, and spring was late for us that year. For some it would never come again.

After the news, welcomed by whistles and cries, came the names of those to be shot the following day. Then messages from the condemned to their families, shouted to those who might be released. Yes, released—because sometimes people *were* released. The first time I heard this I cried, tried to pray. Until then I had always cried when I was hurt or because I was angry, frustrated. Now I wept and couldn't say why. But it wasn't for me. Of that I was sure.

Afterward came the national anthem. I had never before heard the *Marseillaise* sung like that and I don't expect I ever will again. Another night "God Save the King" was sung in honor of some captured RAF men. I knew what that meant. A safe house betrayed, a link broken in the long chain that stretched from Holland to the Pyrenees. And somewhere along that line someone trying to forge a new chain before he too was caught. And another and another . . . and still they came. No wonder the prisons were filled and the wonderful organization of Mr. Himmler swamped by the avalanche of people shouting: Liberation! Liberation! There didn't seem to be enough cattle trains steaming to labor camps in Germany, steaming to what we didn't know.

I wondered if my man with the broken finger was still alive, and one evening that was quieter than others, I decided to yell a message.

"How is the man with the broken finger? The lady with the green scarf wants to know."

The message was no stupider than some others, but it was greeted with jokes and laughter; one man even composed a song, while another whistled, rather prettily, a barrack-room ditty.

"Silence!" someone finally yelled. "Belle dame, l'écharpe et moi, nous partons pour l'Allemagne," and he sounded so happy I was too. Maybe the labor camps weren't so bad after all.

That evening for the first time, during the hush that heralded the night shift, in the dusk of the dying day, I heard one of the purest voices I was ever privileged to hear sing Gounod's "Ave Maria." It rose out of the walls of our women's block, scouring away all the scum from our ill-fed, dirty bodies. It didn't bring salvation or hope. It was an amen of peace for the coming night and courage for the following day.

Three weeks passed—like the proverbial prisoner, I ticked away the days with my spoon in the soft plaster around my window. Then one morning, when the cart with the hunk of bread and the coffee rolled by my door, the guard snapped: "Interrogation!"

My heart turned over. I knew I wasn't ready, that all the things I had planned to say were weak. Interrogation! How can you account for eighteen months of your life, invent lies to prove an existence free of wrongdoing except for the refusal to be interned in German-occupied France? How can one invent innocence? How, when those months lay like a pall over every one of my movements, every one of my actions?

Rue des Saussaies again, the dingy, drain-smelling stairs and finally the room.

The "boss" was a bespeckled individual in civilian clothes. Seen in another place at another time, he might have passed for a schoolteacher. Because his desk was crowded by bulging folders filled with papers, I felt like a child about to be admonished.

"Name?"

I stammered it as I stood, and the blonde secretary, hunched over her machine, typed it without a flicker of recognition. I wondered where Piggy was. It looked as if his one-finger jabs had been a waste of time.

I was questioned for hours, standing like a statue with my arms at my side. It was all my life the "boss" wanted—all the past. Not once did he question the present. But he raised his voice when I was slow—slow because at times I didn't understand his French and slow because I was tired, swaying with fatigue. He smoked constantly. At first it bothered me. In the end, I didn't even notice.

"You were in Greece in September 1939? Why?"

"Visiting the country."

"Where were you before?"

"Budapest."

"And before?"

"Bavaria."

"So? . . . Where?"

"Füssen. It's pretty there. Do you know it?"

There was a pause. I wondered if he was going to hit me in his quiet, deliberate way. If so, I would fall. In a way, it would be a relief. But he didn't. Instead he stood up and pushed me into a sagging armchair by his desk.

Stunned, I laid my hands on my knees to steady their shaking. Oh, God, the relief! For a moment I closed my eyes. It was then that he slapped me. At the same time someone knocked on the door and he went out.

I began to cry. The secretary continued to type.

"I'm hungry," I whined in German.

She looked across at me and shrugged her shoulders. "You'll eat tonight."

"It's not food they give you."

She didn't reply, just continued with her machine. Then the "boss" came in and I never knew if she might have spoken.

Obviously, his conversation outside had concerned me; his attitude had changed. I wondered if he had been talking to the people who had denounced me. One of them knew I had been in Spain—I had sent her a parcel for her children. God, the wickedness of it! I had sent it through the guide, but it had been refused. At the time I had been surprised and then forgotten about it.

"Well . . . Tell the truth now. How did you live?"

"I sold my jewelry. For a time I lived with a man."

"Ah! Where? What's his name?"

"He's dead. He was very old."

"Bah!" And he leaned over, his hand raised.

"I met him in a train on my way to Limoges."

"Why Limoges?" And he made the "g" in it sound like a "ch."

"Because there was still food there and it was cheaper. I planned to live there—stay quiet—lie low."

"There are terrorists there too," he said.

God, yes! Why had I picked that part of France? I had forgotten that the Resistance and the Maquis were just as active there as in Haute-Savoie.

"His name?"

"Jean Durangle. He was very old. I stayed with him six months until he died. He was a retired vet and alone."

He sniggered. Normally I would have been furious at his lewdness, but I was too busy dressing up my lie—too busy finding cloth and color to fit this country vet, grandfather of another liaison officer with whom I had struck up a friendship. One day he had told me sadly of the old man's death in a little village near Limoges where he was mayor. What was the name of it? . . . Something finishing in "ac." But in that region they all finished like that. Oh, God, let me remember. . . . My friend had described it: a high-walled town overlooking a gorge. A place where he had fished and shot rabbits smelling of wild thyme.

"What's the name of the place?"

"Treignac-sur-Vézère," and it came so easily, so smoothly, I knew my guardian angel must be working overtime. How I wish this man wouldn't stare at me! At least when I'd been standing I had looked down at him. Now, sitting in this sagging armchair, it was just the opposite.

And so it went on. At one point I think he was just as tired as I was, but of course not in the same way. Just bored and infuriated.

"Lies! Lies!" he thundered, suddenly springing up.

I shrank away. Here we go, I thought. "You can verify it."

"You were in England."

"England!"

"Yes. You're a spy. You've always been one."

"England," and I burst into tears . . . genuine ones too. Dear England. "England! If I had been there, I would have stayed there, even under your bombs!" England . . .

"Those bombs are nothing compared to what's going to happen. Soon New York will be a pile of rubble!"

I was too upset to register this. Instead I sobbed over and over again: "England . . . England . . ."

It was all he could get out of me, and he cleared his desk, angrily muttering against me and Americans in general. Only six months accounted for. Now, what . . . ? The south of France. Yes, that was good. I had been there. I could draw out my stay and invent an apartment above Cannes where I had lived for a few days.

While he was clearing his desk, his secretary crossed over to a filing cabinet. From it she took a basket with the neck of a bottle showing above the edge. Then, very neatly, she slapped a checked tablecloth onto the boss's desk. Obviously she was a good housewife! She set down a plate of sandwiches and a glass with the bottle beside it. All very bourgeois!

White bread! I hadn't seen that for a long time. My mouth began to water as I watched my interrogator sink his tobacco-stained teeth into it, tearing at it before starting to chew. I wondered if he would give me any. He had so much.

No, he just chewed and so did his secretary while a fly buzzed against the windowpane in the stuffy room.

I began to feel sick, swallowing gobs of sour water, small drops of perspiration trickling down my face. All the while he watched me blandly. I didn't hate him. I suppose I was beyond that. I felt no emotion, only sickness, hunger and disgust at the smell of my clothes and my badly washed body.

"Couldn't you send someone out to order me something? There's a restaurant on the square around the corner." I said it, but God knows how!

He stopped chewing. "How do you know?"

"I often went there before the war."

He sniggered, "Tres chic—very expensive."

"I suppose so. I never had to pay. If you hadn't taken my money, I could pay."

He laughed. "Just watching us is good enough."

And so it went until I gagged into my tear-stained handkerchief.

"Bah!" he shouted, getting to his feet and sweeping his plate away.

"If I could have some water."

"Water! You'll get plenty next time."

Knowing what he meant, I wondered how I could have thought he looked like a schoolteacher.

I suppose it must have been close on four when the paddy wagon drove back into the courtyard of Fresnes. As I climbed down, I noticed it was a wood-burning contraption. They must be getting short of fuel. Six months ago no German-operated vehicle would have used wood. It should have pleased me, because little things like that made a pattern—a pattern that meant the bombings over Germany were having an effect. Restrictions were now the order of the day for the mighty Aryan race! Yes, I should have been pleased, but I was too tired.

Ten of us were standing in the courtyard, but when the guards counted us they started yelling, roughing us up. Someone was missing. We stared at one another and even dared to whisper. Had someone escaped? Oh, it would be wonderful for them. But no, a white-faced woman was dragged out, hair plastered to her skull with dampness. I turned away, frightened. "You'll get water—next time!" The bath! Ducking you until you talked or drowned. Holding out as long as possible and only giving a name on your last gasp. The name of someone not important (as if you could know). The name of someone already in their hands (as if he didn't have troubles enough).

Oh, God, whom could I give? . . . No one. Please, dear God . . . No one.

Another paddy wagon drove up and then another. The women were separated from the men and we shuffled down the corridor through iron gates which clanked shut behind us with a rasping of locks.

On our left was a line of men, their jailers talking in rough German to our women guards. Because most of the men carried bundles and suitcases, I guessed they were newcomers. And then I saw him. Marcel! Shuffling, head down, one hand holding his trousers, a small air-raid satchel in the other. I stopped. Someone bumped me from behind. It was just as well because farther back was Lecoque. In a rush all my doubts returned. The little black book! He had seen me in London. I lowered my head. The men turned away toward the greffe.

My cell was a refuge—even the noise of the key turning in the lock was a relief. Until tomorrow I was safe, alone with my thoughts.

Marcel! Marcel! He hadn't a chance if he'd been caught with his radio. Neither of them did, for that matter. In what branch were they? Escape line, sabotage, espionage?

How should I know, and what difference would it make if I did? And sitting on my bed with my head in my hands, I heard an inner voice reply: "Yes, that's one good thing you haven't got on your conscience!"

"Supposing they saw me?"

Inner voice: "They didn't."

"What will happen to him?"

Inner voice: "That's not your business."

"But I love him."

Inner voice: "You'll get over it. Remember him in the vineyards—the Pyrenees—etched against the blue sky. Don't be soft. You've been a fool You've jeopardized many people. Fight."

"But how?"

Inner voice: "Drink your soup."

"I can't. It's cold," I said, looking at it swimming in the grease of God knows what.

Inner voice: "Selfish bitch! Do you think you're the only one interrogated today? Drink it!"

And drink it I did, shoving it down with pieces of bread in which strands of straw were imbedded. I never found out why there was straw in the bread all through the war years. Maybe there was a surplus of straw. If so, it was the only surplus there was.

Maybe I could get a message to him, I thought, scratching the blackout paint on my window with my thumbnail. Someone before me had already started this and there was quite a sizable cleared spot. In this way, without opening the window, I could see trees, even lilac in the distance. The distance beyond—the distance that was freedom. I opened the window itself only at night to gulp in great gasps of air. (With a bar broken off from my bed, I had managed to pry the nails from the cross-bar that held it.)

Yes, a message. A word that would let him know my thoughts were with him.

Inner voice: "You're such a fool! Don't you think the poor man has enough to think about? Suppose Lecoque recognizes your voice and talks. Shut up. Think of the next interrogation. Think of giving another name. Someone who isn't dead this time."

"Who?"

Inner voice: "Blanc."

"Never. Never." And in my anguish I beat my fists against the wall. "Never. Never."

Inner voice: "You haven't heard from him since the Germans captured the Maquis in Haute-Savoie. Even if he wasn't in your sector, he's probably been caught. He was walking a tight rope the last time you saw him. He knew his luck was out. So did you. Remember the tears in his eyes when he kissed you goodbye."

Never. Never. Not Blanc.

I must have made quite a noise with my fists because I heard thuds above me and tapping in my water pipe.

"Are you all right, Juliette? How did it go?"

"I'm all right."

I longed to tell her more, but I knew it could be dangerous. Stool pigeons were everywhere.

"I have a feeling it will be my turn tomorrow."

Since she had been saying this for some time, I didn't pay any attention. Instead I gave her what little news I had picked up.

But she was right. She went the following morning and there was silence for days. An ominous silence because I knew she was in her cell. The woman in the cell next to her had heard something like a sack being dragged along the gallery one night and then the noise of a door being opened and slammed shut.

From upstairs, downstairs, the ground floor, we tried for days to communicate with her. I even made a few surreptitious signs to the girl on the food trolley. But she looked terrified and thrust me back so roughly my soup splashed all over the floor of my cell.

Then, one evening, just after the "Ave Maria," I heard her identifying taps on the water pipe. She was alive. Perhaps in a day or two she would be able to talk. When I reached the others who wanted news of her, I found I was crying.

They had tortured her, made her undergo the ducking treatment, beaten her. Naturally, I learned this only some days later when she was able to crawl to the "telephone." It was a tremendous relief. They were feeding her. Some of her fingernails had been torn off.

While she slowly recovered I prayed for courage. It was during this period that the prison chaplain visited me one afternoon. An unassuming man with jackboots. I hated him.

"You come to ask me if I need anything!" I spluttered at him. "Go to the cell above me. She needs you more." And then, when he looked embarrassed, perhaps even a little sad, I continued to storm at him. "No, you won't go! You don't want to know what your fellow countrymen do to their prisoners!"

After his departure I found he had left a small, blue book. The New Testament. It was the only good thing about his visit.

Several nights later—I don't know what the time was, but it was dark in the cell—I was awakened by the door being slowly opened. I was terrified and even more so when I saw in the dim light that it was one of the guards—one I had never seen before. Interrogation! In the middle of the night. God, give me courage.

But no command was shouted at me. Instead a parcel was thrust into my hands, together with a crumpled cigarette package containing a couple of cigarettes. I stared at them stupidly.

"Smoke only at night," the woman said, lighting one for me.

"But . . . But the parcel?"

"Food. Eat only at night too. I'll leave two matches."

"Food! From whom? How?"

"Friends! Your family! I will be back. If you see me elsewhere, make no sign. You're au secret. Good night."

And she disappeared, hardly leaving me time to see her face.

I think the extra food must have given me new energy. Oh, there wasn't much, but it was gingerbread, butter, honey and several small cans of pâté, guaranteed pure pork. This last I doubted, but when I pried one open with the can-opener the guard had provided, it was delicious. For the first time in weeks I slept without being hunched up by hunger pains.

I rationed myself. It was easy, but even though I put the butter outside on the window sill, I had to eat it quickly to prevent it from turning rancid.

Putting the butter outside is probably what gave me the idea of escaping. Of course it was a wild scheme, without any chance of success. No one escaped from a cell in Fresnes, even from the first floor.

But one night I started to execute this crazy plan. By digging with my bar into the plaster beside the window I hoped to make the aperture between window and bars sufficiently wide for me to slip through. Then, having tied together my blanket (torn in half) and one of my coarse sheets (changed once a month), I planned to climb down by bracing my feet against the façade the way I had learned in Scotland.

Of course I never even got out of the cell—not even onto the window ledge. I was caught on my third night. I don't think it was the plaster droppings that betrayed me. There were very few and I stored them away in my mattress of corn husks. It didn't make for comfortable sleeping, but if it meant freedom it was a small price to pay. No, it wasn't the plaster that gave me away. It was the noise.

A guard erupted—the tall brute of our arrival. She stormed and ranted, and then, no doubt because she was out of breath, she called a colleague. I might have found their united indignation funny had it not been for the fact that they took my watch. They made no attempt to hit me, although the big one was capable of it and I'd seen her hit someone else when we were filing out for our weekly exercise. No, they didn't touch me. They just shouted and stormed.

The results of this would-be escapade were ten days in a dark cell on the ground floor without soup. Only coffee and dry bread.

Ten days in semi-darkness in a normal life span may seem insignificant. In reality it's like ten years, especially when you have only a thin bar of sunlight for company for half an hour a day, a cold cement floor to lie on, the sounds of a leaky spigot and somewhere far away the shouts of prison guards.

I followed my ray of sunshine, or cold light when the sky was overcast, crawling after it like an animal. When it left me, at some point in the early afternoon, I stretched out, my head propped on my tin bowl. It made me dizzy to lie flat and I got too cold when I propped myself up against the wall smelling of saltpeter. Even my Canadienne didn't keep out the dampness, which penetrated the sheepskin lining and smelled. Of course it was only one odor more and God knows there were plenty of them, no matter how much I washed, standing above the stinking hole in the floor into which the water spigot dripped incessantly.

Lying there, I started to write a book on smells.

Remembering the smells I had known in my life was not very constructive, but it helped to pass the time. I remembered India on a trip my mother had launched us on after she had undergone a cancer operation, and while I was recovering from scarlet fever. What maladies the rest of the family had—sister, stepfather, great-aunt and governess—I don't know. But we sailed from England one dismal January day bound for South Africa via Madeira and Saint Helena.

Madeira was an enchantment, smelling of mimosa and oily rags. A strange combination but connected in my eleven-year-old mind with the sledges in which we used to glide over the black cobblestones. Saint Helena smelled of sulfur and dried rock. South Africa had the odor of eucalyptus and the roses growing in a snake pit in the research farm of Port Elizabeth. There was also Zanzibar, with waving palms that swayed across a garish sunset above a golden beach smelling of hot sand. Oh, yes, beautiful Zanzibar . . .

India was a symphony of odors with certain passages thundering discordantly, like the towers of silence in Bombay. Standing on a hill amid cork trees in which hideous vultures perched waiting for their daily meal of corpses, these towers were odorless. Odorless because the all-pervading smell of Lysol had taken over, ordered no doubt by the cleanly British. They were able to control the smell of death, but they couldn't prevent the sacred cows covered with running sores from wandering through the streets and snuffling at putrid-smelling heaps of garbage.

After Bombay there had been Delhi, a duet smelling of curry and snakes. Curry because the hotel seemed to have nothing else and snakes because, blinded by a lurid sunset, I upset a snake-charmer's basket. Imperturbably a cobra stared at me, swaying gently while other things, brown and ocher like the earth, crawled around my feet. Here then was the smell of horror and fear, sour and pungent.

Did the Taj Mahal have a smell? No, only the fetid odor of stagnant pools filled with water lilies and giving back its shimmering reflection.

Then Benares . . . crowded with monkey-infested temples sprawling along the brown embankments of the Ganges. Everywhere, in and out of the water, small, nimble people helping old and young, covered like the cows with sores, chanting as they bathed. Overhead the pungent odor of incense not quite smothering the acridness of burning sandalwood or the funeral pyres. Sacred Mother Ganges teeming with life. It was horrifying. I preferred to chase a monkey until it escaped up the steps of a temple, where it farted at me with a malevolent leer.

Back in Europe there were less exotic, less penetrating odors. But there was the scent of Paris after a spring shower on the chestnut trees, the reek of garlic and Gauloise cigarettes. There was also the smell of snow falling on a hamlet far from a main road, a village lost by itself and at peace, or so it thought, until the Milice and Gestapo came.

It was close on four when the French commander and I arrived in that once happy place. We had been driving up from Ambérieu in a wheezing "gazogene" to the head of the pass. If I hadn't forgotten my bag, thus delaying our departure, we too would have been in that hamlet when the Milice arrived to shoot all the men, leaving them in huddled groups for the kindly falling snow.

We had left Haute-Savoie because the Germans had surrounded the province, determined to finish off the Maquis and anyone connected with them. And there were many in the cities, villages and hamlets. Everywhere. Haute-Savoie had become a province of France at war with Germany. Of course we had known it couldn't last—that sooner or later the Germans would put an end to it. And of course they did . . . with several divisions. But we made them pay. And we paid too. The Maquis were scattered and broken after fierce fighting in the mountains and gorges. The farms supplying them were burned. There were mass arrests and tortures. Terror stalked through the département; the smallest journey became a risk. What remained of the Maquis was pulled back at night, evacuated down dark lanes into the neighboring département in trucks, carts, anything with wheels. Sometimes the villagers and farmers helped by indicating the hours of the patrols. But it was not always spontaneous aid, because their fear of reprisals from the Resistance was almost as great as their fear of the Germans. But the Maquis were leaving. Help them get out so they could inflict their woe elsewhere. I was very much in the dark about these operations, because I was living in an apartment in a small village overlooking the lake of Annecy and my English colonel had disappeared, leaving me with few contacts. I learned later he had gone farther south into another département where the Germans were attacking the Maquis. He left behind our radio operator, who had seen fighting with the Glières

Maquis before being evacuated.

When it was all over, the commander, known as the "patron," and I left, hidden in the back of a truck; we then crossed the Rhône on foot on a swing bridge made of ropes and cables high above the river. It had been early evening. I didn't know where to look. On the hills, farms were burning and beneath my feet swirled the green and frothy water. Some of the slats on the bridge were broken, and this caused an upward draft from the water which made the frail causeway swing alarmingly. I was never good at heights and it was an agonizing moment. Only the thought of my stocky French officer in his drab, dark civilian clothes and with a price on his head helped me. We had to get across.

And we did. Into the department of l'Ain we went, the patron to gather together the remains of his Maquis and settle them in new camps. But almost as soon as we heard the last of the wheezing "gazogene" that had brought us from Ambérieu, our ears picked up the sound of crying coming from the house nearest us. When we entered it, we learned of the tragedy that had struck this peaceful farm as well as the surrounding houses. Hardly more than an hour earlier the Milice and Gestapo had attacked the hamlet and not only killed all the men but forced their families to witness their execution.

Grief is always a terrible thing. I was stunned for these people, but it wasn't so much their cries that pulled at my heartstrings. It was the grandson of one of the victims insisting that I must be cold and trying to ply me with hot soup.

When some semblance of order had been created by the patron, we learned that the dead men had been left outside. The executioners had forbidden the families to move the victims or risk the same fate. But these people had disregarded the order; risking death, they had carried their beloved husband, father and grandfather back into his home.

The patron wanted to pay his last respects and I went with him to the stable where they had finally laid the dead man.

He had been shot in the back of the neck—a neat hole that left hardly any trace, and I was shocked to hear his family comment upon this with a wealth of detailed wonder. But then these people were rough and simple in their manner of expressing themselves.

He had been an elderly man with fine features. There was something very trim about him; even his mustache was well clipped. In his Canadienne and ski trousers he was still impressive, although he lay on a pile of hay among the cows chewing their cuds.

Of course we couldn't stay. The Milice had said they would return. A half-hour later, after some warm soup, we left on borrowed skis.

Skiing in soft snow is never easy. For the uninitiated it's a feat. Add to this a blinding snowstorm and the effort is a triumph of willpower and endurance. This was true of the "patron," who had probably skied only once or twice in his life.

Oh, we started out well enough, but then the snow in the hamlet wasn't in drifts. Beyond, it was different. The track was obliterated and, to make matters worse, on the basis of the map I had consulted before leaving, I suspected a ravine. Needless to say, if there was one, we couldn't hear the water because it would be flowing sluggishly under a coating of ice and snow.

Between us we had my rucksack, a small duffelbag, a compass and a torch, while in the inside pocket of my Canadienne I had the map, which we looked at as little as possible so as not to get it wet. We dared not use the torch—not because of the Milice: they wouldn't be out on a night like this, but to save the battery.

The patron fell constantly. In the beginning he refused my help, but after twenty minutes or so he was happy to reach for my hand even if he sometimes dragged me down on top of him as a result. And then what a mess of skis, sticks, duffelbag . . . you name it. It wasn't cold—that would come later—but the blinding snow directly in our faces was like freezing water stinging us. I had a scarf over my head, but it was soon soaking wet. Then it must have frozen because my head felt as though it was in a bag of ice.

We had to stop often to take a compass bearing and at times found ourselves gliding willy-nilly down a hill. When this occurred I tried to take the lead so that my companion could follow my tracks. This of course slowed my pace, because the visibility was practically nil for the patron as well as for me. Once I ran head first into a pine tree. I fell and so did the patron. Since we were down, we rested and drank some cognac . . . but not for long. I didn't want that. It was too dangerous to give way to languor.

Toward midnight the snow let up. Then, as the sky gradually cleared, it turned cold. First one star and then another appeared and then the moon came out from behind a mass of high-riding clouds. It was very beautiful and for a time we marveled at it. The patron was falling less often. In fact, what he had just gone through was worth twenty lessons.

We climbed, moving cautiously because over to our right, beyond the stream gurgling through its blanket of snow, we had seen a light.

Finally, well past one, we reached the tumbledown summer hotel that was our destination. Here the patron found some of his men. They were all strangers to me, but very soon a friendly camaraderie was established. It couldn't have been otherwise. We learned that a search party had been sent out for us. I saw that this annoyed the patron, not because it cast doubts on his skiing ability but because of the clearing weather which might bring out patrols.

The following morning I was awakened by breakfast in bed, brought by one of the Maquis couriers. I stared and then burst out laughing.

"How is Boldo?" I asked him. It was the boy from the farm near Chaumont. He had made good on his vow of going into the mountains.

"Waiting to bite you, Madame."

Because the hotel could be searched by the Milice and the Germans, and the patron was short-handed, needing all his men to set up a camp deeper in the woods, it was decided to send me with a verbal message to a village across the valley. I was to deliver it to the owner of an all-purpose shop opposite the bus stop. This was a good arrangement because I could synchronize my appearance with the arrival of the bus. The shop was owned by a woman.

"Tall, gaunt creature with a beard or something like one. Maybe she's a man! Even her cats are queer. No tails. You should see her, patron," said one of the men, older than the rest. He had an efficient Luger stuck in his belt. I didn't wonder where he had got it. Maybe the half-healed scar on his forehead was the price he had had to pay.

"She's a deep one, all right. You really should see her, patron."

"Should I?" was the cryptic reply.

"Some say she's a witch," a younger boy cut in, probably a courier. "When I go there I always think I'm going to see the devil pop out of one of those drawers she's always rummaging in. The people in the village are afraid of her. And then there's the smell."

"Smell?" I asked.

"Yes, Madame. Some days it's intolerable. Even Monsieur le Curé gags."

"Why not? Do you think a curé hasn't a sense of smell?" someone quipped, while the patron's shoulders shook with silent laughter. "And how do you know he gags, your mysterious curé?"

"I was there when he grabbed his handkerchief. Eau de Cologne he had on it. He smelled like you, Madame."

Everyone burst out laughing. How young they were! Like kids. Not even their Sten guns and Lugers held in chapped, chilblained hands could hide their youth. Perhaps their eyes held a wary look, but you had to search carefully to see it. Yet, despite their ruddy skins, their thin faces showed that they were often hungry, and I suspected that the one playing solitaire had a fever; he certainly had a hacking cough.

It was a beautiful day, cold and crisp. Ideal weather for skiing. Only two things marred my joy. The first was an empty feeling in my stomach that a more substantial breakfast would have satisfied; the other—which made me forget the first—was that I couldn't ski as I liked, swiftly with small jump turns. I had to watch everything—the shadow thrown by a tree, tracks in the virgin snow. I also had to listen, standing in the quiet of the pine woods, separating the gentle soughing of the wind from other sounds if there were any. There weren't, but it still had to be done. It was a slow business, but it gave me time to drink in the beauty of the radiant scene. That had been the last time I skied and, lying desolate on the cement floor of my punishment cell, I cherished it as a wonderful memory.

I had reached the village safely and had skied down the main street past the church. I saw the shop, a scruffy little place, and the bus stop opposite it. I went past them until I came to a small square. Here, to give myself the appearance of not waiting for anything, I unfastened my skis to clean them. Would the bus never come? Apparently not. I decided to retrace my steps and go up into the shop without waiting for it. Everything was very quiet. So quiet it made me uneasy. I had a feeling I was being watched. Each house frowning down on me seemed like a menace.

Suddenly the church bells pealed with a clamor that froze on the cold air. It was Sunday. I knew then there would be no bus.

Now from the frowning houses a slow procession of people issued. It reassured me and I decided to join them, hoping they wouldn't notice when I dropped out in front of the shop. My skis on my shoulder—which was not unusual because several people carrying theirs had already passed me—I came to the shop. Would it be open? Yes.

The gaunt creature, witch or what-have-you, who frowned at me from behind her counter was most unprepossessing. And the tailless, mewing cats did nothing to improve the impression. Nevertheless I bought a newspaper, some thread and writing paper. During her search through the cluttered shelves I delivered my message. There was no reaction. Just nothing. This made me wonder if she wasn't deaf. I hadn't expected her to smile, but she could have nodded. After all, we were alone.

No, there was no reaction, so I paid and went out. Now I was really in a mess. The patron had told me I was not to return because I would leave tracks. Instead, I was to board a bus and go to our safe house in Ambérieu. Sunday. No bus. What was I to do?

For the moment I wanted out of the village. Out.

Slipping on my skis, I retraced my steps and it wasn't until I was past the church that I realized I was being followed. And not by one man but several. If the woman in the shop had been unprepossessing, the men walking some distance on either side of me were even worse. They looked like thugs, and the awful thing was I didn't think they were from the Milice or the Gestapo.

They closed in on me after the last house in the village.

"Where are you going?" one of them croaked, grabbing one of my sticks while another closed in, his hand stuck in his pocket. I didn't have to ask what he was holding, but I did wonder if it was a Luger.

"All right, boys! Hold it!" someone called. "Hold it."

At first I didn't recognize him. It had been almost two months since I had seen him. He had always been thin and gangling. Now he was positively scrawny and sporting a beard.

"Elizabeth! What are you doing here?"

"Paul! Paul!" I cried, falling into his arms.

It was the radio man—the companion of my flight from England.

"Hurry! Take your skis off. I have a wounded boy and another who's sick. That's why we're still here. Hurry!"

Their shelter was two dingy rooms over a stable heated by an old stove with a rickety pipe. There was no light, a few pieces of furniture and a broken-down bed. I was horrified because the sick boy lying on it probably had pneumonia.

"He can't stay here. He needs care," I said, looking down at his flushed face. "What have you been giving him?"

"Aspirin. That's all I have. How about the other one?"

"Just a flesh wound. Nice and clean. But this one . . ." I insisted on trying to make the boy more comfortable, and I probably made him worse because he whimpered, his eyes bright with fever.

"We're looking for a safe house. I hope to move him on a sleigh tonight up to a farm."

"My God!"

"The boys are taking turns at making him drink. We'll bundle him up for the journey. It's not far."

Later we talked—that is, I answered questions.

"The patron said nothing else?"

"No. Only the message, and I don't even know if it was heard or understood."

"It was lucky for you I was around. Everyone thought you were a spy. Now, listen . . . we'll move out tomorrow. You'll come with us. If all goes well, we should be with the patron tomorrow night."

"No, no," I protested. "He said no tracks. Even I wasn't going back. When you found me I was on my way to Ambérieu, though God knows when I would have reached there."

Paul shook his head and then shrugged. He had changed. He was no longer the debonair young man who was always teasing me. Only once, when we had sat on a bench between trains in Lyon, overlooking the Rhône, Paul with his transmitter between his feet, had he lost some of his aplomb. Someone had come up and spoken to me, someone from Paris I would rather not have seen. I had tried to play it cool and pretend pleasure, but my heart was hammering. And we had only been in France a few hours. It was my first mission: get Paul to Blanc.

Blanc! In that damp cell his name exploded in my mind once more. He must have been caught. That crystal-cold day Paul had heard nothing of him. If they tortured me beyond endurance, I could give his name. But what of his wife, his children? Would that broken-down old farm light up the night sky like so many others?

Lying for hours on the floor of that cell, I turned over in my mind how best I could save Laurence Blanc until I realized—or wanted to realize—she had probably been taken too. And the children . . .

One morning I woke up tired. I no longer knew what day it was —they just flowed on endlessly in shadow, in darkness or in a beam of sunlight. I had come to the point of no longer caring. This was limbo. I wanted to die.

I found a piece of iron, probably a leftover from the bed that had once been here. With the jagged end I tried to cut my wrist. Finally I gave up, after drawing a little blood. I suppose I didn't really want to die.

And sometime later a Feldwebel came, accompanied by one of the women guards. I didn't bother to get up. Until then I had always preferred to face them standing.

Looking down at me, the Feldwebel kicked me, not roughly,

with the toe of his jackboot. God, those boots! Those trampling boots that had destroyed so much of the world! In a way, it would have been better had he hurt me. This way it was like a contemptuous caress.

"Tomorrow, American! Tomorrow!" he said, grinning down at me. "Juden, ja?"

It made me dizzy to stare up at him and so I concentrated on the buckle of his belt the ray of sunlight picked out: "GOTT MIT UNS."

My old cell on the first floor was like the Ritz.

I went immediately to the window, now securely bolted, and peered out through the peephole. A patch of blue sky, a bit of a tree with fresh green leaves. Oh, it was heaven. I stayed at the window until my legs buckled. Then I crawled to my bed and slept.

It took me several days to recover from my confinement in what was known as the dungeon. Fortunately, another parcel arrived, brought by the same woman. She chided me for my stupid attempt at escape, but she spoke so gently I couldn't be annoyed.

Over the "telephone" I learned that my Swiss friend had somehow injured her knee and that the war news was much the same except that the Allies had started their march on Rome. In France there was increasing sabotage, especially on the railroads. Flights of Allied bombers were a daily occurrence and listening to the sirens wail and the dull thud of bombs was heartening but terrifying as well. We were locked away and our shelter was a prison. Once I saw a plane trailing white smoke against blue sky, two parachutes billowing forth and then a red torch plunging earthward, scattering what must have been incendiaries. Something was definitely about to happen. We all knew it, felt it. Even our guards were subtly changing. They seemed more subdued, often talking among themselves. But every evening the list of names for the firing squad was just as long, and every evening we learned of massive departures for Germany. From the women's block the guards' shouts of "Tribunal! Interrogation!" mingled with "Schnell! Raus! Schnell! Raus!" Some of the women left singing a hymn, beating out the words with their feet. I didn't know if I ought to envy them.

I thought of Marcel constantly. Had he left? Had he been shot? I was often tempted to cry out a message, but something always stopped me. My joy at hearing his voice would only increase his unhappiness.

Somehow the middle of May arrived. How I knew this I can't imagine because I had long since lost count of the days. Perhaps the priest who brought me books had told me. Perhaps simply through the "telephone."

And one morning the words "Tribunal! Interrogation!" were snarled at me with my morning brew of tepid acorns.

Once again the dingy stairs with, I suppose, the smell of drains. I didn't notice smells any more. There were too many.

Surprisingly, and to my relief, the interview was short. Blanc and my phony story of how we'd met slipped into the recesses of my mind. Time. I must gain time. Things were changing.

The "boss" handed me a sheet of paper on which my "statement" had been typed in French and German. After reading the French, I was frightened. Had the same thing been written in German? They could trick me into signing anything.

But no, slowly, word by word, the boss read me the German version while his secretary translated. From the little German I had retained, it seemed to correspond to the French. I signed, marveling at having produced such a mixture of lies, half-truths and sheer imagination.

It was not long after this that the priest came to ask if I would like to take Communion.

"But, Father, I must go to Confession."

"It's not necessary, my child. I will put you down for tomorrow. All are absolved."

My God! They're going to shoot me! But why? They haven't proved anything.

Communion on the top floor of the prison was intensely moving. Just walking down the iron galleries and going higher and higher up the open stairs was an experience in itself. The altar was a small makeshift one. Transportable, like a massage table. Someone had placed some flowers on it. Somehow this made me want to cry. But maybe that was because of the Crucifix above it.

There were about ten of us, including Rolande. Although I had never before seen her, I guessed it was she because she held up her bandaged hands to me. She was an ageless woman with peroxide hair now intermingled with strands of gray.

"Juliette," she whispered, sidling up to me while I watched the guards. "They told me you were tall. I don't believe in this, but the Father has been so good to me I knew it would give him pleasure if I came. I have been condemned."

"To what?"

"To death. Twice, like many others. But I don't know how you can die twice. Perhaps He would know," and she nodded toward the Crucifix. "I have studied all this, but I have no faith."

After that morning, things went very fast. Only I wasn't conscious of it. For me the days dragged. Wind and rain beat against the windowpane; ten, fifteen times a day the wail of sirens, the dull, solid clump of bombs. The Allies were entering Rome, but taking a train in France had become more of an adventure than ever because of sabotage. And I was here! In this stinkhole, trying to compose crossword puzzles and using a piece of plaster as chalk.

"Ils ont débarqué!"

Everything was so quiet, so monotonous I only heard it as a whisper.

"Invasion! Invasion!"

All hell broke loose. Shouts from the men's block. Shrieks from the women's side. Then the beating of spoons on tin bowls. It was deafening and the guards could do nothing.

And afterward, when we were too tired to continue, the *Marseillaise.* If the prison had trembled to its foundation when the bombs were falling in the stockyards behind, now it vibrated from pent-up emotion. Beyond, over hill and dale, from the coal mines of the north, the steel mills of the west, the Alps, the south, the Pyrenees, Brittany, came the cry: "Ils ont débarqué! Ils ont débarqué! En Normandie!"

We were happy for hours. Then came the anguish. Would they keep their foothold? Like everyone else's, my mood passed from ecstasy to despair, so that being called to the Tribunal one morning was a change. But I wondered why they wanted me again.

This time, instead of the paddy wagon, we were ordered to climb into a truck. We were only a few—all women arrested for pilfering, black-market deals or practicing the oldest profession in the world. No one made any bones about anything, talking freely of the news, their activities. Some of them had worked in the prison kitchens and laundry and they seemed a happy-go-lucky crowd. Next to me on the bench was a girl so young she was still a child.

"What are you going to be judged for?" she asked.

"Judged?"

"Yes. I was caught pilfering cigarettes and riding the Métro and giving wrong directions. They always believed me too. But then I took great care when I explained all the wrong changes to them and told them where to find the longest corridors. I hope I made a lot of them miss their trains."

I burst out laughing.

In Paris, the truck stopped somewhere near the law courts and they were herded out. But not me. I and the soldier guarding me rode in stately solitude to the Rue Boissy d'Anglas. There we stopped in front of a large building flying a swastika and guarded by sentries. As I jumped down I noticed it was opposite the Crillon. I was intrigued not so much by the proximity of our Embassy or the famous hotel but by the quarter. I was also relieved to see that the sentries weren't wearing the black-and-silver tabs of the SS. They were Wehrmacht.

The big hall inside was cut off at the back by a partition with a door in it. A wooden bench curved around the walls facing the door. Everything smelled very clean and scrubbed, like the posters of the Bavarian Alps tacked up on the wall. It was also wonderfully quiet.

I wasn't under guard, unless the chubby little soldier hunched over a typewriter was supposed to be guarding me, and I didn't dare ask him what this place was because he wasn't paying the slightest attention to me and I was beginning to wonder if I couldn't escape.

Further to my right—where the bench curved around the opposite wall—was a basket. I slid toward it and ventured a peep. It was full of strawberries. This surprised me so much it cut off my idea of escape. Instead I began to wonder if I couldn't eat them? I was debating this, my mouth drooling, when two soldiers marched in with my Swiss friend hopping on one foot between them.

She had fallen off her cot and hurt her knee. It was horribly swollen and must have been very painful, but all she had been given to ease it was aspirin. Her cell companions, risking the anger of the guards, had demanded her transfer to the infirmary. Their request had been ignored and the poor girl was left with the aspirin—and not much of that—and cold compresses applied by her companions.

I was so shocked I couldn't say anything. And I was to blame for this! Still, I couldn't understand how falling out of a cot could do so much damage. The poor, poor girl.

"What's in the basket?" she asked.

"Strawberries." And I didn't have time to say more because a soldier came from the back, calling our names.

"Let's take them with us."

"Better not. It's so strange I'm suspicious. They might be poisoned."

With her arm over my shoulder and helped by the soldier, we passed through the door in the partition and into an office.

Normally I would have found the place very ordinary, but, coming from Fresnes and the Rue des Saussaies, it was luxurious. It was furnished with real furniture, not beat up stuff like the "boss's." A thick carpet on the floor, a bookcase and two armchairs in front of a walnut desk. Behind this sat a youngish man in uniform. An officer.

"Which one of you is Swiss?" he asked, holding up a passport.

As he hadn't yelled or barked, we stared at him. I began to wonder if I wasn't dreaming. To make matters worse, everything was so clean I became conscious of my disheveled appearance, the stains on my clothes.

"The Gestapo has turned you over to me. I'm a judge attached to the legal section of the Army. You've been in Fresnes since March, arrested for harboring a citizen of a country at war with Germany. Because of your Swiss nationality you'll be released immediately. I'm sure your experience will keep you from infringing again on the laws of occupation." And he smiled, actually smiled. It was then that I noticed he was handsome. Not the blond, godlike type. No, just a nice clean-cut face. His uniform was immaculate and suited him.

"You . . ." he said, pointing a finger at me and shaking his head. "What accusations! England . . . Resistance . . . Parachutist . . ."

"Ridiculous! If I had been in England, I would have stayed there. Who is accusing me?"

"False identity . . . Well, there are plenty of those around. Made for the Jews. Are you Jewish?"

"No."

"I'm glad. But why didn't you want to go to Vittel? No one has ever complained so far."

"The idea of being behind barbed wire frightens me."

He nodded, rustling the papers in front of him. How I wished I could see them. Would the names of my betrayers be on them? Really to believe this horror I had to see it in writing. Those matches and that sixpence had never been in my pocket!

"Do you know Madame D?"

"Not very well. She's a Red Cross driver. We both know her."

My Swiss friend nodded. "She wouldn't do a thing like this. Although she's often obliged to see Germans because of her husband, she wouldn't betray anyone. Besides, she's an American."

"Yes. A very charming lady. She told me you're incapable of doing all you are accused of, Mademoiselle. Your mother is prostrate and says she hasn't seen you since 1942 but that you did have money and jewelry. That you were . . . shall we say, rather spoiled."

I took on my most stupid, vacuous look and decided to remain silent.

"I'm going to send you to Vittel, but not before you've finished serving your sentence."

"Sentence?"

"You forget the false identity card," he said, gently shaking it at me. "Now, let me see. . . . It will soon be three months," and he riffled through the pages of a calendar. I wasn't listening. I was only going to be sent to Vittel? I was free? It was unbelievable.

"Yes, twelve days more. You'll finish them in another cell. No need to keep you au secret. After that, Vittel. Surely barbed wire is better than Fresnes!"

He was benevolent, charming, smiling with pleasure. So was I.

We all shook hands. I even remembered my manners, saying: "You've been very kind. I've been stupid. Perhaps one day I'll be able to thank you."

And I was. Months later, when he was in the fortress of Vincennes, I brought him a food package as well as a list of questions concerning the circumstances of my arrest. I was in uniform, a parachute flash on my sleeve and wearing the ribbon of the Croix de Guerre.

"So it was true?" he murmured sadly, shaking his head. The fortunes of war, and he had been a nice man.

I spent the last two weeks of my sentence in a cell with three other women. One was a girl of my age who said quite freely that she had been arrested because her escape line had been infiltrated by the very German who had later arrested her. Two days before my release she was deported. She never returned. I was told she had died from being given too much food when her camp was liberated.

My other companion was an older woman arrested for peddling false identity cards. Looking at her gray hair and matronly figure, it was difficult to believe.

The third occupant of the cell changed so often we hardly had time to know any of them.

There was only one cot, which we naturally gave to the older woman, and the others and I slept on mattresses on the floor. The warmer weather had brought a plague of fleas. We scrounged for them three times a day, each of us putting her "bag" in her soup bowl and flushing it down the toilet. We wondered when we would have lice.

Because this cell wasn't opposite the men's block and the women in the cells around us weren't talkative, we had little news, but we knew the foothold in Normandy had been established, that other landings had taken place. The sirens still wailed and sabotage was still the order of the day.

When the morning of my release arrived and I heard the key grate in the lock for the last time, my knees were shaking. With my bundle clutched to my chest, I kissed my companions. My last vision of the cell was of the matronly woman sitting on the end of the cot, her fingers in a V sign.

I clattered down the stairs behind my guard, who was racing across the ground floor to the greffe. My slips of paper were snatched from me, and I was given my rucksack, handbag and dressing case. I stared at the case unbelievingly. I had never expected to see it again. There was also a buff-colored envelope containing my money. A few signatures and I was yanked away by the guard—the one who prowled the galleries at night in slippers, the one I had seen slap a prisoner, the one who had ushered us in the night of our arrival.

We stared at one another.

"Frei! Vittel! Gut!" She smiled and then she drew me toward her, whispering: "Don't think too badly of us."

My stomach revolted.

Outside on the perron overlooking the courtyard, two prisoners were drinking in great gulps of air as they watched two men repairing a "gazogene" paddy wagon. Others were talking quite freely as they sat on the steps, ignored by the guard. I joined them.

Suddenly a small, pot-bellied officer approached and began talking, trying to shake hands.

Behind us the guard froze, snapping his jackboots together.

"Who is he?" I asked, stuffing my belongings into my rucksack.

"The Commandant," my guard answered, and hardly had she said the words when he bustled up to me.

"I hope your stay wasn't too unpleasant. But a false identity . . ." He grimaced, his pig eyes gleaming through steel-rimmed glasses.

I thought of Rolande, the man with the broken finger, my Swiss friend with the injured knee, Marcel. Everything. And I was speechless.

"It's not always easy. As compared to our German prisons, this one is old. We do what we can," he continued.

Like hell you do. Then, because I didn't dare say what I thought to this would-be proprietor of a hotel saying goodbye to his guests, I snapped: "My watch! I had it in the cell. It hasn't been returned."

Fingers snapped. A soldier rushed forward.

It just wasn't true! The beautiful Master Race face to face with the changing tide. Bah!

Maybe the man was some sort of nut! And then I saw his eyes, his horrible piglet eyes. They were really filled with concern.

"Pity that in this old prison the plumbing is so poor and you have no plumbers to look after it!"

The soldier returned. He didn't have my watch. I was sorry. It wasn't valuable, but I was fond of it because an intelligence officer in Gibraltar had given it to me to replace my old one.

"We will find it, Madame. We will find it. But you should not have kept it in your cell. I will have it sent on to Vittel."

I returned to my place on the steps to watch the men still working on the "gazogene." Now I noticed behind it the long rows of coffins neatly stacked against the wall of the prison. How efficient they looked. Efficient and definite.

Epilogue

And so it was over, only nothing was the same when the lights went on and the world shook itself like an old dog waking from a nightmare.

Clément Blanc was caught in Perpignan, taken to Lyon, tortured and shot. Laurence Blanc survived deportation only to die some years ago of cancer after turning Les Daines into a home for Mongoloid children. The Blanc children got away to relatives, where they stayed hidden until the Liberation. The "patron" went into some business and is still in it, as far as I know. Until a few years ago I sometimes saw Paul, the radio man, but then I left Paris to live in Brittany. Bridget married and lives somewhere in the States, I think, unless it's South America. The English colonel—the awesome one—lives in England and I'm rarely in touch with him. I have lost touch with Betty and Biddy. My Swiss friend divides her time between her country and France, still living, when she is in Paris, in that cluttered apartment, where she restores old furniture. I have had no word of Marcel since my last glimpse of him at Fresnes. I have had to assume that he was shot.

The people who denounced me went to jail . . . but not for long. Money and influence got them out, but did not prevent their being cold-shouldered in Parisian circles. Now they're old and their behavior is forgotten. Does it matter?

Some years ago I came across a book about Resistance organizations which mentioned people's names. It had only one flaw. The author thought the Austrian brother-in-law—the pinstriped charmer who whammed a lamp on my head—had worked for the Allies. At first when I read this I was indignant and wanted to get in touch with the writer, but in the end I said, "What the hell!"

My mother is still alive, but old and sick. She has turned against me and everyone except her nurses, no doubt because they are useful to her.

For myself, until 1974 I remained in Europe. I tried to write, but soon learned that was no way to guarantee my next meal. And so I went into the advertising business. For the French equivalent of Madison Square Garden: the Vel d'Hiv. It was fascinating, especially because I traveled throughout the country, visiting various stadiums where our firm had billboards and loudspeaker concessions. I was also called on to cover the various fairs, international and otherwise. But in time the advertising business in France changed, became more like Madison Avenue. The Vel d'Hiv was torn down. In its place, huge apartment buildings rose and my office must have become an apartment. Only the Métro, out in the open here, still rushes past, pausing at a station called Bir 'Hakim after a Fighting French victory in the desert of Libya.

Just when I was beginning to look elsewhere for something else to do—without much hope, if the truth be told—I inherited some money. Here's how it happened.

Some time in the middle of the last century a young man just out of law school hung out his shingle in a town in upper New York State and sat back among his lawbooks to await results. They came in the shape of a fire that destroyed everything he owned. He decided to go west, not to join the Gold Rush but to sell implements of every kind to the eager miners. He sold a lot, set up a good many stores, and between his stores and his buying and selling of land, he prospered. In fact, he became one of the wealthiest men in the state of California and, eventually, its governor. His name was Leland Stanford and he was my great-great-great-uncle.

I have always had a great deal of admiration for his energy and persistence and savvy. I also admire him for pushing ahead with the railroad that linked the east coast to the west. But I feel that I see the real Leland Stanford in the man whose only son died in Florence and who then built Stanford University in memory of the boy. That proves to me that he was not simply an adventurer but a man of vision, with a soul that saw beyond the frontiers of money and steel ribbons, reaching out to timeless youth as he once had seen it through his son's eyes. He was the kind of man who made the United States the great country she is and always will be.

Shortly after inheriting this money I fell ill. After numerous tests the diagnosis was multiple sclerosis. I hadn't the slightest idea what that was and was inclined to shake it off. But it didn't shake me. No indeed, it loves me and I've tried to live with it as best I can.

Eventually Paris became too strenuous for me, so I returned to Dinard in Brittany. I never saw the Pyrenees again, and for years I walked with a dagger in my heart, knowing I would never again feel love grow to teasing tenderness. I have had many adventures, but I never married, and today I'm glad of it because I would have hated to impose my disease on my husband. Instead I'm wedded to multiple sclerosis in a stormy relationship.

Friends have told me that Carcassonne has grown a time-worn sheen. If Viollet-le-Duc could return to earth, I think he would spray it with gallons of Mr. Clean!

I hate snow now, and can hardly bear to watch skiing on television—not that my efforts even remotely resembled what you see on the screen. Sometimes I watch people walk and wonder how they can do it and I can't.

I have many friends in Europe, and in the States where I am obliged to live temporarily, I miss them. In this country where I was born, I remain a stranger. Past forty you don't easily make new friends and you long for people with whom you have shared laughter and, sometimes, tears.

I still hate to see chained dogs even though I fully realize the occasional necessity for it, and I still love animals—all animals. For a time I had a hedgehog called Mr. William until he presented me with a family. She loved music, as did a wounded crow

I also had for years. A wonderful, wily old bird who loved to travel. (In those days I was still trying to divide my time between Paris and Brittany.) Perched on the bar of his cage next to my two dogs, the crow would survey the countryside from the back seat of the car. When I stopped in a town, he became the center of attention. Then he would preen himself and stretch out his one good wing and roll his beady eyes, and woe betide anyone who came too near the car! Then his cries would wake the dead. He was also a wonderful weather man. When it was pouring, with no apparent hope of ever stopping, he would suddenly make guttural sounds in the back of his throat and invariably the skies cleared an hour later. He also foretold a change in the weather when the sun was shining. In fact, many of my friends trusted him far more than they did the French weather forecast. He died of a broken heart because he had been relegated to the bottom of the garden when I had to go to the hospital for two months.

One day I returned to Verdun during the uneasy peace that has lain over the world since World War II. It was midsummer, and gorse and heather abounded, but a few paths still meandered up to signs saying "DEFENSE D'ENTRER. DANGER DE MORT."

One of my friends said: "My father's uncle died here."

"And over there is the Ligne Bleu des Vosges, Sedan 1870," her sister replied.

Somewhere behind us a motorcycle sputtered to a stop.

"There was a newspaper story about two Scouts who were killed last month. They went off the path. They say nothing green will ever grow here. Where were the German lines?"

"Opposite," I answered. "Under our feet is Douaumont, which was taken and lost so many times." I was leaning up against a rusted gun, its muzzle still pointing aggressively into space. Nothing had changed.

A noise made me turn.

I froze.

Beside a motorcycle with a sidecar, a slender figure sheathed almost to his ankles in a gunmetal coat.

"Oh, the tactlessness of them! That coat! Will they never learn!" one of my friends exploded.

"What is there to learn?" I mumbled. "He seems too young to have worn that coat."

"His father did."

"And maybe his grandfather before him." I sighed.

With a lopsided smile the older of the two sisters said: "You're very indulgent, Dev. And on this day, of all days! Let's go. Paris is still far away."

I slid behind the wheel. The young German came toward me.

"Are you going to Paris, Madame? If so, may I follow you? I got lost coming up here and I'm in a hurry."

There was a short silence. He spoke excellent French. Should I tell him? He had a nice young face.

"By all means. I'm in a hurry too. I have to be in Paris to receive the Légion d'Honneur."